Praise for [

MW00490171

"*Divine Moments: Ordinary People Having Spiritually Transformative Experiences* is an important contribution to a great awakening that is taking place in the world now. God is reaching out to many people in numerous ways to change humankind. Most people would agree we need a change in human consciousness, and this is exactly what Nancy Clark has researched and presents. Through these testimonies one receives hope and faith that God is involved in this critical and timely spiritual awakening. You have got to be inspired by the love."

—Reverend Howard Storm
Best-selling author, *My Descent Into Death*

"Spiritually transformative experiences are a fact of human history, a driving force affecting individuals and often the course of entire nations. They are quite common and arise unbidden, as a blessing or grace. In each instance they reveal that there is Something More that transcends our mundane, day-to-day existence. *Divine Moments* is a marvelous collection of these experiences that will enrich the life of anyone who reads them."

—Larry Dossey, MD,
Author: *Reinventing Medicine, The Power of Premonitions, Prayer is Good Medicine*

"*Divine Moments* brilliantly demonstrates that spiritual experiences can happen to anyone at any time. Profound transformations in so many once ordinary lives are the result of profound experiences with consistent messages of love, compassion, knowledge and purpose. What becomes increasingly clear is that physical circumstances at the time of the experience are irrelevant. Nancy Clark makes a convincing case that these experiences, therefore, must come from a realm beyond our current understanding of science and reality."

—Yolaine M. Stout, President
American Center for the Integration of Spiritually Transformative Experiences

"Near-death experiences (NDEs), have been increasingly embedded in the fabric of our culture over the 36 years since Dr. Raymond Moody coined the term. Nancy Clark had benefited from her first near-death experience beginning 15 years before Dr. Moody's landmark book *Life After Life*, and has been studying these profoundly elucidating experiences ever since. With *Divine Moments,* she presents the poignant and passionate stories of individuals concerning their mystical experiences transcending our earthly realm - without being "near-death." In addition, she offers her deep wisdom concerning the true value of these phenomena based on her extensive life study. All people have access to these same mystical experiences, which can change their lives in remarkably meaningful ways - through prayer, meditation, loving relationships with animals, the "gift of desperation", or just being open to them under the right circumstances, such as living through the difficulties of human existence.

A profound sense of the true mystery of the nature of *consciousness* has permeated the field of neuroscience and the Philosophy of Mind over the last few decades. This awareness among scientists and philosophers is opening the door to a wider acceptance of the validity of these mystical experiences in the understanding of our existence, and the possibility that mind might exist independently of the brain. The momentum from many different directions is leading towards a fundamental change in human consciousness, offering hope and peace to a troubled world. *Divine Moments* provides a keystone to that global conscious awakening, bringing the mystical and the Divine to all of us - in this life!"

—Eben Alexander III, M.D.
Neuroscientist, near-death experiencer, author
www.lifebeyonddeath.net/

Divine Moments

Ordinary People Having
Spiritually Transformative Experiences

Nancy Clark

1st WORLD
PUBLISHING

Divine Moments

Ordinary People Having Spiritually Transformative Experiences

Nancy Clark

Copyright © Nancy Clark 2012

Published by 1stWorld Publishing
P.O. Box 2211, Fairfield, Iowa 52556
tel: 641-209-5000 • fax: 866-440-5234
web: www.1stworldpublishing.com

First Edition

LCCN: 2011963152
SoftCover ISBN: 978-1-4218-8639-8
HardCover ISBN: 978-1-4218-8640-4
eBook ISBN: 978-1-4218-8641-1

All rights reserved. No part of this book may be reproduced or utilized in any form or by any means, electronic or mechanical, including photocopying or recording, or by any information storage and retrieval system, without permission in writing from the author.

This material has been written and published for educational purposes to enhance one's wellbeing. In regard to health issues, the information is not intended as a substitute for appropriate care and advice from health professionals, nor does it equate to the assumption of medical or any other form of liability on the part of the publisher or author. The publisher and author shall have neither liability nor responsibility to any person or entity with respect to loss, damages or injury claimed to be caused directly or indirectly by any information in this book.

I dedicate this book to the Light of God,
Who is my Source,
For all that I am and all that I will become.

Thank you for showing up when I called upon you
to help me write this book. I am but a pencil in your Hand.
I rejoice in your power working through me.

CONTENTS

ACKNOWLEDGMENTS

I wish to thank all the contributors who shared their experiences and to those who felt this book worthy of endorsement. You are each a jewel in the crown of Divine Light that sparkles in the souls of those who love you.

My deepest appreciation! I LOVE YOU!

My cherished friends, Kenneth Ring, PhD, Joyce Gibb, RN, Mark Lutz, Pat Stillisano, DDS, Randy Snyder PhD, Vernon Sylvest, M.D., William W. Hoover, M.D., PMH Atwater, Josie Varga, Barbara Harris Whitfield, Reverend Richard Dinges, and members of the Columbus, Ohio International Association Near-Death Studies (IANDS), I gratefully thank you for your support and encouragement. You are always present, never judging, never criticizing, never comparing - but just loving me. I am truly blessed to have your friendship and support of my life's "mission."

I wish to thank my editor Paul Bernstein, PhD, Advisory board member, American Center for the Integration of Spiritually Transformative Experiences, who edited the sections of the book written by me. His assistance in improving the manuscript is deeply appreciated. Even though his views on science are not always identical to mine, he has my utmost respect and admiration. Thank you Paul!

I also wish to thank my editor Sue Vail who edited the contributors stories for punctuation while leaving the voices of the contributors in tact. God bless you for this assistance Sue!

Thank you Rev. Howard Storm, Larry Dossey, MD; Eben Alexander III MD; and Yolaine Stout for endorsing my book. Your faith in my service to humanity is greatly appreciated.

My gratitude to Rodney Charles, president of 1st World Publishing who believed I had a book that would help others to recognize that we all have moments of transcendence. His assistance in helping me with my "mission" for the Light of God is deeply appreciated!

My dear husband, you chose to return "home" to the Light of God just as I completed this book. I want to thank you for writing so many wonderful chapters in the book of our personal lives that have meant so much to me. I shall miss our daily laughs together, but I know that one day we will be together in paradise and we will laugh again. I love you with all my heart!

Two of the most blessed angels stepped down from Heaven to be our sons. No words can begin to express how much I will love you for all eternity!

FOREWORD

The privilege of gaining Nancy Clark's friendship began for me with what many would call a "mere coincidence," but what others, including you perhaps, would more appropriately recognize as a "synchronicity." For the last few years of my life, I've been on a spiritual quest, becoming a "seeker" if you will. This is no small thing for a diagnostic surgical pathologist and cytopathologist. Listed on the NDERF (Near-Death Experience Research Foundation) website was a book, Hear His Voice, written by Nancy Clark which sounded EXACTLY like what I was looking for. I bought it, and the "coincidence" came when I flipped to the back cover and found out that Nancy Clark is a *cytyotechnologist*. (Note: Cytology is the study of cells; a cytotechnologist screens slides for hours on end looking through a microscope for things like cancer cells and infectious organisms, marking suspicious foci and sending the slides to a pathologist for review). So, a **cytopathologist** finds a book on mystical experience written by a...**cytotechnologist**(!)...what are the odds? It would be like a cardiac surgeon finding a book written by a cardiac surgical scrub nurse, or an attorney who specialized in corporate tax law just "happening" to stumble upon a book about mystical experience written by a paralegal specializing in ....corporate tax law!

Cytotechnologists are ANGELS to the cytopathologist! These are the ones with the "locator" function, finding the "bad" cells for the cytopathologist. They MUST be grounded and focused, or else people will die from having their cancers missed. This is not the field where one would expect to find a "mystic;" yet, this is where I found "Saint Nancy," but in this case she had used her "locator" skills to help this seeker (me) find exactly what I was looking for! We developed a friendship, and she willingly answered my persistent questions with long, involved, highly insightful and obviously caring emails. I was absolutely flabbergasted that she had spent SO much time answering me, someone she didn't know and from whom she had absolutely NOTHING to gain. The Holy Bible says to judge a tree by its fruit. OK, the point is well taken. How many people do YOU know who would spend such an inordinate amount of time answering the insipid queries of a total stranger? That's par for the course for this modern day mystic. Nancy Clark is the real deal.

Others appear to agree with that assessment, as evidenced by the fact that both of her previous works, Hear His Voice and My Beloved, won national book awards. Divine Moments is her third book, and it builds on that foundation of excellence while taking a new and expanded approach. The author has collected accounts of spiritually transformative experiences for over 30 years. Within these pages are approximately 45 such narratives. They comprise a rich mosaic of human testimony, running the gamut from seemingly ordinary to surprisingly profound. This fascinating collection of diverse anecdotes forms the majority of the book.

The remainder of the book includes several introductory and concluding chapters, all of which are written by Nancy Clark. It is here where she expresses her spiritual understanding in the most explicit and forceful terms yet. This is someone who had *both* a near-death experience and a spiritually transformative experience, which puts her in an essentially perfect position to author a book such as this one. She is intelligent, kind, deeply caring and trustworthy, and her message rings true.

Near-death experiences have long been recognized as highly

significant events that transform people's lives, and the literature about them is extensive and familiar. However, in this book, Nancy Clark describes an equally significant phenomenon, the spiritually transformative near-death-*like* experience. Her voice is now joined by a host of others, in a beautifully diverse and powerful testimony of hope and love. So, if you have ever wondered whether it's possible for "ordinary" people like you and me to experience the Divine *without* approaching death, you have found the answer in this book, and *that* is no mere coincidence either.

William W. Hoover, M.D.
Bettendorf, Iowa
September 11, 2011

The stories in this book were written by ordinary individuals whose reflections are rooted in their belief that their words will inspire us to revere the Life Force that generates life for all of us. Their words show us how the Divine is working through all of us for the good of humankind through our ordinary daily lives. Allow their words to take root in your soul so you can begin to see glimmers of transcendence scattered throughout your own life.

HARVEST
by
Robert E. Blackwell

A harvest is only possible
Through the spread of rain
Upon thirsty seeds.

So it is with words;
Only when given,
Like Heaven's dew drops,
Can one spread them upon
Thirsty minds and souls.

Thus, my sole promise is
The same as always:
To be the wind that
Carries the rain I am given
To wherever the seeds may lie.

Robert E. Blackwell's books of poetry are: Imagine That, My Flying Dreams, Sunshine for the Soul, Sunshine for the Soul Volume 2, and The Ten-Digit Poet. Order directly from the author at: www. randrblackwellbooks.com

CHAPTER 1

SETTING THE STAGE

*"Do not go where the path may lead, go instead where there
is no path and leave a trail."*

—Ralph Waldo Emerson

It is my strong belief that science will never be able to prove
the existence of God, and neither will science be able to prove
that God does not exist. Science will always stand neutral on
the subject. The inner world of experience and spirit is beyond
what we can learn through rational, empirical inquiry. So why
pursue the study of spiritually transformative experiences that I
have embarked upon, a study that points us in the direction of
the Divine?

First, let us define what spirituality is before going any further.
Spirituality is a term used to describe the relationship between
the person and a Higher Being, an experience that goes beyond
a specific religious affiliation. One of the goals of all religions is
the realization of God as having a transcendent uniqueness that
extends beyond the limitations of the mechanistic worldview.
However, religion tends to encourage separation by the creeds,
dogma, and rituals that can differ; spirituality on the other hand,
is being a conduit to serve the Divine by "walking the talk." It is
striving to live the highest ethical and moral existence possible -

living the laws of the authentic Reality through an inner wisdom that unfolds one's greatest potential. A religion of dogma and rituals isn't likely to be very satisfying. If you studied a musical score written on the sheet music you are holding in your hand and even if you memorized all the various notes, it would not compare with actually experiencing what that music sounds like when played by a full orchestra when you are seated near the front row. Spirituality should not be considered a point of superiority, only that it is qualitatively different from <u>thinking about</u> God or morality.

Next, what does transformation mean or more specifically, what does it mean to be spiritually transformed? Well, I'm sure you have had incidents in your life when an event happened that made you change your mind, your opinion, or your belief about something. We all have gone through those moments, transient as they may have been. However, it was a moment that moved us from one position to another.

To be spiritually transformed is similar in nature. The event or experience usually is sudden and has either a subtle or a dramatic effect upon one's values, behaviors, and motivations. This event or experience awakens a powerful inner sense of being that expands one's basis of reality and has lasting shifts of a sense of self and one's relationship to their worldview. The individual has a new understanding of their deepest assumptions about how to live or what has meaning for that individual. Usually the spiritual transformation that takes place within the individual calls them to live specific virtues such as truth, kindness, compassion, love and service. These experiences are varied and include near-death and near-death-like experiences, out-of-body experiences, after-death communications, spiritual awakenings, deathbed visions, religious conversion experiences, meditative and prayerful experiences, and mystical experiences.

It is estimated that nearly 15 million people in the United States have had a near-death experience and similar statistics from other countries around the world are being reported. This would mean that with a population of 6.6 billion people, there would be 330 million cases of near-death experiences worldwide. Even if we cut that statistic in half to mean that not all are spiritually transformed as a result of their experience, that's a lot of people who are being awakened to a new sense of self.

In 2004, the National Opinion Research Center at the University of Chicago found that 50% of Americans polled have had a spiritual or religious experience that changed their lives. This would mean that roughly 100 to 150 million Americans have had mystical, spiritual or religious experiences.

Another religion and spirituality poll conducted by Newsweek magazine in August 2005 found that 75 percent of all individuals considering themselves religious were searching for a more direct, personal ecstatic experience with the God of their understanding. It is not surprising that many religions are addressing this need in various ways using meditation, revivals, prayer, spiritual retreats, and so forth as tools to enhance the process of transcendence.

Evangelicals are looking for this experience in the "born again" or the "being saved' experiences. Catholics have the Cursillo movement. Jews search for it in Kabbalism and Hasidism. In the Islamic mystical tradition of Sufism, many Muslims search through contemplation. Speaking in tongues is a way that Pentacostals seek the Divine Presence more intimately. Buddhists seek it through meditation. This deep-rooted call of the soul to intimacy with the Divine is within every individual no matter what faith one practices.

Subjective, spiritually-transformative experiences are precious to most of the individuals who have them. On the one hand, their experiences have given new meaning to their lives, reverence, devotion, an impetus to humility and loving service to others. On the other hand, many are reluctant to open themselves fully to share those experiences which have such a profound effect upon their lives. They fear their experience will be labeled an illusion or delusion. Some persons are reluctant to share their stories because some scientists theorize that transcendent experiences can simply be attributed to hallucinations, and many other explanations that have been offered by skeptics. Who wants the most relevant, awe-inspiring and emotionally satisfying event of their lives dismissed as meaningless? So they keep these experiences to themselves, quietly moving on with their lives.

I began collecting accounts of individuals who had spiritually transformative experiences as early as 1980. As you will learn in the next chapter, I myself had a near-death experience during childbirth in the early 60's. And then years later in 1979, I had a near-death-like or mystical experience while delivering a eulogy for a dear friend at his funeral service. I began giving speaking engagements a few months after the 1979 event in order to witness to the fact that **there are other triggers besides coming close to death that produce this type of spiritually transcendent experience.** After my talks, there would always be one or two individuals who would approach me, and in a rather reticent manner would tell me they also had had the same type of experience as I while not being close to death at the time either. They too felt their experience was similar to a near-death experience, but they thought their experience "didn't count" because physically their body wasn't in deadly danger at the time. Didn't count? Oh my goodness! The most meaningful experience of their lives and they thought that only near-death experiencers had the credibility to talk about such life-changing experiences.

Thus began my interest in collecting accounts of individuals who were not close to death, suffering from serious illness or physical trauma at the time of their spiritually transformative experience. Cases were not easy to find. Studying experiences such as near-death is relatively easy. You can interview 100 cardiac-arrest patients in any given hospital, collect the data, and publish the findings quickly. Not so with ordinary waking individuals who aren't seriously ill and who haven't been hospitalized. They walk among us. They go to our church, synagogue or mosque; they attend our children's school events; they may sit next to us on an airplane. They are everywhere, but they aren't likely to reveal themselves unless they feel it is safe to open up and share their experience with someone who will understand them. Eventually however, I found them.

In addition to collecting accounts from my speaking engagements, I put several queries in *Vital Signs*, the newsletter of the International Association for Near-Death Studies, Inc. (IANDS). I also submitted a research query in *The Searchlight*, the publication of the Academy of Spirituality and Paranormal Studies, Inc., as well as on my website and by word of mouth. One hundred two subjects contacted me. Of those, thirty-four filled out a questionnaire I had compiled that asked them specific questions about their experience and its aftereffects. I want to be very clear: I did not apply the full range of tools in this research. I leave that to more qualified researchers. My job was to document the anecdotal accounts of those who were willing to share their experiences with me, in the hope that in doing so they would have something of value and importance to teach us.

I have a strong belief that in presenting this information it could alter our understanding of human nature and our spirit consciousness. The importance of such knowledge is to transcend the preoccupation with the ego self, and embrace the greater Self - the Self that experiences the immediate perception of our total unity with the Divine. The subjects in my study deserve to be respected for their willingness to open themselves fully, allowing others to shed their judgments and the walls that create the feeling of indifference and distance to which the rationalizing human mind is attached. The whole idea of this book, is after all about experiencing transcendence. Therefore, it is my hope that what these individuals have to teach us will be seen as beacons of light, in which we can be inspired to transcend our own limited thinking and begin to live from a higher consciousness of the sacredness of all life, and to know we are *all* miracles of being.

Besides the extraordinary transcendent experiences that are documented in these pages, I have also included the ordinary experiences that ordinary individuals have had; for they too, have poignant stories that express how they manage to merge their inner truths with the demands of everyday living. The movement of the Spirit, whether it is major or subtle, is made known to the individual through the human heart. It is a dynamic journey, that prompts the individual to see through the eyes of height-ened consciousness, experiencing everyday life as united with the Divine. I have even included a chapter on animals because they are some of our teachers of unconditional love, one of the most important features of a spiritual living being.

The contributors whose stories appear in this book have been chosen because they are responsible, sane, intelligent, often highly educated people who are acknowledged by their peers. Their stories appear as they wrote them. It is *their* voice I wanted the reader to hear, not an edited version of what they said. They come from all walks of life. They could be your next-door neighbor, your psychology professor, your physician, your public accountant. But they all have one thing in common: a bringing together of their inner and outer worlds, and thereby being guided to a destiny they couldn't have imagined.

Some contributors have elected to remain anonymous for privacy reasons. I deeply respect this need, and I have given them a pseudonym for this reason. Their stories, however, are genuine.

My Findings

As previously mentioned, one-hundred two individuals contacted me about my study. They either spoke to me or wrote to me about their experiences. Thirty-four individuals chose to complete the questionnaire I asked them to complete. Again, I wish to reiterate, this is not a statistically based study; rather, it is a general analysis of what was communicated to me by most of the one-hundred two participants. Some individuals chose to allow me to publish some of their answers to my research questionnaire in lieu of writing out their story, so you will have an opportunity to see some of the questions I proposed to them.

The ages of the subjects ranged from twenty-two to ninety-three years. Many of the subjects were children raised in a traditional religion, although several of them did not continue to practice that religion as early adults. Some could not reconcile a loving Creator with the evils and injustices in the world and, as a result, chose not to have anything to do with the religion they were brought up in. Others simply had vague reasons why they didn't continue to pursue their faith. A few became atheists. Still others, however, felt an increasing frustration with what appeared to be the lack of an authentic search for a deeper meaning and purpose in their lives. As if a dormant, wiser aspect of their being were calling them to begin their search, they simply opened their hearts to find the Divine. Some found their spiritual nourishment in Christianity, Judaism, and Buddhism. Overall, I could find no correlation between an individual's prior religious/spiritual beliefs or practices and their later, spiritually- transformative experience.

The subjects interviewed shared the following assertions about their experiences:

- Was "more real" than physical reality.
- Eludes description - no words were adequate to describe it.

- Ego boundaries, as defined in the ordinary state of consciousness, were transcended.
- A state of ecstatic union with the Creator, angels, otherworldly figures, Light, the cosmos.
- Strong feelings of bliss, joy, peace, and love.
- A feeling of transcending the limitations of time and space.
- What they experienced is said to have come from a different dimension other than the physical dimension.

The transformative effects upon the subjects differ, but generally they included:

- The existence of Heaven, God and celestial beings was no longer a matter of belief, but became a self-evident reality.
- No longer fear death.
- Became more compassionate and loving individuals.
- A stronger desire to help others and finding opportunities in all occasions of their lives to express outwardly into the world, their inner life force.
- Possessing more strength, power and grace to endure whatever was happening in their lives, regardless of the circumstances.
- A certain serenity that enabled them to know with certainty that the Creator's love is with them at all times.
- Some individuals were spontaneously healed physically or emotionally.
- Some individuals brought back knowledge of something they hadn't known about previously (spiritual - scientific).
- Deeper, more intimate connection with Mother Nature.
- Emotional and mental balance.

- Realizing the purpose of one's life.
- Feelings of renewed empowerment, inspiration, creativity and rekindled hope.
- Feelings of interconnectedness with the global community.
- Increased interest in spirituality- reading, studying, joining spiritual groups.
- Common saying: "I'm more spiritual, not religious."
- Acceptance of all religions as a path toward the Divine.
- Understanding that we are more than biological beings; we are spirits of consciousness that continue to exist beyond the physical dimension.
- Greater acceptance of each individual's right to choose or change his or her "path."

Some of the situations or triggers that preceded the transcendent experiences include:

- Being at rest, at work, or at play.
- Praying, meditating.
- Driving a car.
- During a dream
- Accidents, depression, medical issues.
- Watching television.
- Flying an airplane.
- Talking on the phone.
- Hearing a voice.
- Being struck by lightning.

The individuals in my research considered themselves to be more spiritual than religious. They regard everything as an important facet of their spiritual life. "Everything" includes not only prayer, sacred texts, and places of worship, but also family, friends, work, service to others, nature, and all aspects of one's daily life.

In other words, the Infinite cannot be put in a "closed box," to be opened only by adhering to the dogma and rules of certain religions. For my study participants, I found over and over again, it's as if their experience opened that box, and then they began to know the transcendence or the nearness of the Divine in their daily lives. They know that life is a continuum, and there are other realities more "real" than the physical one we inhabit. They know that the shift in their personal identity was not transitory, but permanent.

For most of the participants in my study, a "new" person evolved from this experience. A change in their sense of who they are affected everything else in their daily experience. When your sense of self expands, your heart expands. What happens in spiritually transformative experiences, is the ego releases itself, the veil has lifted, and one sees Reality as it is. The Reality of one's true self is beyond one's ability to make others fully comprehend what one has experienced. How can one begin to explain a consciousness of one's inner world to someone who has never experienced it? We TRY, and we do the best we can!

What causes spiritually transformative experiences? In my opinion, I believe it comes to us by Grace when we are ready to receive it and act upon the responsibility that accompanies it. I believe it is brought about from the deeper and truer part of our Being, the Light within, the guiding greater Wisdom and Intelligence of life itself. I believe in a benevolent evolutionary process that guides us toward our highest potential as human beings. I say this because I personally have experienced the transcendent Reality, and can therefore speak from a perspective of knowledge, rather than speculation. Because the transcendent spiritually transformative experience is a path "home" to our innermost true self, the richness and indescribable beauty of

STE's come by Grace when we are ready to receive + to act on the accompanying responsibility.

Reality blossoms, and one realizes that everything is held in God's tender embrace. Irrespective of our religious beliefs, we remain a part of the universal spiritual energy that is the true basis of reality.

I've written this book to show not only the many different situations that can connect one to the timeless spiritual dimension, but also to look at the ways in which the world of spiritual *meaning* may open up to us. As our spirituality deepens, we begin to live out our highest ideals, because we come to recognize that we carry within us the seeds of latent qualities that awaken us to our meaning and purpose in life. The individual who is truly transformed will be working out a part of the Divine Plan through Divine attributes that are brought through consciousness from soul perception - which is more lasting and real than any bodily experience. In the end, the only conclusion we can make regarding one's spiritually transformative experience are the words written in the Bible: *"By their fruits ye shall know them."*

CHAPTER 2

TWICE AT HEAVEN'S DOOR

The Author's Experience

"Everything is shown up by being exposed to the light, and whatever is exposed to the light itself becomes light.

—Saint Paul Ephesians 5:14

True stories can entertain people with their associated drama, especially when those stories deal with life after death. Who doesn't want to know what lies beyond the beyond? A natural curiosity abounds, and we are drawn to such stories, hoping that one day we will each transcend this earthly realm, and find the reassurance that our faith in an afterlife was correct after all. Or, that our cynicism and disbelief were in error.

Without directly experiencing a Heavenly realm for ourselves, we are left to read and listen to the stories of those who have gone before us. That is why I am putting to paper my own journey to Heaven, with the hope that it will inspire others to think deeply about their own mortality and more importantly, that in sharing my experience with others, it may help to build a bridge in understanding that our mortal and eternal lives have meaning and purpose.

I do not wish to *entertain* you with my story. I wish simply to share what happened to me. Nor do I wish to preach to anyone, or try to convince you that I have all the answers to life's most difficult questions. I don't, and neither does anyone else. What was ultimate truth for ME, may not be your truth. I ask only that you give me respect for my personal interpretation of my own experience. After all, I was there! Therefore, I am my own expert on my own experiences. No one else can be that expert on someone else's experiences, no matter how learned that individual may be.

Where do I begin? I guess at the beginning. In the early 1960's, I died while giving birth to my son, and I had a near-death experience. I developed eclampsia of pregnancy characterized by high blood pressure, edema, and convulsions that resulted in my death. My physician was going to admit me to the hospital one month prior to delivery because I had already begun to have serious symptoms, but he ultimately changed his mind, thinking I would be safe enough to wait until labor began. Obviously, I was not alright.

Once labor began and I was admitted to the hospital, something apparently went very wrong. Though my eyelids were shut, I witnessed the medical staff in the hospital trying to revive me. But I had no interest in what they were doing to my body lying motionless on the delivery table below. By then, my spirit-self had lifted out of my physical body and had entered a dark void. The darkness did not frighten me, because I was experiencing the rapture of a love so pure, radiating from a Light Source streaming down toward me. I felt ecstatic at seeing this Light, and I felt drawn to it like a magnet. "Yes, yes! I want to go with the Light, wherever the Light would take me," I thought. Bliss was the only feeling saturating my spirit-body as the Light's love was streaming toward me. How could I want anything more than this? Never! Never!

The nurse kept pounding on my chest shouting "Come

back, Nancy, come back!" I absolutely did not want to come back to my physical body down on the delivery table. The Light was calling me upwards, toward itself, with a love that shatters one's imagination.

Over and over again, the nurse kept pounding on my chest shouting, "Come back, Nancy, you have a son." I listened to her incessant voice, and I felt no desire to return. She was interfering with my bliss, and the journey with the Light that I so wanted to continue to follow. I felt no connection to the physical body of "Nancy" below. In fact, I viewed the body as if I were looking at a coat I no longer needed or wanted. I was still very much alive, although in a different form and reality. I made a very painful and reluctant decision to return back to my physical body, solely to stop the nurse's incessant nagging!

When I regained physical consciousness, the immediate awareness I had was lying on a cold metal surface with a sheet covering my entire body. I pulled the sheet down over my face and glanced to my right where I saw another body lying motionless on a metal gurney with a sheet covering its entire body the same way I was. I believe I was in a morgue. I blacked out at that point, and regained consciousness later, in a different hospital room. After questioning my physician about what happened, (I didn't tell him what I'd experienced because at that time, no one spoke about near-death experiences. The term hadn't been coined yet. Had I mentioned to my physician what I'd seen, I would have been sent to the mental ward. So I kept quiet.)

My doctor refused to tell me what had occurred. When I persisted in questioning him, he said, "Look, I'm an excellent physician. If I tell you what happened, it would cause such severe psychological trauma that you would never, ever want to have children again. You want to have children again, don't you?" he asked. "Hmm, yes," I replied. "Okay then, from this moment on, move forward with your life and don't look back. Forget what happened," he told me sternly as he patted me on my shoulder.

From that moment on, I knew it was useless to talk to him, so I did what he told me to do and never told a soul after that.

Years later I had my medical records reviewed and discovered that they apparently were altered (I presume), to report that I had a "normal delivery;" no mention was made that anything was amiss. But I know what happened, and no one can take that truth away from me. I think it was easier for the hospital to report nothing out of the ordinary than to risk a law suit. That is my personal opinion. Remember, this was during the early 1960's when we didn't have the privacy acts and regulations that we have now. I am suggesting that it was relatively easy to cover up this incident. I say that because what I experienced **happened**! It is still as vivid today as if it had happened yesterday. It was no hallucination; or a story conjured up by me.

Years later, I had another Heavenly experience, this time deeper, richer, and more extensive than my first near-death experience. What I shall describe from this point on, is the most sacred and transformative experience of my entire life. I believe that my first near-death experience "opened me" in some deeper, more sensitive manner to prepare me for this second experience. This time however, I did not have to die first, or suffer from illness or physical trauma, in order to have this most sacred experience. The Light apparently wanted to come to me again with a purpose, and this time I was ready to receive the Light without interference by anyone or anything.

Near-death experience researchers call this type of transcendent experience a "near-death-like" experience, or a spiritually transformative experience, meaning that an average, healthy, and fully conscious human being can have the *identical experience* as someone who was close to death at the time of their transcendent experience. PMH Atwater, one of the world's leading near-death researchers, said on her website that my experience "was every bit as light-filled and wondrous as the most amazing of near-death experiences. Technically, her episode would be labeled a "near-death-like" experience." There are many triggers to this type of mystical experience, coming close to death is only one trigger.

If this sounds bizarre to you, it is only because the general public has very little information about near-death-like experiences. But in fact throughout history, there have been reports of saints, mystics, prophets, and others who had this type of transcendent experience without coming close to death. The historical literature is filled with these accounts.

My particular experience is often compared to the Apostle Paul's experience on the road to Damascus. A Heavenly Light appeared before Paul and commanded him to begin a life of spiritual service. Upon seeing this Heavenly Light, Paul was forever transformed, and began his ministry without reservation, not fearing what others would think or what they would do to him. It is this supernatural power of the Heavenly Light that raises the individual's own personal power to transcend all obstacles in one's path, because the truth of that encounter with the Holy One supersedes any perceived limitations, doubts, or fear. What ultimately becomes the "mission" of the one who has touched the hem of the Beloved, is loving service to something greater than oneself. This is precisely what happened to Paul and this is precisely what happened to me.

Remember this please: When the Divine wants to intervene in our lives, it is done in a supernatural way, so powerful, so truthful, that our finite minds cannot dismiss it as a hallucination, wishful thinking or something similar. No, the experience is REAL, more REAL than the physical reality we presently inhabit. Unless one has had this experience, one cannot understand this. But for the one who has had it, no words can adequately express it.

I was taken up into the Heavenly Realm on January 29, 1979. During that event, I experienced the identical components of a classic near-death experience, with the exception that I was not close to death at the time, suffering from serious illness or physical trauma. I was merely delivering a eulogy at a friend's funeral.

I was perfectly healthy, thirty-eight years old, and not taking drugs of any kind. I was not mentally unstable. In fact, for many years I was working at a major university teaching cytology, the study of cells and doing cancer research. Later on, I went into clinical diagnostic work. Someone who is functioning at such a high level of intelligence and living a healthy and happy life at the time of the experience isn't someone you would consider mentally unstable. The opposite is true of someone who is mentally unbalanced. The person is usually depressed, has difficulty with human relationships, often has difficulty holding a job and usually doesn't see their life to be fulfilling in any way.

This is my true story and I have not deviated once from this account nor have I embellished it in any way. It is the same factual story I told in 1979 to friends, family, researchers, during my speaking engagements, more fully in the book I wrote, _Hear His Voice_ and to anyone who will listen. Only the words will change in describing the experience, but the content remains intact. I am about to show you that there is another trigger mechanism other than coming close to death that produced the same experience as a near-death experience. It is the term, near-death experience that is misleading since other triggers can produce the identical experience!

As I stood at the podium delivering the eulogy, the Light that I had seen years before during my near-death experience during childbirth appeared again. My physical body and physical consciousness continued to all present to be performing the task of speaking the eulogy. But another aspect of my consciousness, the part I call my spirit-self, lifted out of my physical body, entered into the otherworldly dimension and into the consciousness of the Light of God.

We already know from years of scientific research in the study of near-death experiences that the soul, higher self, spirit, or consciousness, is not dependent upon the physical body for its survival. It has been shown that even when the physical body has experienced clinical death, the consciousness of the individual continues to exist outside of the body. Individuals have witnessed, and described in great detail, events that were taking place while they were clinically dead. These events including the conversations that others were having were later confirmed as having happened as described.

This is strong evidence that one's consciousness continues to survive **independently of the physical brain and body.** Therefore, it is probable to conclude that one's consciousness can also transcend the physical body and continue to exist and experience one's conditions as I did while delivering the eulogy.

The moment my spirit-self entered the otherworldly dimension, I became aware that the physical reality I had just came from was an *illusion*, and the otherworldly dimension I just entered was the REAL reality. That was an awesome light-bulb realization.

As hard as I try to convey the image of the Light to others, I cannot do it justice. Words are inadequate. Brilliant, luminous, all-embracing- pick an adjective and it is pale in comparison to the wholly mystical illumination I was perceiving. My physical eyes did not see this Light; it was my soul's eyes that beheld the majesty of an ineffable glory. It was a moment of great beauty and ECSTASY permeating my whole being. I saw myself in my true radiance, as a precious gem, and most certain of my Divine heritage.

Unconditional love was pouring into my soul, the likes of which I have never experienced. No love on the face of the earth can compare with the unconditional love of the Light. Healed in a nanosecond of all illusions I'd previously held about myself- the low self-esteem, guilt, an inability to love myself fully - I now received the most precious gift from the Light: it showed me how LOVED I am, with no strings attached! The awesome realization was that I was loved no more and no less than anyone else. Children of the Light were loved EQUALLY - no strings attached!

The Light infused itself into my being, so that I became one with the Light; there was no separation. We were ONE. I knew "who" the Light was. It was as if my soul-memory had revealed that knowledge the instant I saw the Light. I understood at my soul level that it was the Light of God. I was back in the loving arms of my Creator! How ecstatic I felt to be "home" again: the place I had come from and where I will once again return when my life on earth is through. I entered the ultimate destination of my true being, and the JOY I felt cannot be measured.

All the while I was merged into Oneness with the Light of God, communication took place telepathically, and everything was happening simultaneously because time as we know it was absent. Traveling at a tremendous rate of speed, the Light and I traveled through the dark universe and I witnessed at least 11 dimensions that are quite different from the physical world of matter that we live in. I have no words to describe this.

As the Light and I passed through the many different dimensions, we arrived at the beginning of the creation of the universe. Infused into my consciousness was the understanding that the Light was the Supreme and sole Creator of the universe. I understood that the Light was the starting point of everything ever created. To my amazement, I learned that the Light was living *energy,* the sum total of and infinite energy of the created and uncreated cosmos. Until that very moment, that knowledge had not been part of my belief system. I had always envisioned the Creator to be a male with a long white robe and a long white beard. The Creator that I was merged into oneness with was an infinite loving Being of *Light energy* that cannot be conceptualized. It proved to me that humanity has an extremely limited view of who or what the Creator is.

The Light showed me that the very first created form emerged from the Light as a spark of itself, and that all of creation - everything - from the atoms, molecules, quarks, has at its core, the spark of the Creator's Light. This spark is a very pure and perfect form of *spiritual energy, or Divine Love*. It's power is greater than our limited awareness can imagine or comprehend. I had a vision of seeing mankind in its current evolutionary state of being symbolized spiritually as being in the caveman era. Just as the caveman discovered the energy and power of fire and ultimately evolved to a higher state of being, I saw that mankind today has the potential to discover lying within themselves, the ultimate energy and power of Divine Light and Love. Discovering and utilizing this knowledge would be the catalyst for a new evolutionary world where Heaven on earth will be realized. This knowledge was a profound lesson that the Light was teaching me. I thought, all we have to do is to *awaken* to the realization of who we are at the core of our being - LIGHT and LOVE, and express that outwardly, unconditionally, into the world. That message resonated loud and clear. I understood that was the bottom line. That was humankind's destination! What a powerful light-bulb moment was for me.

My deceased friend (for whom my physical body was delivering the eulogy) stood beside me, held my hand and let me know he was alright and very happy. I had no reason to grieve for him any longer. All took place through an enhanced perception apart from my physical body and physical consciousness. My spirit-self which is all knowing, saw that my deceased friend was still alive, although in a different form, invisible to others living in our conventional reality.

In that Heavenly realm I comprehended everything that was communicated to me by the Light as absolute truth. I didn't have to question or doubt anything that was said or what I was experiencing.

I was given a life review. Prior to this experience, I believed that when we die- since God has been keeping a record of our good and bad deeds-if we have been very bad we would go to Hell. If we had been very good, we would go to Heaven and be loved by God.

My life review was so different from those expectations. The Light of God was loving me through all the scenes of my human life without casting judgment. <u>I was judging myself</u>, as I witnessed events in my life when I had not loved myself or others. The most important criterion for judging my life review was this: how well had I used my life to love myself and others? Was I a Light bearer, or a Light extinguisher?

Comprehending that truth was crystal clear as I began to learn that humans have the spark of the Light/God within every soul. It is the releasing of that Light energy or Divine love that makes a holy difference in the world, one person at a time, in each person's little corner of the world, through their relationships with one another.

My life review was rather painful, as I witnessed ALL the times when I'd withheld my love from others because of anger, frustration, vindictiveness, or apathy. I realized I'd had so **many opportunities** every single day to be a vessel of Light and love but failed. I also saw the times when I hadn't loved myself. As painful as that was to me, the Light of God was loving me throughout this life review, knowing that I was learning a great lesson realizing the importance of loving myself and others. "I will try not to make the same mistakes again, now that I know better," I thought.

"God, I want to stay with you forever!" I shouted. I knew I had to disconnect from my physical body, that woman who was delivering the eulogy at the same time my spirit-self was embraced in the arms of the Beloved. So I contemplated giving "Nancy" a heart attack.

Q: How well h t used my life to love myself t others?
Light bearer or Light extinguisher?
opportunities e day

"NO, No," I heard the Light of God firmly telling me. "You can't stay, you have to go back and tell others what you learned while you were here with me." At that point, I was ready and more than willing to return back to the physical dimension in order to fulfill the purpose to which God was calling me. In fact, I was deliriously enthralled to be able to use my life to bring honor and glory to the One who'd called me to Heaven's door to bear witness to this miraculous encounter with the Beloved. The love I had for God during this experience was so enormous that I wanted to do anything the Light told me to do…anything! Using my life to fulfill this service to God would be my gift back to my Great Teacher. "YES, YES! I will gladly return to the earth plane to embark upon my mission for you God, YES!" I breathlessly cried out.

"Wait a minute, dear child. Before you make your decision, you must know what your life will be like, should you accept this calling," I heard my Great Teacher tell me. I was then given a life-preview of what my "mission" would be, the details of my work for the Light. Yes, it would certainly be challenging, as I viewed this life-preview. But I was reassured that the Light would never leave me, and we would work together as a team in getting this "mission" completed. I was told, *"As long as you hold onto my hand and don't let go, I shall lead, you shall follow; the path ahead of you shall be prepared for you."*

I was so lovingly embraced by the Light's unconditional love and with the promise of faithfulness to me and to the work I would carry out for God that I had no hesitation at all in making my decision. My soul was bursting with passion to serve the One who had gifted me with new life, new purpose, and new love which I carry with me to this day.

When I made my decision to go ahead with this endeavor, the Light flooded my consciousness with ultimate knowledge. I knew everything there was to know, past, present, and future. Every word and every thought that was or ever will be spoken or written was made known to me. I was not permitted to remember all that knowledge upon my return to the physical dimension, however; only parts of it. This is what all near-death experiencers report as well, in the thousands of cases that have been studied by researchers. This is one of the classic, across-the-board, similarities in over thirty years of scientific research, revealing this common thread among experiencers.

With regard to this issue PMH Atwater, noted near-death experience researcher, wrote an article: (*When NDE "Truths" Are in Conflict...* in the International Association for Near-Death Studies, Inc. publication, "Vital Signs" Vol. XXVIII, No 4, 2008) in which she states, *"no single experiencer* can supply all the answers! The power of the near-death phenomenon and what it can tell us can best be found through a synthesis or summary of the many. True, just being around an experiencer, or reading experiencer books, can be life-changing. I grant you that. But transferring to any experiencer the role of speaking for everyone else or being the best speaker or having the most to say or holding the record for the most harrowing case or being the most angelic or gifted or blessed or verified or stunning, is tantamount to self-deception. Guess who is fooling whom?"

Atwater recognized this ego-inflation among - and I quote - "some of today's new crop of near-death experiencers who are far too willing to come across as blanket authorities on the subject, and they are equally much too anxious to present 'one-size-fits-all' answers to life's greatest questions." She added, "It's a tricky day when we allow others to determine what is right for us. That can only be determined by you through a process of prayer, meditation, deep thought, testing (questioning), and letting go or surrendering to what many call 'The God Within.' I couldn't agree more with Atwater, as this is exactly what was revealed to me during my experience with the Light of God.

I respect Atwater's investigative work immensely in this field of consciousness study. So I support her opinion on this particular topic of ego-inflation. You see, my Great Teacher taught me something that Atwater apparently senses as well, and what apparently led her to write the article. Let me explain.

One of the greatest light-bulb moments during my experience occurred when I learned that *the smallest acts of kindness were immense* acts, spiritually speaking. Why? Simply because the ego is not involved in those acts. We do them simply because we are motivated by our "inner voice" to do them. It is the **loving thing to do!** We do not expect a pat on the back, or any type of reciprocity for doing that small act. In fact, we don't even think we are doing anything of any great significance when we do it. This is a HUGE, HUGE, spiritual deed and something my Great Teacher, the Light of God wanted me to help people realize. Because when we unselfishly do this, we are expressing through us, the Light into the world. The LIGHT!!! Every day there are countless ways of elevating ourselves to a higher and a more Divine Light-embodied soul-being, simply by responding to the love within us through doing small acts of kindness.

As I said earlier, during my life review I was shown ALL moments in my life when I'd chosen not to express loving kindness. Please, please don't make the same mistake I did! It is painful to review such moments, when we should have acted lovingly but didn't.

On the flip side, I was also taught by my Great Teacher that the ego is self-serving. Ego wants to be top-dog at any cost. Ego wants to elevate itself to a superior position over someone else, and ego will find all sorts of ways to trick self and others into believing this is fine. Ego will always try to pull one **away** from God, because its interest is serving **self** first and foremost, even though the individual may think he/she is not acting from an ego nature. Ego wants to shine. It wants to puff itself up by claiming to know more than others when it comes to spiritual truths. Ego wants praise and attention from others. Ego is a sly thing!

This was also such a light-bulb moment for me during my experience. Apparently my Great Teacher felt this ego stuff was very important for me to comprehend and to then tell others about, since our culture is so wrapped up in it and we aren't aware that ego should have no part in developing our true spiritual nature. Our "true self" is selflessness, that Divine aspect of ourselves shining into the world as LIGHT. I was taught that our lives here on earth are meant to learn how to express love unconditionally, without ego-attachment. So when we have our life reviews, we see those moments when we allowed our egos to be top-dog, and did not live from the LIGHT, expressing our authentic Spirit-self into the world.

Again, this knowledge is what I experienced as MY truth as revealed to me by the Light of God. I do not intend it to be everyone's truth unless it rings true, deep within yourself. I am simply passing on what my Great Teacher revealed to me to share with others.

Another interesting facet of my experience was the appearance of twelve guides who collectively chose to assist me with my "mission" upon returning back to the Earth dimension. All were seated around a long wooden table, and all were dressed in what appeared to be monk's robes. All but three had their hoods pulled over their faces so I could not see who they were. However, the three to my right had their faces exposed to me. I had never seen these three individuals before. However, a fascinating thing happened after I returned from my experience. A few years later, synchronicity would draw these individuals to me. Upon seeing them, I "recognized" them from my experience, but never told them about their promise to help me fulfill my calling for the Light. Why? Simply because I knew that their souls knew what they had promised to do, and when the time was right, they would help me in whatever way they were called to. If I'd told them about their part in my life's mission, their egos might feel obligated to help me in some way. No, I knew their ego-less souls knew what to do, when to do it, and how to do it without any interference from me. That is precisely what happened over the years since my experience. It was truly amazing to witness this "plan" unfolding in my life, and to be grateful for all the help they did indeed give me without realizing they were part of my Heavenly experience to begin with.

I never told these three individuals until very recently that they were present during my experience. I felt they should be thanked appropriately for all the help I was given through the ensuing years. I don't know if the other remaining guides have appeared in my life to help me with my calling. Certainly, I have felt some strong connections with some people, and thought perhaps they may have been part of this plan for my life. But since their faces were not revealed to me during my experience, I have no certainty at this time that they were with me during my experience. Strong suspicion, but no proof. I hold all twelve of these guides in my heart and soul for all eternity. What greater gift of love can there be than to come to this earthly realm to help someone in this way? To choose to leave Paradise for this earthly realm to help others is the utmost sacrifice I can think of. God bless all those who have chosen to do this!

The experience was winding down at this point, and as the Light and I were still merged into oneness we began to travel back to the Earth. I was allowed to witness all the chaos in the world, but I understood that everything was working according to some greater plan that humans did not comprehend. I understood that even the most horrendous acts had meaning and purpose. Don't ask me to explain this; I can't, because I left the spiritual realm and I'm now back in the physical realm with all the humanness that living here on this Earth plane encompasses. I too, have questions…big questions about suffering, and why things happen to good people. But I must say, while I was merged into oneness with the Light of God, I truly did understand that everything makes perfect sense on a spiritual level. **Every experience we have**

is a stepping stone toward our greatest good and our ultimate spiritual growth. Yes, even the tragic experiences. That recall helps me to not dwell so much on the answers that would make sense of this suffering, for I know that when I return to that Heavenly Realm, I will once again understand EVERYTHING and why those tragic experiences were needed! Until then, I will be patient and trust in a Higher Power who loves us through our suffering, who cries with us, and who gives us the strength to move through it.

Gradually, a separation between the Light of God and me began to occur, as I felt my spirit-self beginning to return to my physical form - which was still delivering the eulogy. Before the separation was completed however, the Light of God spoke one last word to me: "Book." Immediately placed deep into the innermost part of my heart was the knowledge that part of my "mission" here on earth would be to write a book, and to communicate all that my Great Teacher taught me during those fifteen minutes I journeyed to the Heavenly Realm. Passion beyond passion was infused into my heart to fulfill the promise I made at that time to God to write that book.

Then, the greatest sorrow of my life transpired, as I watched the Light distance itself further and further from me, allowing my spirit to re-enter my physical body to finish up the last sentence of the eulogy. I cannot describe the intense sorrow I experienced knowing the Light was leaving. But at the same time, I understood that this parting was only temporary, that one day I would once again reunite with the love of my life, the Light of God, in that Heavenly Realm I had just journeyed to. And this time, I want it to be PERMANENT!

What happened following that miraculous experience? Well, just as my life preview showed me, I lost all my friends because they thought I was crazy. My family didn't believe me either. Some people mocked me as I told them about my experience. A Baptist minister told me never to speak of this experience again because Satan was working through me. He quoted the Biblical passage, "Satan can be disguised as an angel of Light." Did that stop me from sharing this story? No way! I have to answer to someone greater than my ego-self. The Light of God is all that matters to me. Fulfilling my calling is my gift back to God, no matter what I have to go through. The skeptics and nay-sayers will one day enter that transcendent realm, and they will find out for themselves that what I tried to tell them was true after all. Other parts of my life-preview came true as well, and for those parts I am extremely grateful.

The aftereffects of this miraculous life-transforming experience were felt immediately. I was filled to overflowing with love for everyone as soon as I finished speaking the eulogy. Perfect strangers were perceived as my family, that's how intense my love for everyone was. Rather than experiencing myself as a separate physical form apart from all the rest of creation, I felt the illusion of my separate self simply melt away. I loved everyone and everything with an immense transformed consciousness. Shortly after I finished the eulogy several people came up to me and told me that while I was speaking, they witnessed a white glow all over the outline of my body. I didn't tell anyone what happened to me except my family immediately afterwards, and to my dismay, they didn't believe me. To be honest, I don't think I would have believed someone who told this story either. But it DID happen.

I should note that at that time, I had never heard of Raymond Moody, M.D., his book, *Life After Life*, or the term 'near-death experience.' Also of note is my lack of any knowledge pertaining to religion, the Bible, philosophy, new-age material or mysticism. My main interest at that time in my life was being a wife, a mother, a cancer researcher and community volunteer. The only thing I knew for certain was that the Light and I merged into was the **SAME LIGHT** I'd encountered during my first near-death experience years earlier. That was absolute! There is only one *true* ←
reality that all beings will eventually experience. Everyone will

only one TRUE REALITY + all will eventually experience

experience that true reality after the biological body expires. But since I experienced that reality twice, once upon my death and the other during normal awakening, I am in a good position to compare both - and there is no difference. Ultimate reality is the same, no matter what trigger releaser brought one to it.

My life changed dramatically following my experience. The Light of God became the center of my being. In reality, the Light never left me. I still have the acute awareness of the Divine Presence within me; I feel a thirst for the Divine that is unquenchable. I became very passionate in fulfilling my "mission" for the Light of God, by writing and speaking of what my Great Teacher taught me while I was on the other side of the veil. However, I am not a "religious fanatic." I do not pressure anyone into believing or accepting anything that does not feel appropriate for them or feels genuinely meaningful to them. I merely share what happened to me, and what I learned while merged into oneness with the Light of God. I respect a person's free will to believe, or not to believe, that which comes from the deepest part of my heart and soul. This so-called "mission" was what the Light instructed me to do, and I promised I would do this until I draw my last breath.

I no longer fear death; I have an appreciation for the beauty of life and feel very close to nature, especially animals. I have a loving concern for others and a desire to help others. I founded the Columbus, Ohio Friends-of- IANDS group in 1984, (International Association of Near-Death Studies) and continue to serve as its president. It is a wonderful organization dedicated to providing individuals with support, information and research about near-death and similar experiences. There has also been an increase in my psychic development, including the ability to heal. Writing became a wonderful gift I received afterwards, no doubt to help me with my so-called "mission," to share the realizations I was gifted with while enshrouded in the ecstasy of the Light of God. My first two books both won national awards.

Before this experience, I had never had any desire to write, nor did I have the ability to write. All gratitude goes to the Light of God, who inspires me to write in order to serve others in the manner I was instructed.

I give presentations to help educate the general public about the many different triggers that can produce near-death and near-death-like experiences. I lost interest in materialism, and I cherish personal relationships. Rather than pursuing my ego needs, I have relied mostly upon the Divine Presence within me to guide me through life, and this has resulted in a very stable and meaningful life for me. Humility and gratitude are huge features of my daily life. I can honestly admit that most of the time I am in a state of joy and peace even through the trials and tribulations of daily life.

Through my transcendent mystical experience, my soul has revealed its true identity, the revelation of the Divine Presence within. While it is true that I have walked forward into a new life, a life of JOY, a life of peace, a life of grace, it is my hope that we can all walk together with our arms around each other's shoulders, and allow ourselves to feel the Spirit within ourselves. There is no separation; there is only oneness. Let pure love guide us to new levels of Light, for Light **IS** God.

CHAPTER 3

NEAR-DEATH AND NEAR-DEATH-LIKE EXPERIENCES - WHAT'S THE DIFFERENCE?

"We can easily forgive a child who is afraid of the dark. The real tragedy of life is when men are afraid of the light."

—Plato

For over thirty years, researchers have studied the near-death experience to the exclusion of many other trigger processes that resemble the near-death experience. Coming close to death is only *one* means of having such spiritually transformative mystical experiences. This book will show you many other triggers.

During the months following my near-death-like experience, I began to notice media reports about people who had very similar experiences to mine. The only difference was that they were close to death at the time. Theories about the cause of this experience, termed a near-death experience, were coming from physicians, scientists, theologians. It seemed that everyone had a theory or the answer to what caused this transcendent phenomenon, and the theorizing still continues. Each time I heard someone determine that the cause of a near-death experience was due to either a dying brain, lack of oxygen to the brain, anesthesia, other drugs, I wanted to scream, "foul-ball!" **It can't** be due to those factors since I am living proof that I had the identical experience and I wasn't close to death at the time! My brain was functioning clearly; there was no lack of oxygen to my brain while I was delivering the eulogy. I didn't have anesthesia, and I wasn't taking any drugs whatsoever at that time.

There must be some other theory to explain this type of transcendent, mystical experience! I suggest the cause of the experience is not a product of brain activity as many neurophysiologists contend. Mind or soul is outside the brain. It's not related to brain function at all. It is non-physical, cannot be known by the senses, nor reconciled with science or reason. Spirit or mind is more intrinsic to reality than matter. The Greater Mind/God/Source/Creator cannot be put under a microscope for our finite ego minds to dissect and comprehend its nature. No human being can know the mind of God, only that which the Creator itself reveals.

Although *true reality*, as experienced by mystics, near-death experiencers, and others is mysterious, we have the benefit of learning from their wisdom and their experiences. They tell us that our true nature is one with the Infinite, the Supreme, and it is our birthright to discover and learn that truth. Why? I believe the individuals who have such spiritually transformative experiences are the pioneers of a new humanity, ushering in a new awakening that eventually will bring heaven upon earth. It won't happen overnight, in fact, it may take centuries, but I do believe one day we will all live in peace. Perhaps that is wishful thinking, but on the other hand, I have to acknowledge that there are transformations taking place in the hearts and souls of millions of people who have had these spiritually transformative experiences. There must be a reason for this massive escalation toward the development of higher consciousness. Perhaps, it is the Divine plan after all, the foundation of which is LOVE.

William James, M.D., one of America's most eminent psychologists and philosophers (1842-1910) once said, "In order to disprove the law that all crows are black, it is enough to find one white crow." Well folks, I am, or my near-death-like experience is a white crow. If you look carefully at it and compare it to the other black crows (near-death experiences), you will see that a white crow flies the same as black crows, eats the same foods, nests the same way, has the same blood coursing through its body, etc. The only difference is the *color*. But that color difference (or the triggers that can spark transcendent experiences) do not make all crows different. **All** crows are the same! Science has studied the near-death experience for over thirty years now, but little attention has been focused on the many other trigger mechanisms that allow the same type of experience to occur in many individuals. Too often, the scientific method has ignored or brushed aside the crows who are white, only to focus their attention on black crows.

I must however, mention a few praise-worthy researchers who included the subject of near-death-like experiences in their books. Kenneth Ring, PhD, considered the world's eminent near-death experience researcher, wrote about my experience in his books, *Heading Toward Omega*, (1984), and Lessons From the Light, (1998). To quote Dr. Ring from the Foreword he wrote for my book, *Hear His Voice*.

"When Nancy went on to describe the aftereffects of her particular experience, they were identical to those that had been reported by the near-death experiencers I drew on for my book [Heading for Omega]. Thus, Nancy had, seemingly inadvertently, provided just the sort of evidence I needed to make the argument I was then developing in this book (Heading Toward Omega), namely, that one didn't have to be near-death to have the kind of spiritual insights that are typical of near-death experiences, and that, furthermore, the transformations that follow them, as Nancy's case showed me, can also occur without coming close to death. Therefore, as

Nancy rightly claims in her own book, the trigger or releaser for the experience is irrelevant. What happens to you during the experience is what matters, not what brings you into it."

Several other near-death experience researchers also described my experience in their books. Charles P. Flynn, PhD, author of *After The Beyond* (1986) and Barbara Harris Whitfield, author of *Spiritual Awakenings*.

PMH Atwater, another renowned near-death researcher also wrote of my experience in a chapter on the near-death-like experience in her book, *Beyond The Light*, (2009). At the chapter's conclusion, she writes, *"When we take a deeper look at the phenomenon we are investigating, it becomes apparent that there is a great deal of information current research does not address."* I agree with Atwater, and that's why I am writing this book in order to get this information out to the general public.

Also in her book, *The Complete Idiot's Guide to Near-Death Experiences*, (2000), she has a chapter on "Near-Death Look-a-Likes" and in her updated version, *The Big Book of Near-Death Experiences* (2007), and in her latest book, *Near-Death Experiences: The Rest of the Story*, (2011).

I commend these researchers for bringing attention to other triggers which launch near-death-like experiences. But more work needs to be done in this field. The general public has very little information that experiences that mimic the near-death experience can be triggered by ordinary events such as meditating, walking, sleeping, praying, etc. Individuals who are brave enough to share this type of experience with others are too often regarded as crazy or fanatical. The gifts they wish to share with us are stifled.

Do you recall what it was like for near-death experiencers before Raymond Moody, M.D. brought that phenomenon to public attention? Experiencers were afraid to tell anyone, for fear of being labeled deluded or even mentally ill. It wasn't until we educated the public about such experiences that it became easier for near-death experiencers to share their stories. The media went wild trying to get the latest stories to broadcast and publish. Suddenly, it wasn't a "secret" any longer.

I can recall a telephone call I received one day following a newspaper article written about me and the experience I'd had. A 97 year old woman read that article and felt she had to contact me. She spoke softly on the phone, and told me that she had had a near-death experience during childbirth, and I was the first person she had told. She had been afraid to tell anyone what she experienced. She wept as she recounted the love of the Light and what she had experienced. I wept with her. She told me that after all these years of keeping that experience to herself, she could now close her eyes for eternity with the peace she now felt after telling me about it. Bless her heart. I will never forget her or the validation she received in knowing that others experienced what she did, and that she was finally able to tell another human being about it without being judged crazy.

My point is this. There are many other non-near-death experiencers who have had similar experiences but who are afraid to speak about them. They are in the same boat that early near-death experiencers were in facing ridicule and skepticism when little information was available to the general public about such experiences. It would be wonderful if we could embrace all those who can bear witness to the transcendent nature of reality, so that no one gifted with those experiences would have to be fearful of ridicule any longer. That is the reason we must get this information to the public. Ordinary people are having these spiritually transformative experiences, and they aren't crazy.

Science and the media have spent a great deal of time focusing upon the events leading up to the actual moment of the near-death experience, to lend support that this experience is authentic. And because of that, a lot of interest has been shown in this type of transcendent experience. There is a lot of drama associated with the near-death events that occur while the individual is still present in the physical dimension. Medical procedures, crash scenes, drownings, heart attacks, etc., all play a part in our curiosity of what it would be like to nearly die. What lies beyond death, if anything? But the events that lead up to a spiritually transformative experience **are not** the experience. *The "experience" occurs at that moment when physical consciousness transcends the confines of the physical dimension and enters into another greater, or "more real" dimension. It isn't the event leading up to the experience that's important, it's the experience itself!*

Once the individual has been granted entry into that transcendent reality, no matter how invited, our studies should include all those experiencers who bring back to humanity their gifts of heightened consciousness and the mystical perspective of seeing life united by the Divine. In that way, in addition to what near-death experiencers tell us, others who have also passed through the thin veil by other means will also be able to tell us more about the mystery. Each camp is but a piece of the mysterious puzzle we have before us. No single piece of the puzzle will yield the overall picture, but each piece is an important contribution to the whole. Black crows as well as the white crows!

This brings me to an interesting statistic. In 1992, the International Association for Near-Death Studies, Inc., researched the phenomenon of near-death experiences by sending out a questionnaire to its members asking how the individuals came to their experience. Two hundred twenty-nine individuals replied. Of those, 23% had an experience during clinical death, 40% during serious illness or physical trauma, and get this: 37% had their experience without coming close to death, suffering serious illness or physical trauma. Clearly, this tells us that the *lowest* percentage are those who have had a near-death experience! There is relatively little difference between the other two groups.

In other words, this legitimate research by the world's foremost near-death experience organization, has confirmed what so many within our population have experienced - spiritually transformative experiences, or mystical experiences.

By now you are getting a better idea of my intention for writing this book. What lies beyond the quantum comes from the mouths of those brave souls who have been invited through those doors and who witnessed for themselves the existence of unseen worlds. They tell us what they have experienced so that humanity will begin to perceive that we are all an integral part of this multi-layered creation. What is needed then, is the willingness to humbly admit that the mysterious is unknown and unknowable, at least for the time being. If we lose our sense of the mysterious, we lose our sense of awe for the creation of the universe and our part in it. What transcends the world of the senses is offered so that experimentalists have further frontiers to explore.

WORDS OF WISDOM

"God sleeps in the rock,
Dreams in the plant,
Stirs in the animal,
And awakens in man."

—Sufi teaching

CHAPTER 4

CAN SCIENCE PROVE THE UNSEEN?

"I try to believe like I believed when I was 5...when your heart tells you everything you need to know."

—Lucy Liu

Before science came to be, people relied on folk wisdom and their own common sense and logic to explain how the world works. It wasn't until Galileo and Isaac Newton four centuries ago, that observation and theory brought about the scientific method. Basically, the scientific method involves the following:

- Observation: investigating; collecting data
- Hypothesis: trying to figure out what this data means; an educated guess
- Testing the hypothesis: finding ways either in the laboratory or in the real world to test the hypothesis
- Acknowledging reliability: is the hypothesis on target or not reliable enough?
- Replication: is the same information able to be repeated by other investigators using the same hypothesis?
- Scientific law: when it appears the hypothesis is 100% reliable, at that point, it becomes a scientific law

Yet, science is still problematic. The more questions that are answered, the more those answers raise more questions and possible answers again. Remember we were told we live in a three-dimensional universe in which everyone's perception of space and time is identical? Then along came Einstein, and science revealed that we live in a four-dimensional universe in which everyone's perception of space and time is not identical. Today, the theoretical physicists are talking about something called *string theory*. That proposes that we live not in a three or four dimensional universe, but in ten or more dimensions!

Some researchers do not stray far from the prevailing orthodoxy in their given fields. For instance, psychologists or psychiatrists may focus on psychological explanations for the cause of transcendent experiences. Neurophysiologists may want to explain it in terms of brain function, etc. During my own mystical near-death-like experience, I understood that consciousness creates matter, not the other way around. This is of course scoffed at by many hardcore science reductionists who believe that our physical universe can be understood by reducing everything to their basic components: molecules, atoms, quarks, etc.

Science is all about physical reality. It can't tell us anything about consciousness that extends beyond the physical reality. The thinking of reductionists is that consciousness is nothing more but brain chemistry, period.

Now in support of the scientific method in which I was rigorously trained, I understand the need for skepticism and for being cautious about data that does not support the known laws of physics. But notice I used the word "known." Theoretical physics is gaining an increasing audience within the larger scientific community concerning hypotheses about invisible multiuniverses that may be right next to our own in other dimensions or right on top of our own, interspersed within the space we inhabit. There are many well-known and prestigious physicists from accredited universities at work on these theories. Their proposals are accepted as plausible by science, while the experiences of the mystics and others who have *actually encountered* those transcendent or supernatural realities are either not being believed or are being ignored.

However, it is my opinion that innovations are made through free inquiry when we can open our minds to other perspectives outside the narrow confines of the scientific mainstream community. I propose that the answers will be derived from the experiencers themselves, who will lead us on our search for the answers about the mystery of our true human nature.

I am suggesting that science does not always have the bottom line when it comes to knowledge about the mysterious workings of the universe. There will always be scientists who will debate others' observations. What we know today, may change tomorrow. William James, M.D., noted philosopher and psychologist said, *"First, you know; a new theory is attacked as absurd; then it is admitted to be true, but obvious and insignificant; finally it is seen to be so important that its adversaries claim that they themselves discovered it."*

For the most part science, and many of us in fact, use external measures like our five senses - what we can see, hear, taste, feel and hear, as our reality check. We have a hard time believing that there is more to our reality than our five senses. In fact, there is a lot of seemingly and unfounded prejudice voiced from intelligent and scientifically free-thinking realists who contribute to the overall debate concerning the subtler, nonphysical aspects of reality. To speak of the higher worlds of ascension and multi-dimensional reality, is for some, simply too much to fathom and is considered insanity. To speak of God, religion, spirituality and faith is considered akin to believing in superstitions, and is thought of as being practiced only by weak believers who need a crutch.

Regardless of where you are on your own personal journey,

I believe that we can all agree that there is a mystery at the heart of the universe that we will never be able to fully comprehend. Mystery is beyond the capacity of the intellect. In the Talmud there is a saying, "Teach your tongue to say, 'I don't know.'" We don't have to understand how everything works in order to accept its reality. We have all seen for ourselves, the results of various phenomena. We know they work! We accept them and integrate those mysteries into our lives.

Take for instance, the internet. I cannot understand how I can email someone across a vast ocean and in minutes, receive a reply back. Back and forth, we can converse through typed words appearing on a computer screen, and with a click of a button that message reaches the far-distant shore of another person whom I have never met before. I did not physically cross the ocean, knock on that person's door to be welcomed inside, but yet, some aspect of my presence was with that person seated at her own computer. Perhaps that person was happy to receive the words I wrote. But they were only words on a computer screen in front of her. They were intangible letters that made up words. They did not physically enter her brain. Yet, her emotions which are non-physical, were stirred and were real.

Non-material things are real. Can you see, hear, smell, taste, or touch a memory, intuition, joy, sadness, ideas? What about the hole in a piece of Swiss cheese? Is that a physical thing? No, but we accept those things as part of our reality. We move through our everyday lives dependent upon things that cannot be seen or understood.

Saint Augustine offers us a gift of perspective and humility when he said, *"Understanding is the reward of faith. Therefore seek not to understand that thou mayest believe, but believe that thou mayest understand."*

While this book contains anecdotal stories written by ordinary people, these brave and wonderful souls have put themselves on

Teach yr. tongue to say "I don't know"

the front lines so to speak, and they realize they may be judged negatively for what they experienced. I am so honored that they shared their experiences with me for this book, because I believe it will help others who have had similar experiences to know they are not alone. Aside from that, it is my hope that the scientific community will not denigrate anecdotal stories that have given so many experiencers meaning and purpose to their lives. It is wise to focus on what can be learned from observing actual cases. Vernon Sylvest, M.D. wrote in his book, *The Formula: Who Gets Sick, Who Gets Well, Who is Unhappy, Who is Happy and Why,*

"There is a tendency in the scientific community to dismiss accounts such as these as anecdotal and thus invalid as evidence. To do so is a mistake. By definition an anecdote is the account of a little known fact or happening. Large case studies are made up of numerous anecdotes. Even randomized, double-blind studies are collections of many anecdotes. If science is to go beyond itself and explore new ground, it must look at evidence that is beyond the experience of large randomized studies. Then it can use this new information to develop and fund large prospective or retrospective studies to gather together a body of evidence upon which our culture can rely in order to make good decisions. We must not disparage the anecdote; it is an important first step and often may be the only step available. If the established scientific community does not respond, it may be that the grass-root anecdotal experiences of the general public will direct the choices of our culture for its own good.

Science disparages the anecdote in an attempt to protect us against fraud. Too often this disparaging of the anecdote comes from a need to be "right" and an unwillingness to change perceptions and shift to a new paradigm. The premise that science has operated on in the past is that there is an objective reality independent of consciousness, that consciousness is a secondary phenomenon operative only in the limited confines of the rules of that objective reality. In fact, there is no objective reality independent of consciousness. Physical reality is a subjective experience. This understanding must be incorporated into the design of scientific studies if science is to be of most benefit in guiding us to our fullest potential for benevolent dominion over our experience."

WORDS OF WISDOM

"I maintain that the human mystery is incredibly demeaned by scientific reductionism, with its claim in promissory materialism, to account eventually for all of the spiritual world in terms of patterns of neuronal activity. This belief must be classed as superstition...We have to recognize that we are spiritual beings with souls existing in a spiritual world as well as material beings with bodies and brains existing in a material world."

—Sir John Eccles
(Nobel Prize-winning neuroscientist)

CHAPTER 5

MYSTICAL EXPERIENCES

"The spiritual life is part of every man's life, and until he has realized it he is not a complete human being."

—Evelyn Underhill, Practical Mysticism

At the University of Chicago, in conjunction with the National Opinion Research Center, Dr. Andrew Greeley found that 18 percent of Americans report having had a mystical experience once or twice in their lives. Twelve percent report having had several mystical experiences, while another 5 percent have had mystical experiences often. This brings the total up to 35 percent!

What then, is a mystical experience? Any discussion of enhanced states of consciousness with awareness of the Divine must include the subject of mysticism. According to Webster's Dictionary, the word mysticism is defined as, "The doctrine of belief that direct knowledge of God, of spiritual truth, etc., is attainable through immediate intuition or insight, and in a way differing from ordinary sense perception or the use of logical reasoning." And Webster's Dictionary defines the word "mystical" as "manifesting an individual's direct communion with God through contemplation, vision, an inner light or the like; as mystical rapture." A mystic is therefore, one who follows a mystical way of life.

So in layman's terms, simply put, mysticism is an experience of direct union of the soul with the Divine. Saint John of the Cross said that those who have those moments with the Divine enjoy *"a certain contact of the soul with divinity; and it is God himself who is then felt and tasted."*

Mystics have been with us since the beginning of time, but they have often been misunderstood in their attempts to provide us with what they considered to be higher states of awareness of the Divine. For instance, during the Inquisition, people were killed because of their beliefs. Take for instance Joan of Arc. She claimed to have heavenly visions and voices that, for her, were strong evidence that God was calling her toward a cause. With guidance from her visions and voices, she led the king of France's army. Because she could not prove her visions were real, she was burned at the stake in 1431.

The Salem witch trials were yet another example of the terrible period in our history when fear that such individuals were possessed by Satan led many of them to be burned at the stake. Also, Jesus was crucified because he was a threat to those in power at the time.

William James, M.D. wrote a classic book, *The Varieties of Religious Experience*. It was first published in 1902 and has remained in print ever since. He proposed four criteria to define the mystical experience:

- The experience is ineffable or beyond words to explain it.
- There is a noetic quality, meaning a state of deep, inner knowing that transcends ordinary intellect.
- The experience is transient, meaning it doesn't last very long, rarely more than an hour, more often, just a few minutes.

- The experience is a passive state. In this state, one feels grasped by a power greater than oneself.
- Mentioned elsewhere are bliss and a sense of union with all things.

Notice how these qualities are so similar to the accounts described by near-death experiencers and, as you will soon learn, by others who were not close to death at the time of their experiences.

Another timeless book written on the subject of mystical experiences is *Cosmic Consciousness*, by Richard Maurice Bucke, M.D., written in 1901. It is a classic book today and has been referenced by many who have studied mysticism. Bucke, a Canadian psychiatrist, had a mystical experience twenty-five years before he wrote his book. The experience suggested to him that the universe is interconnected with all consciousness, and that cosmic consciousness is a mystic state of being above and beyond self-consciousness, the natural state of man's consciousness.

Bucke's book, *Cosmic Consciousness*, describes the lives of individuals throughout the last three thousand years of human history who have experienced mystical illumination. He believed cosmic consciousness was slowly beginning to spread throughout humanity as the next stage in human development.

The lives he examined as having an advanced state of consciousness are reported in his book and they are well worth reading. For now, I will simply list some of them you may be familiar with. They include: Gautama the Buddha, Jesus, Paul, Plotinus, Mohammed, Dante, Bartolomé Las Casas, John Yepes (called St. John of the Cross), Francis Bacon, Jacob Behmen, Willian Blake, Honore de Balzac, Walt Whitman, Edward Carpenter, Moses, Gideon, Isaiah, Socrates, Roger Bacon, Blaise Pascal, Benedict Spinoza, Swedenborg, William Wordsworth, Ralph Waldo Emerson, Alfred Tennyson, Henry David Thoreau.

By no means are all of the above-mentioned the only individuals in history who experienced the transcendent mystical
illumination and whose lives were transformed afterwards. I
will describe others who prior to their experiences were ordinary people. Some were downright dreadful, but following their
experiences all dedicated their lives to the Beloved and to helping
others to deepen their understanding of the Divine. Some of
them were made saints after their deaths. I am including some of
their quotes as well.

In the first century A.D., Saul of Tarsus was a Roman citizen,
a Jew who persecuted the Christians. On his way to Damascus,
he fell from his horse, blinded by the Light, heard the voice of
Jesus and his life was transformed. He converted to Christianity
and became one of the most important Biblical figures in history, having founded the Christian church. Today the Christian
religion has more than 1.9 billion members.

> *"God has put us who bear his Message on stage in a theater*
> *in which no one wants to buy a ticket. 1 Corinthians 4:9*
> *(The Message)."*

In A.D. 610, Muhammad, an Arab merchant, was praying
in the mountains when he had a vision of the angel Gabriel who
told him, "Recite!" Muhammad was afraid he was being possessed by demons. However, on the third command by the angel
Gabriel to "Recite," he began to speak beautiful words that were
not in his vocabulary at the time. Over the next twenty-three
years Muhammad believed he was being divinely inspired to
write what we know as the Qur'an.

> *"The creation is as God's family; for its sustenance is from*
> *Him: therefore the most beloved unto God is the person who*
> *doeth good to God's family."*

In 1936, Bill Wilson, an alcoholic for many years, had reached bottom. He found himself on his knees crying out, "If there is a God, let Him show Himself." Suddenly the room filled with a brilliant white light and he was overcome with ecstasy and the conviction that he was in the presence of God. From that day forward, he never drank again. As a result of how this experience transformed his life, he went on to found Alcoholics Anonymous.

> *"Thus I was convinced that God is concerned with us humans when we want Him enough. At long last I saw, I felt, I believed. Scales of pride and prejudice fell from my eyes. A new world came into view."*

In 1937, Simone Weil, a French philosopher and social activist whose writings were based upon radical politics, experienced a religious ecstasy in the same church in which St. Francis of Assisi had prayed. The experience led her to pray for the first time in her life. A year later, she had a more powerful mystical vision in which Christ appeared to her. Following these mystical experiences, her extensive writings became more mystical and spiritual in nature.

> *"It is only the impossible that is possible to God. He has given over the possible to the mechanics of matter and the autonomy of his creatures."*

In the twelfth-century, Hildegard of Bingen had mystical visions of light beginning at the age of three.

> *"The visions which I saw I did not perceive in dreams nor when asleep nor in a delirium nor with the eyes or ears of the body. I received them when I was awake and looking around with a clear mind, with the inner eyes and ears, in open places according to the will of God. But how this could be, it is difficult for us mortals to seek to know."*

Hildegard became a Benedictine nun, composed beautiful music and wrote books on spirituality, among others. She called herself God's mouthpiece, a "small trumpet," a "feather on the breath of God."

Born in 1347 in Siena, Catherine of Siena had a vision of Christ seated with the Apostles Peter, Paul, and John. She made a vow one year later to give her whole life to God. She became a Dominican nun and on Shrove Tuesday, 1366 while praying in her small room, she had a vision of Christ, His mother Mary, and the heavenly host. Mother Mary took Catherine's hand and held it up to Christ, who placed a ring on her finger which solidified her faith in Him. The ring was always visible to Catherine, though invisible to others. Her greatest mystical writing is the book, *The Dialogue of St. Catherine*, also known as *The Book of Divine Doctrine*. It is believed that she dictated this work under the inspiration of the Holy Spirit.

> *"Everything comes from love, all is ordained for the salvation of man, God does nothing without this goal in mind."*

In 1473, Catherine Fieschi of Genoa had a mystical ecstasy experience which set her on a devoted life of close union with God. While kneeling in a confessional, she received the ecstasy of God's immense love. She spent her life working with unselfish service to the poor and the sick, and eventually became the director of a hospital. Her writings convey the necessity of the person to be in perfect humility to prepare the way for God's perfect love to penetrate one's soul.

> *"The soul becomes like gold that becomes purer as it is fired, all dross being cast out. Having come to the point of twenty-four carats, gold cannot be purified any further; and this is what happens to the soul in the fire of God's love."*

In 1538 after joining the Carmelite Order of nuns, Saint Teresa of Avila began to receive visions, raptures and ecstasies from Christ that changed her life forever. Saint Teresa of Avila wrote of her experience:

> *"It was granted me to perceive in one instant how all things are seen and contained in God. I did not perceive them in their proper form, and nevertheless the view I had of them was of a sovereign clearness, and has remained vividly impressed upon my soul... The view was so subtle and deli-cate that the understanding cannot grasp it."*

Her written works include *The Way of Perfection*, *The Interior Castle*, and the *Life of Teresa of Avila*.

> *"We need no wings to go in search of Him, but have only to look upon Him present within us."* Saint Teresa of Avila

In 1522 Saint Ignatius of Loyola experienced a vision of the Virgin Mary and the infant Jesus while at the shrine of Our Lady of Montserrat. After that, he began praying seven hours a day and began writing his famous *Spiritual Exercises of St. Ignatius*. He became the founder of the Jesuit priests.

> *"Teach us to give and not to count the cost."* St. Ignatius of Loyola

Julian of Norwich was thirty years old when she had a series of intense visions of Jesus. She is considered to be one of the greatest English mystics. She wrote about her visions in several works, the best known, called *Sixteen Revelations of Divine Love*, (circa 1393)

> *"Between God and the soul there is no between."*

John Yepes, better known as St. John of the Cross, became a Carmelite monk in the 12th century. Together with his friend St. Teresa of Avila, they worked for the reformation of the

Carmelites. However, he was imprisoned for two years by the unreformed Carmelites who were opposed to what he was doing. During his years in a tiny cell in prison he experienced episodes of Divine Light, and began writing about his illumination by describing the soul's journey toward God. He wrote several works but his most famous one is *The Dark Night of the Soul*. St. John of the Cross is recognized as a leading authority in Western mysticism.

> *"God is always in man, and very commonly the soul is aware of His (passive) presence. It is as if He slept in the soul. If He wakes up only once in a man's whole life the experience of that instant affects the whole of life. If the experience of that instant should be indefinitely prolonged what soul could bear it!"*

Jacob Behmen was a German Christian mystic and theologian who had many mystical experiences. One day in 1600 he had a vision while looking at a beam of sunlight reflected in a pewter dish. He understood this vision to reveal the relationship between God and man, and good and evil. He wrote many books on the subject during his lifetime.

> *"Spiritual knowledge cannot be communicated from one intellect to another, but must be sought for in the spirit of God."*

Saint Francis of Assisi was a Catholic friar who founded the Franciscan Order. While Francis was praying on the mountain of Verna in 1224, he had a vision which his Brother Leo is said to have said, *"Suddenly he saw a vision of a seraph, a six-winged angel on a cross. This angel gave him the gift of the five wounds of Christ."* Francis received the stigmata of Jesus Christ. He is known as the patron saint of animals and the environment.

> *"Remember that when you leave this earth, you can take*

with you nothing that you have received - only what you   ←
have given."

In 1946 Mother Teresa said that she "heard" God ask her to work with the poorest of the poor in the slums of Calcutta. She was hesitant to leave her work at a girl's school to go and work in the slums, but she heard God ask her, "Wilt thou refuse?" The rest is history, as Mother Teresa accepted God's invitation to help those poor people in Calcutta.

"Not all of us can do great things. But we can do small things with great love."

The examples of the mystics I mention above serve to remind us that these individuals weren't born this way, they were ordinary people who had life-transforming spiritual experiences and their lives were changed forever. They left humanity with enormous contributions to human life, which gives us insight into the eternal questions: Who am I? Why am I here? Where am I going? What is the purpose of life?

All mystical and transcendent experiences have always been the same in their essence. Early prophets and seers reported these transcendent experiences in terms of whichever conceptual, cultural and linguistic framework that individual had available to him/her at the time. These individuals or prophets were usually alone at the time of their revelation. The person experienced his/her Truth about God, morality, the universe and identity from within, usually in a swift and sudden movement of experiencing this Truth as a supernatural revelation.

Then what happened was that an organization needed to be set up in order to make those mystical revelations accessible to everyone else so others could benefit from these teachings. Churches were formed, and people became loyal to the church's version of the prophet's revelations. Now the problem comes when you have these ancient prophets and mystics who try as best they can to describe something that is ineffable (goes beyond words) to others who have never had such an experience. Communication breaks down, because there are no words in the human language to adequately convey the Truth that came from these prophets and mystics.

So now you have groups of non-experiencers or non-prophets and non-mystics who set off to try and convey to their followers the original meaning of the prophets and mystics, and the essential original meaning gets lost. What happens then is that many people tend to regard the church or the organization or its leaders as more important than the prophet and his/her revelations that started the whole process to begin with.

The awful part is that eventually the leaders of the church or organization set themselves up as authority figures, and made a heresy out of the mystical experiences and even persecuted the mystics themselves. This is still happening today! Mystical experiences are the same yesterday, today and tomorrow. The revelations that ordinary people are experiencing today are just as relevant today as they were in ancient times. We all need to understand one another, to get along, and to love one another. It may be that a Divine Power is preparing humanity for a deeper role in the history of religions as well as preparing each individual to take responsibility for their own personal relationship with the Creator and with one another. Love is the only power that opens the mind to greater clarity, making the wholeness which already exists come forth.

WORDS OF WISDOM

…and the day came when the risk it took to
remain tightly closed in a bud was more painful
than the risk it took to bloom….

—Anais Nin

Love is the only power t opens the mind to greater clarity.

CHAPTER 6

ORDINARY PEOPLE SHARING THEIR SPIRITUALLY TRANSFORMATIVE EXPERIENCES

Reading about the transcendent experiences of ordinary people is a good way to gain insight into the universality of the spiritual process. A spiritually transformed person is one who has had a change of heart from the old self to a new one; it is akin to a heart transplant to a person with a diseased heart. However, please do not get the idea that in order to become spiritually "awakened" one has to have visions, or that someone has ultimate truth as a result of their experiences. There is only one absolute truth and that **must be directly experienced**, not told. Each person has their own unique way of viewing the same truth. But truth is only truth when you have learned to live it.

At the deepest level, our hearts believe what our minds cannot explain. This kind of faith moves us beyond the senses into the mystical, the process of growing into God who reveals truths the eye cannot see. It is like a small trickle of water on the vast side of a wooded hillside that finds its path by flowing through little clearances and openings as it meanders and zigzags downhill gaining momentum. It doesn't "steer" itself, it just follows the next opening that appears in its path until it joins up with a larger flow of water where it will continue on its path to larger streams and rivers and eventually to the ocean.

It is my hope that the ordinary people who share their experiences in this book will give us insight into those same eternal questions. Why am I here? Where am I going? What is the purpose of life? Please open your hearts and minds to these beautiful souls who articulate their experiences for us with the hope of moving us more deeply into the life of the Spirit.

WORDS OF WISDOM

"God is like a mirror.
The mirror never changes,
But everyone who looks at it
Sees a different face.

—The rabbis of Midrash

THE VOICE

Barbara Bachner, Massachusetts

I was raised in the Methodist Church, and when I was about twelve years old, my father became a Methodist minister. Despite this, I ended up not really believing in God. I think I wanted to believe in God, but I kept trying to do so with logic, and that never worked. Then one day while on the treadmill reading *Endless Light: The Ancient Path to the Kabbalah* by David Aaron, I came upon this statement, "I don't believe in God, but what I believe in I call God."

That had great meaning for me, and I was so happy to have found it. I think the difficulty I had been having was that I could not believe in God the way He had been being presented to me; I had to go about it from a different direction, so to speak. Anyway, it was a start, and that made me very happy.

Then one February morning in 2003, my husband noticed his leg was swollen, and I insisted he go to the doctor. A few days later, he was discharged from the hospital with a diagnosis of cancer, but we didn't yet know it was lymphoma. When we came home from the hospital that day, we thought he had some primary cancer that had already metastasized to his lungs and liver. My husband, a doctor himself, thought he might not live through that first weekend.

When we came into the house and settled down on the sofa, I said, "What we need is a good sermon." (We had heard Rev. John Claypool while at Chautauqua Institution and had ordered a number of his sermons on tape.) So I grabbed for a tape, any tape since just hearing Claypool's voice always seemed so calming. As I put the tape in the player, I had no idea which sermon it would be or whether it would be at the beginning, middle or end. Out poured these sweet words to heal our hearts: "Go now, go with God, be not afraid. Let God go before you to guide you, behind you to protect you, beneath you to secure you, and beside you to befriend you. Go now, go with God, be not afraid. Amen."

My husband and I looked at each other, and our mouths dropped open! What a blessing! What a perfectly placed miracle that benediction was in our lives. It gave us something to hold on to as we kept putting one foot in front of the other over the next few weeks and months.

Soon after coming home from the hospital, my husband wanted to get some near-death experience books from the library. He read them, returned them, and was through. I read them and kept wanting more! I had read Moody's *Life After Life* in the '70's with great interest, and now, I had even more reason to be interested. I began to order books from Amazon, and it seemed that each book led me to another. Then, one day while reading one of them on the treadmill, I suddenly realized I believed it! I really and truly believed that we don't die, that God oversees it all, and that much of what I was reading, strange as it sounded, was probably true! That was a great moment in my life, but my husband had not shared it, so it was a delicate balance for me to enjoy my new interest and talk to him about it, without turning him off by pushing for him to believe it too. (Eventually, he came to it in his own way.)

I found God by starting with, "I don't believe in God, but…", but I experienced the 'miracle' of the benediction. Who knew you could become a believer by reading, not the Bible, but NDE books? Then something wonderful happened to me that added depth to my new faith.

In April 2005, my husband was in the hospital being treated for lymphoma, and he was having a very bad time of it. On one particular occasion, it was 3:00 AM before I could leave the hospital to drive home, and as I drove I was telling myself to stay awake and keep my mind on my driving rather than on my husband...focus, focus, focus. Then, suddenly, I heard a Voice, sweet, gentle, calm. It came to me from the direction of the passenger seat. It was a male voice, not an elderly person and not a child. There was no accent. It wasn't muffled, raspy, or in any way difficult to hear or to understand. It was so very clear it made me think of a mountain stream of clear water. It was not a voice I recognized, or that I had ever heard before, although I would hear that same voice again and again over the next few days, always while traveling alone to or from the hospital.

Most of us are familiar with "that still small voice within," but this Voice was so very different from that, there is no way I would ever confuse them. It wasn't 'within'; it was perceived as an audible sound coming from a direction to the right of my body. It seemed to me that I was hearing it exactly as if a person had been sitting there next to me.

The first time this happened, I immediately assumed it must be God or, if such things existed, a guardian angel, but having had time to give it much more thought, I now believe it was probably God, Jesus, or Holy Spirit.

The mood that always accompanied the voice was one of complete calm and peace, so much so that I never experienced one second of fear despite the fact that what was happening to me was completely unexpected and new.

I heard this Voice several times over a period of a week or two, even as my husband's condition improved day by day. Each time I heard the Voice, I again knew wisdom had been imparted, and one interesting detail is that they always seemed to be bits of wisdom that were familiar to me! As the messages were spoken, I took them in, recognized their value, noted that they were familiar, and then immediately I couldn't recall a word of them! I think I wasn't supposed to get focused on words when the real message was something far deeper and grander than mere words!

I believe what I was supposed to remember is that I'm not alone, that when I'm going through tough times there is Another who will be there with me, whether or not I hear His Voice.

About Barbara Bachner

Barbara is a retired medical office manager.

MEETING THE LIGHT

Mary Baker, Oklahoma

I grew up in the impoverished hill country of "Bible Belt," U.S.A., but I must explain that only about 15% of Bible Belt residents troop to churches, Bible in hand, every Sunday. Most people believe the Bible is the word of God, and that Christianity is true, but attend church rarely if at all and are largely ignorant of the Bible. Most in my neighborhood could not read beyond a second or third grade level, and several could neither read nor write at all.

My father was fully literate and mama could read pretty well and write fair. Both were Christians, but mama attended church maybe two or three times a year. Daddy attended alone wherever he was but worked away from home, first in the Civil Conservation Corps, then on a railroad section gang, living in boxcar barracks and coming home only for Christmas and vacation.

When I was three years old, they managed to purchase fifty acres of steep, wooded hills with a two room, dirt floored log shack four miles from a small town. It was too hilly for cash crops but there was enough flat surface to grow vegetables. We had a flock of free range chickens for meat and eggs and kept two cows.

We had no electricity nor running water and no transportation. Neighbors who had either a wagon and team or an old jalopy took us to get groceries once a month and to the doctor in emergencies. Otherwise, we walked. This partially explained why mama, though living the Christian ideal, wasn't churched, but perhaps more relevant was that she was a spiritually private person who did not read the Bible aloud, nor discuss religious matters, nor pray aloud unless daddy was home. He encouraged

bedtime prayers for the adults (though children did not participate). Daddy read a chapter from the Bible and led the family
in a hymn at bedtime but otherwise, did not teach nor discuss
religion with us children. Consequently, I grew up pretty much
a "heathen."

I believed that people either went to Heaven or Hell,
depending on whether they were "saved," but had never inquired
how to be saved. Since getting saved seemed to involved obeying
rules, I decided in my early teens that I'd postpone that until old
age and in the meantime, be free to do whatever I could get by
with. I considered myself pretty clever and a good liar, therefore
capable of getting by with much.

My "pal," a year older than I, was of the same mind. Unlike
me, she didn't go to school. She was already sexually active and
smoked and drank when dating. She also cussed like a sailor
openly defying her mother and stepfather. They did not object
strongly as long as she worked hard.

I'd never heard of "religious experiences," certainly was not
a likely candidate for one nor was I by any means seeking one.
However.......

Just before my fourteenth birthday my pal and I, along with
her parents and other neighbors, were doing field labor for daily
wages, when her step-father scolded us for talking more than we
were working. She cursed him loudly, and I reminded him that
he was not my boss, but we did go to work because we needed
the money. After awhile my back begin to tire so I stood to rest
a minute, enjoying a refreshing breeze that blew over me, and
then, incredibly, blew through me, penetrating every cell of my
body, cleansing me completely.

Immediately, or perhaps simultaneously, I was aware of an
invisible but very real "Person" slightly suspended in the air
before me. I perceived great power, but also loving compassion
and holiness in this person and the puzzling awareness that I

knew this person well, had always known him, and had seemingly forgotten him until that instant. I trusted him completely as
he entered into my mind communicating in a manner that could
not be misinterpreted because it by-passed human thought patterns or language, imparting pure awareness. This inner awareness was accompanied by visions, the meaning of which I understood from the spiritual communication.

I saw a form that I understood represented me, though it
did not resemble me as it was short and dumpy, mostly tummy
and supine, whereas I was a tall, skinny girl standing erect. There
was an odious sore on the left thigh of this form eating away the
flesh. I understood this symbolized sin destroying me.

The Person communicating to me offered me spiritual
healing if I would choose to follow a path of love and peace. The
vision now showed a footpath through a wood with a light like a
spotlight shining down upon it ahead of me symbolizing "His"
presence continually guiding me. Then I was told that at the end
of my path, "You will come to me."

Suddenly, I was immersed, surrounded, embraced in golden,
oceanic, Light, full of peace and love, joy, fulfillment, of being
Home. I felt so sorry for every unkind thing I'd ever said or
done. I realized we are all very precious to God and should love
one another.

When the vision ended, my face was drenched in tears. My
heart changed. My ultra-tough pal, similarly affected, was also
weeping. We apologized tearfully to her parents saying God had
spoken to us.

On that day over sixty years ago, I began studying the Bible,
attending church and praying, beginning my journey. In scripture I found explanations for much of my experience and descriptions of similar events. Then in the seventies, I read Moody's
book, "Life After Life" and similar works. I was not alone. I find
my chosen path to be the right one for me.

"I am the light of the world. Whoever follows me will never walk in darkness, but will have the light of life."

Questions and Mary's Answers from my research questionnaire:

Q. Did you experience a feeling of lifting out of your body or something other?

A. No. I had no sense of leaving my body but of being oblivious to my surroundings throughout the experience.

Q. Did you see or sense any other beings or entities present during your experience?

A. I sensed very clearly God as He communicated to me. He was invisible but very much distinctly real. Nothing ambiguous about His presence. There was no other entity.

Q. Did you experience any frightening or negative feelings during your experience?

A. When I was shown the vision of the form representing me with the "sin sore" on it, I was revolted by the hideousness and vileness of the sore but was immediately relieved of this feeling as God told me how to escape its destruction.

Q. Did time or space seem altered to you in any way?

A. I was oblivious to all except the experience. I was unaware of time passing, but it must have as I had tears all over my face when I came to myself, and it took time for the tears to flow down my face. The experience seemed to unfold very rapidly with no time for reflection, but it was all very clear as it happened as I was mentally/spiritually understanding without need of language or words.

Q. Did this experience seem real or dream-like or a hallucination?

A. It was, as I often say, **AS REAL AS A ROCK!** Nothing at all dream-like or like a hallucination and I have had both and know the difference.

Q. Following your experience, do you consider yourself to be more spiritual than religious? If so, how would you explain this to others?

A. I do not make a distinction between the two. I am both more spiritual and religious. True religion is an expression of spirituality. Otherwise, it is a meaningless ritual and not really religion.

Q. Did you talk about this experience with anyone? How did people respond?

A. Yes, within minutes I shared with Polly's parents. They were supportive, and she said, "Hold on to Jesus!" even though they were not very religious and seldom went to church. My family were also supportive. I have often related this to friends and in church during testimony services and was well received most of the time but did have one friend laugh at me and say my imagination ran away from me. I have posted it on internet forums with mixed reactions-some very hostile from "New Age" and other anti-Christian elements.

Q. Do you feel this experience is sacred or holy in some way?

A. Of course! How much more sacred can anything be than to be in the presence of God?

Q. Following your experience, do you have more, less or still the same feelings of an inner sense of Spirit or of the God of your understanding?

A. More. Before I had very infantile concepts of God as a kind of super Santa Claus, keeping records of who is good and bad, deciding who went to Heaven and who didn't. He was "up there" someplace, and I was glad to have some distance from Him. I thought I would settle with him when I got old. After this experience, I felt and knew God as a real Person and such a wonderful Person, central to my life, with me always. My Heavenly Father.

Q. What is the single, most important bit of wisdom you wish to tell others who have not had a spiritually transcendent type of experience?

A. A real, living, loving God exists. Knowing Him is the most important thing in life.

About Mary Baker

Mary Baker retired from various menial jobs; farm labor, shoe & garment factories worker, retail sales clerk, housewife and cattle ranching with late husband. She can be reached at her email address: Janecontrary@yahoo.com

THE LIGHT

Joe Robert Ballard, Kansas

In 1969, I felt this world and myself were both very negative forces. I simply thought that this life, this world, was all there was. Sitting on a lonely Kansas road late one October night, I was to learn - experience, if you will - a piece of the reality I was blindly longing for.

For months my friend, Dennis and I had been driving around South-Central Kansas discussing and wondering about the terrible state of the human condition. A very trying event for two nineteen year-old children. Our lives were simply at dead ends, going nowhere that we could see. We were looking for something real, beyond what we had experienced in this physical world. I guess you could say we were in deep depression without much hope.

As we were sitting in my car on a dirt road, Dennis noticed something moving across the wheat field. As I looked, I could see a wave of energy floating, if you will, above the ground. Naturally, we became frightened, so I started my 1968 vehicle and started to run. As we did, I turned back to look once more. Before we could go a hundred yards, the vision came across the field in a blink of an eye. Within a few feet of us, it became the most beautiful Light and energy form!

As others say, I can only try to describe it in earthly terms. I felt as if the Light was entering my body or soul as well as staying on the outside for us to see. I was overcome with ecstasy, that something wonderful and glorious was about to happen. At the same time, I felt the most peaceful feeling, that everything was going to be just okay, no matter what happens in this life. I looked into the horizon, and the trees were rising up and down on the horizon. I knew at that moment we were in touch with what religions call God.

My friend Dennis, who has passed on since that time, was scared beyond description. I felt I wanted to stay with the Light, and also tell everyone I knew of this wonderful Light. It was not my time to go on with the Light because I drove away, headed for the nearest town to tell everyone I had been with God. The more people I told, the more I began to realize that people thought I had just gone over the edge. I was consumed with the idea of spreading the wonderful feeling the Light showed me. Simply no worries, free from all fears. Just a magnificent feeling.

I have learned to pick people and times to discuss the Light. I feel that in my own thoughts the Light is helping me overcome the biggest fear of all, death, helping me to see clearly through this physical stress that we create for ourselves, thinking that we need to suffer to find love.

About Joe Robert Ballard

Joe is a handicap bus operator and has written an article for the International Association Near-Death Studies, Inc. (IANDS)

PERSONAL EXPERIENCE OF MYSTICAL STATE OF CONSCIOUSNESS

Boyce Batey, Connecticut

Originally published in the 1980 conference Proceedings of the Academy of Religion and Psychical Research (ARPS) © and reprinted here with permission.

In the summer of 1954 when I was twenty-one years old, while I was in the house of my father in Miami, I was reading aloud <u>The Prelude</u>, the beautiful poem by William Wordsworth, in which he describes the growth of consciousness in the mind of a poet. As I read, I thought I would conduct an experiment in my own consciousness and attempt to be totally aware with all of the senses. As I sat in a chair with my feet on a hassock, eyes closed, I tried to be totally aware with all of my senses, first starting with the sense of touch - the feel of the chair on my buttocks, my arms on the chair, my shoes on my feet, the air touching my skin, the clothes on my body, the feel of my heart, my lungs, the organs in me, trying to be totally aware with all of me of the sense of touch, the totality of what touch is and the individual components of touch. And then, when I reached the point where I felt I had totally in consciousness that which was coming in through the sense of touch, I tried to hold that in consciousness while moving on to the sense of smell - the smell of the frangipani and the gardenia outside the window, of the new-mown grass and of the tar from the sun-baked road, the Aqua/Velva I was wearing that day - what was coming in totally through the sense of smell - the totality as well as the individual components. And then, when I had reached a point when I was aware in consciousness of that, trying to hold that in consciousness as well as what was coming in through the sense of touch, I moved on to the sense of hearing, the sound of the engine of a far distant airplane, of cars passing on the roadway, of back door slamming and cars passing, of the wind in the fronds of the palm tree in the back yard and of my own inspiration and expiration and trying to be totally aware of what was coming in through the sense of sound while holding in consciousness what was coming in through the sense of smell and touch and then I opened my eyes and tried to be totally aware of what was coming in through all the other senses and then what was coming in through seeing - the totality of seeing that which is normally unseen, peripheral vision, far vision, near vision, colors, textures, the beauty of the fold in my pants, the relationship between colors and textures.

While I was in the process of doing this as an experiment in consciousness as an active will of my mind, all of a sudden without my trying, without my knowing what was happening, I was functioning in another level of awareness, my consciousness was in another plane or dimension of reality and a great white light surrounding me and was completely with me, functioning, beating, pulsating with me. I was that light, that light was I, everything out there was in here and everything in here was out there, and I was part of that and that was part of me and everything out there was part of me, and I was God and God was there and here and there, too. And there was in my being a sense of peace and joy and exultation in dimensions and quality that in consciousness I have never before nor since experienced. And I was aware of all of the laws and the meanings of existence, of feeling as though the drift of the Cosmos ultimately was toward good, and that there was only good and no evil in the Universe, that there was no death and that all was life and life in God and that I was that. This experience lasted for only some 6 to 8 seconds but was the most profound experience of my life, an experience which ever since I have sought to regain through studying kundalini yoga, through myriad eclectic forms and types of meditation, but never since have I realized that which happened then and it transformed my life. I was twenty-one at the time, but it is the single most important event in my life. It took me weeks to begin assimilating all of the meaning of it, though I knew what it was at the time.

Research Questions and Boyce's Answers From My Questionnaire:

Q. Did this experience seem real or dream-like or a hallucination?

A. "<u>More real</u> than conventional every-day reality."

Q. Did you experience a sense of oneness or unity with everyone and everything?

A. "Yes. I was one with God and everything and God and everything was one with me."

Q. What was the most relevant and meaningful part of your experience?

A. "The whole experience - not just a part - radically changed my world view."

Q. Following your experience, do you consider yourself to be more spiritual than religious? If so, how would you explain this to others?

A. "More spiritual and less religious. I viewed myself, others and life itself from a higher perspective. I'd been an acolyte in the high Episcopal Church and accepted the rituals and ceremonies of the church as meaningful. After my mystical experience, the ceremonies and rituals and belief systems of the church became less important because I felt deeply that I'd been in direct contact with God."

Q. Did you talk about this experience with anyone? How did people respond?

A. "Yes. My father, mother and later, my wife. They were very accepting of the experience although my parents may not have understood it. When I described the experience to my mother-in-law, an atheist, she said, "You just overloaded your circuits and blew a fuse!" Later, I shared the experience at conferences and in adult education classes I taught."

Q. Have you lost interest in materialism and competition to achieve a higher standard of living?

A. "Yes, to some extent, but spiritual values became more important."

Q. Did this experience lessen your fear of death?

A. "Yes. I understood that all is life."

Q. Do you feel this experience is sacred or holy in some way?

A. "Definitely. The experience of being one with God is, for me, the epitome of life's experience."

Q. Following your experience, do you have more, less or still the same feelings of an inner sense of Spirit or of the God of your understanding?

A. "More. I feel God is more within me than without."

Q. Do you have a greater desire to read, study, share, or discuss matters of a spiritual nature following your experience?

A. "I have had, ever since this mystical experience in 1954 and am adverse to small talk."

Q. Following your experience, are you more accepting of all people's different religious beliefs or less tolerant?

A. "More tolerant because I view different religious belief systems as different paths to the same reality."

Q. In retrospect, do you think this experience happened for a reason or to help you in some way?

A. "It has helped me perceive and live from the perspective of an enlightened state of consciousness."

Q. What is the single most important bit of wisdom you wish to tell others who have not had a transcendent type of experience?

A. "In this life, seek to attain a mystical state of consciousness through meditation and other psycho-spiritual disciplines. By doing so, you have everything to gain and nothing to lose."

About Boyce Batey

Author's Note: I have known Boyce Batey for many years and can vouch for his authenticity and loving service to humanity. Boyce is the Executive Director of the Academy of Spirituality and Paranormal Studies, Inc. For more information about the Academy, please go to their website at: www.aspsi.org Boyce Batey can be contacted at bateyb@infionline.net

A NEAR (ETERNAL) LIFE EXPERIENCE

Bill Bingham, Texas

My experience came about as a result of emotional trauma- a big fight and splitting up with my wife. She came from an affluent, high academic, and musical background. She was pretty, talented, and cultured. I was middle class. Six years after our eventual divorce, she showed up again. She told me what she was up to back then and that she was taking psychiatric treatment now.

I loved this woman, but I also knew at a deep level that she was not good for me. We fought a lot, and I couldn't figure out why at the time. The night of the separation fight, I was torn by conflicting emotions. I wanted to go get her and bring her back, but I knew it would just be more pain. So, I picked up a book, forced myself to sit down in bed and read, trying to get her off my mind. I could barely see the words; I was so wrought up. But I forced myself to read one word at a time. I was constantly skipping back to read words or sentences over because thoughts of her kept pressing on my mind. Eventually, I fell asleep.

When I awoke, I picked up the book and started reading again one word at a time. There was divine order in the timing; I was teaching in college, and we were just starting the semester break when the fight erupted, so I had two weeks off. I spent that time wrestling with my mind and emotions, pushing her out. The forced reading went on day and night, ignoring all outside distractions, for several days before I began to experience some peace. A few more days all thought of her was gone.

Years later, when I was heavy into the practice of Zen Buddhism, I realized that I had become very one-pointed through the forced reading. This is a state that Zen strives mightily for.

Zen can also bring you to surrender.

Then I had the thought, "I wonder if I dare think of her now?" Well stupid, that was a thought of her. Immediately a rage rose up through my previously profound peace; "How could she do this to me!! I loved her." Instantly, a totally commanding voice spoke: "But did you love her totally?" So powerful was this voice that I felt I had been caught in sin on some cosmic scale. Instantly, a radical surrender descended on me, a surrender of body, mind, and soul. It cleared the way for a river of living light and glorious emotion to race down through me with the force of a fire hose. It knocked me down. I lay on the floor in total awe. For several minutes the brain did not think, the body did not move. I could only experience the amazing feeling and light flowing through me. It is impossible to exaggerate the intensity of this feeling. It's like being electrocuted with joy. For me, it changed entirely my understanding of what the body and mind are capable of, virtually of what the mind and body are.

After several minutes of the light and outrageously glorious feeling, my being began to settle down to a state of merely extreme bliss. Then I started to see the history of my life go by. My emotional state now was one of what I then knew to be - unconditional love. The love was coming toward me from everywhere. The room (probably the universe) was filled with love. It was like a force of nature just there for everyone. My mental set was, "This life had been exactly the way it was supposed to be." Supposed by who or what I didn't know. Again, the brain wasn't thinking this. The mind just knew it. It was as if it were placed there by some external power. Someone might look at that and say there is a plan for the universe or all creation or something. I certainly know there must be some plan for my life with all its ups and downs, success and failures, or how would it be as it was "supposed" to be with no hint of condemning judgment.

After that, I started to see magnificent displays of knowledge. I had "understanding" of things in ways that we just don't possess in our everyday lives. That's why it is so very hard to describe these episodes. I'll just say that whatever I focused my mind on, I had complete knowledge of its nature, the history of its existence, its place in the universe, etc. Again, I did not calculate or think these things, they just sort of showed up in my mind without me asking or wishing for or expecting them. It was all very complex and yet simple. Simple in a sense that it was somehow familiar.

Then I felt a slight physical jolt against my shoulder, the first awareness of the envelope of my physical body since the "light being" came down. Then the first self generated thought was, "What was that?" Not very profound. But immediately I got a mental transmission: "All fear of death has left." I knew that this was true just as all this had a sense of certainty about it. This is <u>Truth</u>, everything before has been a type of illusion. I was left in a state of bliss for 6 months later.

During that time, I had two more experiences, higher than bliss, with visions. I understood these were powerful experiences of forgiveness and then acceptance. Later life lessons and extensive reading showed me these are major, recurrent steps in spiritual healing: <u>Surrender</u> (temporary ego death), <u>forgiveness</u> and <u>acceptance</u> in that order.

It hasn't exactly been all gravy in the many years since my experience though I have been blessed many, many times. Though money meant much less to me after my experience I made money and retired early. Though my religiosity did not improve, my interest in the spiritual life exploded and I have spent much time reading the mystics of all religions and going to church and temple. Even the rough spots haven't seemed so rough. They all turned out to be good learning experiences. God's love is there for us all, without judgment. Going into my near-death-like experience, I was agnostic. Ever since, I've been changed. Although I was not near physical death, it was like a peek into eternity. Certainly, I had contact with a higher consciousness or power. Certainly, I was converted. I had - and I have - no doubt that there is a higher consciousness, that life is eternal at least in consciousness and that death is nothing to be afraid of.

About Bill Bingham

Bill worked as an engineer and manager, taught school, etc. but only got lucky when he started a one man business. Having made enough money, he retired at 47, glad to be free of the spiritually toxic atmosphere that hangs over most of the military industrial working complex. In 1992 he started and ran an IANDS near-death/near-death-like support group in Houston for 16 years. The group created the book, "When Ego Dies" published in 1996 by Emerald Ink. Bill was also the co-chair of the ground breaking 2006 IANDS 4 day conference held at a world famous Cancer hospital in Houston.

Bill can reached at: bingtx@hotmail.com

THE CLOSENESS OF GOD

Roger Bowlus, Ohio

I enlisted the day after Pearl Harbor in the United States Army Air Force and sent to Biloxi, Mississippi for basic training. There, I applied for and was accepted to be sent to pre-flight-flying cadet training in San Antonio, Texas. I was 23 years of age in 1941.

After completing primary, basic, and advanced training, and graduating as a USAAF pilot, commissioned as a second Lieutenant, I was sent to Fort Worth, Texas to be trained as a four-engine, B-24 pilot. B-24's had a flight crew consisting of pilot, co-pilot, bomb-bedier, navigator, gunners and a flight engineer.

Upon completing the B-24 training and awaiting further assignment after graduating, I was asked by my instructor if I'd care to accompany him on a training mission where he had one student who had not qualified in night landing. It was dusk where your depth perception for a short time has not acclimated itself to the near-darkness, and the student undershot the runway which sheared the landing gear, and we slid down the run-way on the belly of the plane, in a shower of sparks - the force of the crash ruptured the gas tanks and when the plane stopped at the runway intersection, we quickly evacuated via the emergency exit from the flight deck. We had no more cleared the wreck than the plane exploded! Right then, I felt that the Lord had been with us and saved our lives!

After graduating in late summer of 1943, I was retained as an instructor in B-24's and operated in that capacity at Fort Worth until early 1945 when the latest consolidated B-32's were introduced to the flight industry, and I was assigned to be an instructor in this new advanced aircraft.

Being raised during the depression, my father was a salesman, and we lived in different cities. I attended many schools, but the family never established on-going contact with any church. We were, however, constantly reminded of God's presence.

After the escape from the burning aircraft, it seemed to me that I felt the presence of a guardian angel or a Divine presence from that moment on. Flying at night in SW Texas during WW-2 with NO moon, the darkness is about as intense as I have ever experienced. SW Texas in that period was NOT populated and there were few if any ground lights, so it was DARK!

My "experience" was not one where I saw anything, experienced any "touching," etc., rather, I had a "mental feeling" of being close to God. This was not a one-time occurrence. Whenever I was flying at night under similar conditions, I "felt" the same closeness and "close" is the only word that expresses the feeling. That feeling gave me confidence to perform my duties and impart the best of me to my students, who, soon would face the ultimate test.

To this day, I converse with the Lord - not at any given time but when I feel the need to ask for guidance or just to talk! Mainly, to thank Him for granting me great health at my age of ninety-two.

I served a bit over four years in WW-2, followed by twelve years in the USAF Reserve. I flew just under three-thousand hours of Air Force flight time in various Air Force planes followed by over forty-two years of employment in the former Bell System and of utmost importance, fifty-two years of a solid, fully enjoyable marriage to a super lady who fought and lost, a valiant fight to ovarian cancer.

It is not of my origination, but I have found, that God works in ways that are mysterious to us and as time passes, we find that in most cases, if we take the road He has opened for us, things will work out.

This is not the country I grew up in. Greed has replaced pride of attainment, living together, and creating off-spring outside of marriage is fully accepted. Observance of established laws and living within one's financial means has been lost, as has total control of off-spring by parents, and more and more people have grown dependent upon the largess of government, supplied by taxing those who diligently work. For a large part, we have lost the association and guidance of the Lord which has led to taking the least desirable choices.

About Roger Bowlus

Author's Note: I have been privileged to know this young-spirited man of ninety-two years of age through several years of email correspondence when he first contacted me after reading my book, *Hear His Voice.* An intelligent, warm-hearted gentleman, he asked many questions about near-death experiences and the after-life knowing that he would soon be heading for "home" one of these days. Recently, he told me that because of our correspondence, he can now face his ultimate destination to the afterlife without fearing it. *This is precisely why these spiritually transformative experiences need to be talked about and shared with others! This knowledge can bring hope and comfort to others in knowing that life is a continuum.*

IN THE PRESENCE OF GOD

Sandy B., North Carolina

Her account is documented in the questions and answers from my research questionnaire.

Q. At the time of your near-death-like, mystical, or spiritually transformative experience, were you close to death, perceived a life-threatening event or experience serious illness or physical trauma?

A. No, I was depressed, and I wanted to die, but I was in no danger of dying.

Q. What was your age at the time of your experience?

A. Twenty-three years.

Q. Describe what you were doing at the time of your experience.

A. I was asleep at the time of my near-death-like experience. I was depressed for a long time and wanted to die because I gave up on life, but I made up my mind never to commit suicide. I was just barely getting through each day.

Q. Did you experience a feeling of lifting out of your body or something other?

A. When I first discovered that I was in a place that was very different than Earth, I didn't even realize that I was not in my physical body. I did not realize that I was out of my physical body until I returned back, and it took me quite by surprise that I was somehow being "poured" back into my body, still laying on the bed. It was only at that moment that I realized that my spirit/ soul had been separated from my physical body.

Q. Did you have a sense of traveling through a dark space, void, tunnel or something else?

A. No, I had no awareness of how I got to that place in the Light or how I came back. I didn't see any travel going to or from the Light. I was just instantly there and then instantly back again.

Q. Did you hear any sounds during your experience?

A. Yes, I heard the most beautiful music that doesn't even compare to music that we know on Earth. This music was perfect and free with flowing emotion that was more like a type of communication. This music flowed through my spiritual body like the wind. I did not hear it with my ears, but I heard it with my whole essence. It's difficult to describe what this was like. The music was communicating with me and trying to soothe me at the same time as it was reflecting my own excitement and awe. I felt that the music was emanating to me (from God) while I also felt my own contribution to the music. It was like a musical dance of emotion flowing toward me and through me and also flowing back out from within myself, coming from my own emotions. Both sources (from God and from myself), intertwined and mingled together to make the most beautiful music!

Q. Did you see a Light? If so, did you see the Light from a far distance, in front of you, beside you, behind you, or merged into oneness with you?

A. The Light was all around me and coming from the ONE who was in front of me, identified to me, (with an "otherworldly" type of communication), as Our Father, Our Creator. This Light was so bright that there could be absolutely no darkness or no shadow in this place. I didn't look at myself, so I have no idea if I looked like a being of Light. All I know is that I was in the Light, completely surrounded and submerged in the Light.

Q. If you saw a Light, who or what did you perceive the Light to be?

A. The Light was connected with Our Father, the Divine Source of Life.

Q. Did this Light have any immediate impact upon you? If so, describe.

A. Yes, this Light was brighter than if I were to be a tiny gnat caught inside the filament of a light bulb - yet this intense Light did not hurt my eyes to look within it. It was brighter than if I were to look at the sun. I was amazed by its intensity.

Q. Did you see or sense any other beings or entities present during your experience?

A. Yes, I sensed other beings behind me, but I didn't turn around or focus my attention to look at them. I didn't want to distract myself away from seeing Our Creator because nothing else mattered to me at that moment. I was completely mesmerized and in awe of finding myself in the presence of God. Even though I did not look at the other entities, I could feel/sense their presence and their loving thoughts radiating out toward me.

Q. Did you experience a feeling of love or intensified feelings?

A. Yes! Every emotion that I felt, whether from the Divine Source, the other entities, or even from myself emanated with intensified feelings. I was overwhelmed and overjoyed with this intense feeling of love, acceptance, and security.

Q. Did you observe anything frightening during your experience?

A. Nothing was frightening even though I did not know what to expect next. I just loved God with my whole being, and I felt God's love encompassing every speck of my essence. There was no other emotion felt other than from the purest feeling of love. It was ecstasy!

Q. Did this experience seem real or dream-like or a hallucination? Explain.

A. Not at all! This experience was more real than my life on Earth. Even though I can distinguish between being asleep or awake, it was as if life on Earth is also a type of dream state and that my near-death-like experience was the real life. And now it's as if I am back on Earth, still stuck in my dream, and I can't wake back up!

Q. What was the most relevant and meaningful part of your experience? Why?

A. The most relevant and meaningful part of my experience was God! I never would have believed that it was possible to be in the presence of God if I hadn't experienced it for myself. I couldn't imagine that God would be so concerned or interested in being with me. I feel like a nobody, nothing important, but God showed me that no one is insignificant to God.

Q. Did this experience increase or decrease your spiritual or religious beliefs or practices in any way? If so, in what way?

A. Obviously, I no longer have any doubts about the existence of God, but I did come away understanding the difference between what I found and experienced in the Light which differs from what religious beliefs and practices teach about God.

I felt the love of God firsthand; therefore, I know better than to follow what people teach which doesn't resonate with God's Divine love.

Q. Following your experience, do you consider yourself to be more spiritual than religious? If so, how would you explain this to others?

A. Yes, I do consider myself to be more spiritual than religious following my near-death-like experience. Before that, I was religious-minded and very conscientious about God and very active in my church. I listened to what religious leaders taught because I didn't know what to expect about God, and I wanted to please God. But after my experience, I found out what to expect from God by actually **witnessing** Our Creator interact with me. My experience showed me how people from all religions misunderstand the Divine nature of Our Creator.

Q. Do you feel more, less, or still the same in areas of compassion, love and acceptance of others? Explain.

A. I have always been a compassionate, loving person who accepted people for who they are but after my "awakening" experience, I did become more open and confident to embrace all Divinely inspired religions under God. I came to understand the unity of all religions while at the same time understanding that most followers of any of these religions don't fully comprehend their own scripture in its truest form of guidance without human distortions or without human misunderstandings being incorporated into them.

Q. Do you feel more, less, or still the same in your desire to help others? Explain.

A. Ever since I was born, I had a sense of helping others. Even so, I have come away from my experience wanting nothing else but to help people to better understand the unity of all life with a better way of coexisting with a diversity of cultures, etc. I learned of my mission during my awakening, and I had an intense desire to fulfill this mission as best as I was able.

Q. Did you talk about this experience with anyone? How did people respond?

A. I shared my experience with family members and a few close friends. My family members believe me as they well know that I am a truthful person and would not make up such a tale. My husband and children have witnessed the strong effect on my life that my near-death-like experience and awakening has had on me which strongly impacted and changed my life in many ways. Other family members had difficulty embracing what has happened to me for what it actually was. They prefer to believe that I had some sort of strong dream, and they don't want to even entertain anything that doesn't agree with their already established religious belief.

Q. Have you lost interest in materialism and competition to achieve a higher standard of living? Explain.

A. I never was a very materialistic or competitive person who craved a rich lifestyle. I didn't want to be poor but preferred to live with enough ease and comfort not to have to struggle in hunger and poverty. After my near-death-like experience, I have become even less materialistic about a higher standard of living. I came to understand that there is a higher purpose to life than to just live for a life of comfort. Life was about learning and evolving into a higher consciousness of morality and acquiring virtues. Most of these virtues are gained by enduring difficult challenges and overcoming problems. I realize that our trials and tribulations are the means to bring about the challenges that we need to go through to learn and evolve into our higher consciousness.

Q. Did this experience lessen your fear of death? Explain.

A. Absolutely! I don't have any fear of what will happen to me at the death of my physical body because I KNOW that I will continue to live in the spirit.

Q. Do you have a better sense of self-acceptance? Explain.

A. I do have a better sense of self-acceptance. I used to be a person who beat myself up for my mistakes. I used to feel that I wasn't good enough or smart enough or accomplished enough in life. But now I realize that God accepts me for who I am and that I don't have to be an accomplished person by human standards. God's ways are not our ways. God doesn't judge us by our credentials or academic accreditations, certificates or social status. God knows us for who we are in spirit.

Q. Do you feel this experience is sacred or holy in some way? Explain.

A. Definitely! It bothers me to share my experience with negative skeptics and debunkers. People who don't understand what it was like to experience what I did disrespect the sanctity of what I experienced. Those people didn't feel the awe that I did, so my experience means nothing to them in regards to them respecting the sacredness of the Divine, and so they ridicule, insult and mock Divine things. This is difficult to tolerate because it is as if they are desecrating the goodness of the holy and they have no idea what they are doing. It is like giving pearls to the swine because they trample the goodness underfoot. They don't see or acknowledge the precious treasure of spiritual insights and knowledge.

Q. Following your experience, do you have more, less or still the same feelings of an inner sense of Spirit or of the God of your understanding? Explain.

A. I have a much better understanding of God after my experience; therefore, I KNOW that we have a physical and spiritual essence.

Q. Do you have a greater desire to read, study, share, or discuss matters of a spiritual nature following your experience? Explain.

A. After my experience, I couldn't stop thinking about it. I hungered to find more insights about spirituality and how other people experienced spiritual things. I read, studied, shared, and discussed matters of a spiritual nature from anywhere and any place I could find it. I was no longer tied to one brand of religion because my mind opened up to understand the core of interconnectedness of all religions and all things back to our Original Source.

Q. Are you more sensitive to sounds, light, allergies, electric or electronic malfunctions, etc.?

A. I don't like loud noises or large crowds. I have noticed that the light bulbs in my house blow out pretty often. I don't know if this is related to me, but this seems to be a noticeable difference that I hadn't noticed before my experience.

Q. Do you view life and humanity's purpose on Earth any differently now?

A. Yes, I do realize that there is more to life than our life on Earth. We don't stop living when our physical body dies. We continue to live in the spirit, and there is a sense of purpose.

Q. In retrospect, do you think this experience happened for a reason or to help you in some way? Explain.

A. Both. This experience gave me back my life when I was

suffering from depression. It has renewed my life with a sense of purpose and mission. My near-death-like experience and awakening has helped me to discover many spiritual truths that I couldn't have known without discovering it firsthand, and I am so thankful to be reassured and confident of many spiritual things without having so much insecurity and doubt as I had before. Spirituality to me is no longer based just with faith, but is now set upon a foundation of KNOWING it by **witnessing it**. I have no more doubts about the existence of God because I know that God exists!

Q. What is the single most important bit of wisdom you wish to tell others who have not had a transcendent type of experience?

A. There is so much to share about spirituality and the Divine, so this is a difficult question for me to pinpoint to just one bit of wisdom. I want to say that life is about discovery and change, and we must learn to always be flexible in our hearts so that we may be open to discover new, mysterious, and amazing things that we didn't previously understand. Life is a gift to be enjoyed with freedom to explore higher states of consciousness. If we block our minds from discovering ethereal insights, then we will miss out on the richness and beauty of life's purpose.

About Sandy B.

Sandy is a homemaker, wife and mother. She has had several spiritually transformative experiences, and is working on writing books about her experiences. Sandy is a member of Aciste,org and Aciste.ning.com (Experiencer only website). She may receive messages through these sites.

MY SPIRITUAL ODYSSEY

Eunice Brock, China

When a teenager I read the following poem written by a college student:

I do not ask for ease.
The tender years gave me that -
That and the feeling of swift wings
Toward the sun.
I only ask that the hill
Be high enough and steep enough
That at the summit
I may look into the sun
And yet turn back
Beholding what little I have done
To find it good.
I ask for a song at the top
And a torch against
The darkness going down.

At the age of ninety-three I feel like I'm on top of a high mountain with a song in my heart. From this high point, I look backward into the past and forward into the future. So let me share with you some of my feelings and thoughts from this high point in my life. As I look back, it has been my spiritual odyssey that has been the most important thing. My odyssey began a few days before my fifth birthday. My parents were on furlough in America and were raising money for the mission at a religious camp meeting in North Dakota. The evangelist preached about his horses running away, upsetting his carriage and causing many broken bones. He told how God saved him and healed all his broken bones. I was so delighted that God had healed that man's broken bones that when the altar call came, I headed to the altar.

At the altar an evangelist for children asked me what I was praying for, and I told her the whole world. She told me I should ask Jesus to forgive my sins. I responded that I hadn't done anything bad so didn't need to ask for forgiveness. I asked God to bless a few more people and went back to my seat. This of course didn't fit the "born again" experience the missionary community held, but I was sustained by knowing that Jesus had blessed little children and said they belonged to the Kingdom of Heaven.

I was born in China in 1917 of Christian missionary parents and grew up in China during a period when the nation was in turmoil. In Bunching Fu, now called Liaocheng in Shandong Province, there was almost constant war between war lords and a three-year famine caused the death of about 8,000,000 people. The lords were not anti-American and the danger to us was from stray bullets and shells that sometimes landed on mission property. As communism began to arise, it brought with it strong anti-Western feelings. When I was nine years old, this anti-Western feeling was so strong that the American consul ordered all Americans to leave the area where we were living and go to Tsingtao, a port city, where American war ships were stationed. I do not remember if my near-death-like experience occurred before we went to Tsingtao or after our return to Tungchang Fu a year and a half later when anti-Westernism seemed to be less dangerous.

The missionaries where I lived always held prayer meeting every Saturday morning which met in another compound across the street from where I lived. I knew the missionaries had some anxiety about the rising anti-foreign feeling, and that south of us some Westerners had been killed. It wasn't Saturday and my parents had gone across the street for a special prayer meeting. I was out in our yard when I heard the roar of an angry mob that had filled the street. I had heard throughout childhood the story of Christian martyrs who had been beheaded by the Boxers, and I knew the mob could easily break through our gate and cut off my head. At that moment, a wall of fire shoulder high surrounded me and radiated such a profound peace I knew if the crowd broke in I would face beheading with serenity. The mob finally disappeared without doing damage. The peace that passeth understanding has remained. Someone once asked me what color the wall of fire was that surrounded me. I do not remember the color but only the profound peace it radiated. I had no fear of death.

For me, Jesus is a powerful spiritual being who can inspire one's life. I have tried to understand the historical Jesus. I have read that near the time of his birth an uprising of Jews was put down by the Romans who crucified two-thousand of them. What hatred must have resulted! And then Jesus came along and told all those hate-filled people they should love their enemies. Jesus taught that the love of God and what was like it, the love of man, was the essence of spiritual life. Jesus saw love fulfilling the law. Law was meant to prevent murder, theft, etc. Love of others would prevent such acts. The Jews learned in their early years that they were very special persons as God had chosen them out of all the people on earth to give them His sacred law.

The gospel of love threatened the beliefs of the Jews, so Jesus was killed as a heretic by the Jewish religious leaders. Being a devout Jew, it probably never entered the mind of Jesus that his followers would create a break-away religion from the Jewish faith. Jesus preached about the Kingdom of God as a spiritual Kingdom and not about forming a church. The word church mentioned in the gospel written in Greek was not in the Aramaic language used by Jesus.

Like Jesus, I am not a Christian. I believe that love is the essence of spiritual life and that the spirit lives on beyond bodily death. I also believe the laws of God are universal and applicable to all advanced intelligent beings everywhere in our multiple dimensional universe. Some religious beliefs currently held seem tribal or limited to our planet. Because of the strong evidence for reincarnation, I have recently come to believe in it. So I believe my odyssey will continue after death and in other incarnations. Incarnation answers some questions and raises other questions. I also believe our individual consciousness is a part of some larger consciousness.

In my forties, I had my third mystical experience. On one occasion in a very beautiful spot in sexual union with my husband, I experienced a profound oneness with the nurturing universe - a oneness with the yin energy at least as I define the female nourishing energy of the universe.

For me the ultimate stuff of the universe is Divine Cosmic Consciousness. Just as water can take the form of a solid, a liquid, or a gas each with its different attributes so I believe God creates from His-Her -Self, all the forms that make up our multidimensional universe. For me, that seems that every quark and every galaxy and every form of life or spirit are a part of God. Like the poet I believe: "Flower in the crannied wall could I perceive you all in all I would know what God and man is."

As I consider God to be the creator of all, He-She is directly or indirectly responsible for all we perceive as good or evil. It seems to me that the purpose of life in the four-dimensional part of the universe is for spiritual development and that comes about from working to abolish evil, a never-ending problem as solving one problem often lays the foundation for another problem. We may think of diseases as evil and if we abolish them, what happens to the population problem?

It is interesting to me that some who have had a near-death experience find answers to all their questions about good and evil which they promptly forget when they are resuscitated. I tend to humanize God by thinking that the universe is God's cosmic game. Earth is one of the stages for drama in which we play our part. What would drama be like without villains? In our theaters and TV shows don't we enjoy the conflicts between the villains and heroes? How flat life would be without marches for peace, caring for the ill and dying, building houses for the poor, entering the political arena for a cause, etc. Every stage is the evolution of man offered challenges. As I see it, this is the nature of the Divine plan.

I believe that God not only enjoys the drama of exploding stars and colliding galaxies but also enjoys the dramatic evolution of life and human society. Our senses evolved to meet the requirements of our four-dimensional world, but in addition, humans developed curiosity about the abode of spirits. The first signs of this interest were when they started to buy practical objects with the bodies of the dead. Tribes utilized shamans to deal with the spirits and souls of the ancestors. As I see it, there is a great difference between the Near East religions and the Hindu and Buddhist religions. The Jewish, Zoroastrian Christian and Muslim religions taught about sin and salvation provided by God, whereas the Buddhists and Hindus taught that God and Nirvana were reached by one's own spiritual growth and development that usually required many reincarnations. Hell for the Buddhists and Hindus were temporary and to teach the person that wrong doing had negative consequences whereas Hell for the Zoroastrian, Christian and Muslim was eternal, and personally, I see no useful purpose served by the latter. Our knowledge of God, ourselves, and the universe is very limited. Each has a bit of knowledge like the blind who knew what the elephant was like only by the part they grabbed hold of.

To prevent religious conflicts we need a uniting faith for our Global Village. It may well be science and technology that will bring this about. I will briefly mention several things that may weaken the dogmas of the various religions. A Gallop Poll indicated that 15, 000 Americans have had a near-death experience. Important research has been carried on in the U.S.A, Europe, and other countries. Studies have shown that many of those who have had a near-death experience have sought to live a more spiritual life, and they have become far more liberal in their religious beliefs. I want to see China start research in this field. Much research in consciousness is being done in some of our major institutions and in organizations for that purpose. Research in Princeton indicates that mind can move matter. Research at Stanford indicates that mind can change the radiation rates of chemicals.

For two thousand years or more the Hindu and Chinese doctors healed the ailments of their patients by treating the energy of the body, the life-force the Hindus call prana and the Chinese call qi (chi.) This energy rising from the base of the spine to the crown chakra produces a powerful experience called the kundalini experience. Yogis sometimes experienced this after years of meditation, but it can happen spontaneously and is doing so more often. There is no reason why some form of equipment can't be invented to stimulate this experience that sometimes profoundly increases the knowledge and ability of the person. Physicists have mathematically devised a ten-dimensional universe made up of vibrating strands of space. The 20th century science mainly explored our four-dimensional world and look at the changes it made. This century other dimensions will be explored and just as great if not greater changes will result. What will happen when we have equipment that will make it possible to see and talk to those living in the dimensions on the other side of death? Why not a conference on theology with Zoroaster, Jesus, Mohammed, Buddha being the speakers?

About Eunice Brock

Author's Note: I am including a rather lengthy bio for Eunice Brock because I feel she is a remarkable woman who left a beautiful mark on my soul in the several years we have been emailing one another. I would like the readers to learn as much as possible about this amazing woman and her life that I have come to cherish.

Eunice graduated from Vanderbilt School of Nursing. After graduation, she married a Southern Methodist minister and helped him serve the rural churches in Georgia. She became the first woman local preacher and later the second ordained woman Southern Methodist Church minister. During the Second World War, she also taught high school and did some nursing.

Eunice and her husband became increasingly liberal and no longer believed that Christianity was the only way to know God so they left the Methodist Church. Her husband became a social worker, and Eunice obtained a M.S. degree in psychiatric nursing and worked as a nurse until she retired.

Her dream of returning to China to help its people never died, so she wrote Mr. Chen of the China Youth Development Foundation that builds schools in China. She told him she wanted to live in a very poor village and build a school. She flew to Beijing in September, 1999 and had several conferences with Mr. Chen. He felt that she should live near the area where she grew up, so what little Chinese she remembered would be understood. He went to the area and found Mayor Liu of Liu Miao Village to sponsor her. Mayor Liu showed her the village, its homes, and schools and asked her if she would donate computers to the primary school since the village didn't need a school.

Eunice decided to live in the village and donate computers, asking only for a translator and housekeeper. Mayor Liu held a high position in the "chicken factory" and Pat, a college graduate who spoke English and worked for him, was asked to work for

Eunice. Together, they moved to their village home. They were greeted on the street by a large number of villagers, and soon after, there was a ceremony in the school yard in which through the China Youth Development Foundation, Eunice donated computers to the school.

Local TV was present, and when the ceremony was shown on TV, it sparked the interest of other news media probably because of her age and the fact that she had chosen to live in a village when Chinese desire to move to cities that are more progressive than rural areas. She received a number of trophies including three trophies as a news maker, one in Liaocheng, one in Jinan the capitol of this province, and in Beijing. Last year she was honored by being given a Green Card by the Chinese government that allows her to live in China. This year the Woman's Federation in Liaocheng celebrated Women's Day with a program in a theater holding two to three thousand people. Certificates were given to ten men for their contributions to Liaocheng and then trophies and flowers to fourteen women who had made contributions. Eunice was given a trophy for providing a spiritual (humanitarian) model for Liaocheng citizens.

Eunice has been engaged in researching biofeedback and psychedelic drugs that may prove useful in helping certain types of mental illness. The Liaocheng International Peace Hospital where Eunice is Honorary President, is within several years building a 150 bed hospital for the mentally ill. She is preparing a doctor to work in the hospital using new techniques and drugs. Now at 93 years of age, she has developed a severe life-threatening problem with her aortic heart valve. But she told me she faces death with tranquility as her childhood experience permanently wiped away the fear of death.

For over two years, Eunice's major project has been writing a book for her Chinese friends entitled *Search for a World View That Will Harmonize the Scientific Concepts of the Physical and Spiritual Realms*. Eunice told me that this will be a very controversial book as much of it deals with the research of near-death experiences, after-death communication, reincarnation, and other psychic phenomena and also practices leading to spiritual experiences. Polls indicate 50% of the Chinese are atheists. The Communist Part of China (CPC) requires its members to be atheists, and it is the party that controls Chinese government. The woman translating her book into Chinese thinks it will not pass the CPC censorship.

However, Eunice told me that China is undergoing rapid changes. This decade they ended teaching that religion is the opiate of the people. Many thousands of Chinese study abroad and sooner or later, Eunice feels, their scientists, because of quantum mechanics, will become interested in consciousness research which is so prevalent in America today. Religions are also growing in membership in China especially the Christian religion. There are now 23 million Christians in China. A number of provinces are largely populated by Muslims or Buddhists. Unknown are whether Taoists are increasing in numbers, but Chinese Traditional Medicine, which they developed, continues to be used as well as their rites in weddings and funerals.

Eunice hopes that her book encourages the Chinese to contribute to the united spiritual power needed to overcome the crisis mankind and Earth faces.

CAROLYN'S STORY

"Carolyn" wishes to remain anonymous

I was thirteen years old and preparing for confirmation in the Catholic Church. We had to study our religious doctrine so that we would be able to answer the Bishop's questions on our Confirmation day, should he choose to direct questions to us. (It was very intimidating to even think of the Bishop asking us a question!) So I was studying very seriously.

One Saturday afternoon, I was lying on my bed. I closed my eyes, and I do not know if I was asleep, but I saw a bright light going up to the sky from me - upward toward a figure who had arms outstretched. The figure was Jesus, and He was bathed in the bright warm light. He communicated to me that I could go to Him right then. I felt so loved and warm and welcomed as never before and I wanted to say "Yes." But it was clearly my decision, and since I am an only child, I began to feel sorry about leaving my parents. So, very regretfully, I said (or thought) "I can't go now, I want to, but I can't leave them." Jesus seemed to relate to me that He understood.

The feeling of peace and protection and love has never faded from my memory, or has the visual - light going upward very high to the Christ-figure with arms open at His side. The light was an energy-like connection between us, and communication between us seemed very real.

A GOLDEN LIGHT

Anthony Chipoletti, Pennsylvania

Sometime around 1995, I was looking through the book-shelf at my local large chain grocery store. My sister worked there, and I was comfortable spending time browsing through the titles. One title, *Beyond The Light*, caught my eye. It covered research into near-death experiences. The author, PMH Atwater, included her contact information, so I bought the book to try to understand my own near-death experience which had happened fifty years before that day.

I invited PMH Atwater to Pittsburgh, PA to speak about her research. She gave me three names with phone numbers, and insisted that I call each person before she would visit me. The first man I spoke to on the phone had hosted small groups of near-death experiencers in his home for many years, but he claimed to be a skeptic and declared his disbelief in any super-natural events such as near-death experiences.

The second call was with a young woman who had a ten-year old son. She claimed to have exaggerated an experience that she and her son had in order to get public attention.

The third call was to Nancy Clark. Nancy never mentioned any details of her experiences except to say that she died during childbirth and woke up in the morgue. However, she asked about my family, and she related details about her family. We agreed to keep in touch. As soon as I hung up the phone, my bedroom was filled with a golden light. It seemed to be the presence of my mother who had died about six months before that date. I sat back down and waited until the light was gone, which happened after about thirty minutes. The light had filled the room, about twenty feet by twenty feet, maybe nine feet high. It did not seem to be anything physical but appeared to be in a spirit realm, meaning the light was not the same as my light- bulb within the room, but the light appeared to me to an awareness of a spiritual presence.

When PMH Atwater and I contacted each other, I asked her if I should tell Nancy what had happened, but she said that many people who had spoken to Nancy experienced similar events, so it would be no surprise. Many months later, Nancy asked me to provide some brief information about the light. Now several years later, Nancy has again asked me to write a short description of my light experience which happened after Nancy and I talked on the phone in 1995, This account is the result of Nancy's request.

While I still believe that the light included the presence of my mother's spirit, and that Nancy was the catalyst to allow me to have that experience, my ideas about life have changed considerably since 1995. This year, 2010, has altered my ideas about many different topics. But every year since 1995 has been very enlightening to me. In 1995, I became a research interviewer for the Drug Abuse Treatment Outcome Study, which produces a white paper report for the President of the United States of America.

After 1995, the experience as a DATOS interviewer was way too stressful for me, so I moved on to other adventures. My Internet presence became a catalyst for many of my new ideas, some of which I recorded and uploaded as audio pod casts. The most enlightening pod cast which I recorded was about the tau neutrino. About the year 2000, the tau neutrino was the last of twelve building blocks of matter to be discovered. The electron had been discovered about 1897, so I named my pod cast The Tau Neutrino and the Century of Science, The 1900's.

Since 1995, I have decided that the human point of view is only one of billions of possible point of views. I believe that we are experiencing our HOW and not a WHO. We have an eternal awareness of every point of view, however, I feel that our human point of view is so distracting and localized that we simply have no comparison to our abilities to experience REAL TIME. I define REAL TIME as the infinite set of experiences which include the local human point of view, however, also includes every other point of view.

This infinite awareness, I believe is our true reality. We are aware of every aspect of existence; however, it is impossible for our human point of view to encompass the infinite mind. I believe we have existed forever as a spiritual awareness. No one created eternal.

In Nancy Clark's research questionnaire, she asked the question, "In retrospect, do you think this experience happened for a reason or to help you in some way?" I answered, "Yes, simply to acknowledge the spiritual awareness of love and peace." This interpretation is still the one which I believe, is our spiritual awareness, it has existed forever and will continue forever, simply as it is now, an awareness of infinite and eternal existence. Our experiences are also infinite and further, I believe that we exist for the purpose of communicating within our spiritual awareness forever.

About Anthony Chipoletti

Anthony is a story writer and co-owner of the movie script, *The Graviton Ring and the Structure of Everything.* He has also published a short story, *Android, Age One,* published only on the web. His email address is: graviton ring@gmail.com

I AM NO ONE SPECIAL

"Christine" wishes to remain anonymous

I am no one special. I have always known that the earth is not my home. Being raised in a strict Catholic home, I never questioned the existence of God. In my late twenties, I felt the need to seek God more sincerely. This seeking has brought to me mystical experiences, the first of which I share here. I think all of us are trying to find our way back Home. It is just that some of us are aware we are on the journey, and others are not.

It was the year I made a sincere request to God about helping me to find my way back. I had just given birth to my first child that year. Perhaps that experience made me feel closer to God and want to have Him more in my life. Creating new life is quite a miraculous thing. I had always been a religious person, a devout Catholic, raised in a strict Catholic house with two sisters and four brothers. My mother converted to Catholicism when I was a young girl. My father's family has always been Catholic. At this time, I was asking to know the Truth. Perhaps I was sensing that there was more to God than the trappings of church traditions and rituals. Looking back, I realize it was a time of innocence…a child asking her Father for advice.

One night as I was falling asleep, two entities (I could not see them), used their energy to accelerate me at a high rate of speed upward where I had an encounter with Jesus. He was not configured as a person, rather he was a flowing stream of consciousness. I just knew it was Him. He asked me, "Do you love me?" I burst into tears and said "Yes." Then out of the stream of consciousness came an arm (His arm) to embrace me. I was then shown a symbol made up of three letters that were whiter than any white we have on earth. They were "ISH."

At the time I wasn't sure what they stood for but I remembered having seen them before during my religious education when I was a child. I then "fell" at a high rate of speed back into my body. The next day I looked up the meaning of "IHS." It is a contraction derived from the Greek word IHSOYE, Jesus, used as a symbol or monogram. It later became understood as a Latin abbreviation, IHS, meaning Jesus Hominum Savior - Jesus Savior of Men.

Shortly after this, I was exposed to *A Course in Miracles* after it was first published. Other texts and experiences came along. For example, I was invited to attend a teaching session with Elisabeth Kubler-Ross to observe the work she was doing. I no longer questioned how something comes to fall into my experience. I realize I live by Grace.

As the years rolled by, I concentrated on raising my children, following my husband to further his career. I do have degrees in education and have taught school along the way. I care deeply for children. At one point not long after this experience, I opened a Montessori school which still exists today. I know it has helped many children receive a good start. I continue to nourish my soul with spiritual material. The mystical experiences have become fewer. But I am expecting them to happen again at some point. I feel I have some work to be done before I am finished living here. My intuitive sense became stronger over the years, and I have acquired an abiding Knowing that all is OK.

I am no one special. I just had a sincere desire thirty-plus years ago to return Home. I wanted this to the exclusion of all other things. God hears the yearnings of our hearts and He responds. Have no doubt about that.

Questions and Christine's Answers from
my research questionnaire:

Q. Did you experience a feeling of lifting out of your body or something other?

A. "I did not sense anything unusual in my body that particular night but over the course of a few months during which the experience occurred, I developed what felt like a thickness in my throat. I went to see a throat specialist who could not find anything, but I could really feel a lump-like structure. Years later while reading metaphysical literature, I discovered writings about the chakras and felt that it may have had something to do with my throat chakra opening up. It subsided over time. This was about the same time my heart would burn too - with love I think. I haven't researched that yet to this day. I actually have rather forgotten about it until you asked this question. At this time, I also occasionally would feel this tremendous love for a person (perfect strangers) I saw on the street. Not everyone, just some - like I knew them before or some part of me knew them before, and I felt very drawn to them by love."

Q. What was the most relevant and meaningful part of your experience? Why?

A. "Being in Jesus' presence and being asked by Him if I loved Him. It has given rise to questionings within myself about my thoughts, attitudes, and behaviors ever since then. All these years hence, I have contemplated what it means to love Him. What a wonderful teaching technique! It's like the Socratic Method. I am still wondering if I was or am behaving in such a way that is pleasing/acceptable to Him. As the years have gone by, I've come to realize what a precious gift/opportunity I was blessed with. I also believe that I could be with Him again if I so wanted."

Q. Did this experience increase or decrease your spiritual or religious beliefs or practices in any way?

A. "It increased my spiritual beliefs and practices immensely. I became more motivated than ever to seek out Truth. Books and people cross my path. I am open to learn and expect to be shown the way. I felt like I was given permission to investigate/ study other spiritual sources emanating from other places than the Catholic Church."

Q. Do you feel more, less, or still the same in areas of compassion, love and acceptance of others?

A. "I have more compassion and acceptance of others because I know they come from the same Source as I come from. This understanding was not instantaneous. Some things I know intellectually from reading and studying, and some things I have learned by using my heart. I cannot explain this."

Q. Did you talk about this experience with anyone? How did people respond?

A. "I have never told anyone of this experience but you. I have always felt that it was too Holy and Sacred and personal to share. I still feel that way to some extent. I do have an awareness that I will need to share more and more as I grow older."

HEAVEN AND HELL

Matthew Dovel, Nevada

I've had two near-death experiences. One experience was pleasant and the other was unpleasant. Both have had deep and lasting personality transformations.

At the age of twelve, I drowned and went into the white light coming face to face with God almighty, and as He grabbed me by the wrist, He told me that I had work to do, so I had to go back. Upon my return, I immediately was acutely aware of just how evil this world was having suddenly spiritually emancipated. I also noticed I could now feel and see other people's emotional state of mind making it very difficult to be around other people especially large groups. When others were at their peak emotional states, from anger to love, I would become overwhelmed, and it wasn't long before I found temporary relief in alcohol and drugs.

At the age of twenty-five, the alcohol and drugs stopped having the desired effect, and I was once again unable to cope with my gifts, so I remembered that the only time I have ever felt complete and at utter peace was when I was in the presence of the Lord. Hence, I decided to return to heaven and leave this hell, what I perceived to be hell, behind me. I attempted suicide and had my second near-death experience, but this time I didn't go to heaven.

I was dropped into the pit of hell for three days where I was shown the nature of my sins times seven. However, that was nothing compared to being shown a vision of eternity in hell if I didn't change my ways. While I was being delivered from hell, I was told I still had work to do, and I couldn't do it if I was drinking or doing drugs. Trying to describe hell and for anyone to fully comprehend eternity in hell would be like trying to describe a color to a blind person. I will never forget these two near-death experiences as they are etched permanently in my mind.

From the day I returned from hell until now, I have yet to take a drink of alcohol or a mind or mood altering drug having quit a thousand dollar a week drug habit cold turkey. Also, I have dedicated my life to helping the suicidal and the survivors of suicide.

After the second near-death experience, I experienced even more spiritual enlightenment, opening my awareness to this world and the afterlife. Still able to see and feel the emotional states of others, I had new awarenesses that allowed me to help others overcome their emotional peaks.

These near-death experiences were the two worst experiences of my life and if it were up to me, I would have liked to have kept them a secret until my last breath, but God has other plans for me continually placing me in situations that give me no other choice but to share them. God's voice is loud and clear to me now, so when God told me to write a book about my experiences, I was very resistant at first. Having no writing ability or desire to be an author, I wrote a letter of query to the first publisher who I could reach just so God would leave me alone. Once again, God showed me His will by having the publisher want my manuscript, "My Last Breath."

With over twenty thousand books being published each month, and with the worst publisher in the world, just imagine my surprise when ABC's "Good Morning America" and "20/20" wanted to interview me about my experiences. Nothing I do, or have done can be claimed as my own ability or talent. It all comes from the one and only true source of power, God.

In 2006, I founded ISP (International Suicide Prevention) a 501(c)(3) public charity with the goal to help those that are suffering from suicidal thoughts, and families that have lost a loved one to suicide. I have developed a new methodology that is unique and effective for identifying the highest risk for potential suicides and removing suicidal thoughts. I'm proud to say that ISP has been called upon to work with public schools, police agencies, mental health professionals, international groups, and military.

Coming in contact with the creator has great responsibility, as nothing happens by accident, and there is a reason for everything that happens to us all. Being chosen to share what is next after this life cannot be changed or forgotten. I should know, as hard as I have tried to just be, I'm searched out, found out, by those wanting to know what is next for we will all know soon enough, and near-death experiences are God's way of preparing us. The choices we make today will echo for eternity.

About Matthew Dovel

Matthew is a suicide prevention expert who lives in Las Vegas, Nevada. You can read more about his experiences in his book, *"My Last Breath."* Check his websites: http://www.supportisp.org and http://www.mylastbreath.com

THE TWO WEEK MIRACLE

Christine Duminiak, Pennsylvania

In 2000 my dear dad, my best golfing buddy, was called Home to the Lord. Although this was a difficult time for me, I felt very blessed to have my mother, his soul-mate, still a part of my life. Four years later on Leap Day, my mother, the heart and soul of our very close-knit family, was also called Home to join him.

There was a deep pain and longing in my heart from losing the physical presence of my last surviving parent. Not only were we losing the last of our parents but the house full of memories of past holidays, birthdays, anniversaries, and all types of celebrations, as we would be selling their house soon too.

In spite of this, I believed that God, my dad, and my mother all wanted me to be happy again. I certainly longed to be happy again, and I knew that it would be difficult for me as a Certified Grief Recovery Specialist, who specialized in spiritual bereavement recovery, to be "up" for my clients unless joy returned to my heart once more. So I turned to Jesus and specifically asked, "Dear Jesus, please replace my heart's sorrow with Your joy."

These were the only words that I could barely utter to God in my time of deep pain and loss. I would mumble those same words every time the profound pain would wash over me.

I believe that my fervent prayer to Jesus got His tender loving care and attention toward healing me, as my mother came to me two days after her passing. She played in my mind one of the hymns that she wanted sung at her upcoming funeral. The hymn was "Loving and Forgiving Are You, Oh Lord." I felt that this particular hymn was also a message from her letting me know just how loving and forgiving God truly was.

I was also treated to a special vision of many silhouetted spirits wearing hats as they stood in front of a bright light with spiritual fireworks going up all around them. It was as if a grand celebration with the whole gang was taking place in Heaven because my mother was now there with them. Again, joy filled my heart seeing this special vision.

After just two short weeks of asking Jesus specifically to replace my heart's sorrow with His joy, a miracle happened. The pain in my heart suddenly left me. Yes, I still missed the physical presence of my beloved mother, but I was no longer in pain. Joy actually replaced my heart's sorrow once again, which is what I had specifically asked for. I was happy again!

For anyone who is suffering pain and sorrow from the physical loss of a loved one, from my own personal experience, my advice would be to call upon the Great Physician to heal you. Believe that you are very loved by God as one of His special kids, and you too will be amazed at the wonders that God can perform to heal you.

God bless you all. In Christ's Love.

About Christine Duminiak

Christine lives in Bensalem, Pennsylvania and is a Certified Grief Recovery Specialist, Founder of Prayer Wave for After-Death Communication. Radio Co-Host of "Ask the Angels," Author of *Heaven Talks To Children* and *God's Gift of Love: After-Death Communications*. Christine's website is: www.christine-duminiak.com

VISITS TO PARADISE

William Fechter PhD, USA

My three visits to paradise occurred while in a dream state, but they were not your commonplace dreams as I can remember them in great detail two decades after they occurred. I learned years later that some refer to these types of dreams as "visitations," but whatever they are called, they change the way you view reality.

My prior beliefs about reality before these dreams occurred were materialist leaning toward atheism, but with a hope or interest that something more exists after this physical life ended. With a PhD in a science field, my beliefs were much in alignment with materialism, and my belief that this physical world is the only reality. I was approaching fifty years of age, and I was asking the universe on a regular basis if anything existed beyond this life. These dreams appeared to answer that question.

Two of those dreams occurred just a few nights apart, and the third dream occurred several nights later, and this dream met at least in my mind the qualifications of a visitation dream. The first two dreams, I later learned, are called garden or paradise dreams. In both dreams, I was floating above a magnificent display of glorious landscapes, forests, lakes, and they were beyond anything that the beauty of this physical earth has to offer.

The third dream I met an entity on the other side, and this woman in a light gray robe was standing about 15 feet from me and had this gentle smile that radiated from her face. A smile that showed love and compassion that I cannot fully describe, her smile revealed a knowing beyond knowing about the struggles, hardships, and what I perceived as my personal failures that had occurred in my life. Then I realized I was receiving a life review as our minds were connected perfectly.

During my life review, she not only had knowledge, but she had complete understanding of each and every significant emotional event in my life. Until one experiences such a level of understanding from another, which I experienced in that life review, it is impossible for me to try to explain these feelings accurately to others. After several years of reflection, I could only best describe this level of knowledge and acceptance as divine understanding and compassion.

After this life review, I floated toward her as she opened her arms and then we hugged; then from the moment we touched which created a reverberation of vibration in our bodies that was pure ecstasy. It was like I could feel all of her energy every "ounce" of it. It was awe-inspiring and again beyond any words that I know of to describe this experience. Nothing, absolutely nothing, I have experienced in this life even comes close to this wonderful awe-inspiring hug. Then when we had almost merged together the dream ended instantly.

The most significant part of these dreams was the life review with telepathic communication and the spiritual hug that can only be described with such words as ecstasy, bliss, or rapture. The difference between our existing communication using words compared to telepathic communication can be compared to the difference between light and darkness. The understanding and compassion during the life review is something that I have never experienced in this life. Now I know beyond any doubt that compassion is more than sympathy or empathy- it is a deep and profound understanding combined with unconditional love and acceptance. It cannot be defined with mere words; it must be experienced.

The sense of realness was so absolute that I remember these dreams in almost full detail 20 years after these dreams occurred. I had never before had a dream like these dreams nor have I had any dreams like them since. These dreams helped me to begin a personal journey that has lasted for two decades to discover truths and seek deeply, very deeply into the mysteries of life. I am now writing a book with a co-author about several of these mysteries of life.

These discoveries and experiencing such compassion has given me the ability to see with clarity that we are not broken, we have not separated from God, likewise we have not fallen from the love or grace of God. We are unique expressions of God, and this uniqueness means that every soul reveals its unique attributes of God. We are but pioneers on an evolutionary journey of enormity, not in wealth and power, but an enormity in creativity, divine love, and compassion.

Once we have experienced such divine love and compassion that was revealed to me in that third dream, we have an enduring hope for our future, a longing to love all, a faith and trust that all of God's creation is perfectly imperfect for a divine reason.

As a retired consultant and college professor, I now can look back on my life and see how fate including those dreams has played its hand in my life. Those series of dreams helped to open the spiritual door to make the decision to become a sincere seeker of spiritual truths. I became intensely focused not only if life after death existed but into these mysteries of life such as suffering, ignorance, innocence, and the meaning of creation.

The most important bit of wisdom this dream meant to me might be summed up by a simple but profound quote of a Chinese sage: "The ways are but two: love and the want of love" Mencius 300 BC.

Once we have experienced this level of love and compassion that this woman in the gray gown revealed to me and if we sincerely seek to understand, not just know about but understand, then this simple but deeply profound bit of wisdom by a Chinese sage I believe will give us a greater longing to be able to respond with love and compassion to saints and the Hitler's alike- indeed to all life in the world.

About William Fechter, PhD

William Fechter, PhD is a retired university professor and consultant. He has just completed a book with co-author, Josie Varga, entitled, *Original Innocence: The Three Mysteries of Life Revealed*. If you would like to contact him, his e-mail address is: oureternalinocence@cox.net His website is: www.oureternalinnocence.com. Josie Varga's website is: www.josievarga.com

A PERSONAL STORY OF TRIUMPH

J. Paul Foreman, Utah

I spent twenty-two years of my life studying and searching for religious truth and finally came up against a wall of complete disappointment, even after going to Catholic elementary school, attending a Catholic priesthood seminary in Santa Barbara, California, and later graduating from a Catholic university. I erroneously concluded that God was an aloof, humanistic entity who paid little attention to the sufferings or to the personal concerns of men. My impatience led to anger because of my personal spiritual lacking at that time and because of the ineffectual ways I had committed myself in the pursuit to find God. My desires were in the right direction, but my methods proved to be unproductive.

I brooded over my failure for five years after leaving college, and when I could no longer stand myself being an atheist, I set out again to find religious truth. I moved to Utah and allowed some missionaries from the Latter Day Saints Church to visit and to talk with me about God. I was very touched by what I saw in this particular teaching; nevertheless, at the moment I had suspicions about organized churches generally, and I hesitated in giving my endorsement.

Art had always been one of my best subjects. I respected its power to uplift an artist's awareness to higher levels of perception and to gain a purer state of thought where work might truly begin. I began pencil sketches for a large composition of the crucifixion of Jesus Christ upon a cross. My interest to know more of the substance of God quickly revived as I engaged with this newly designed method of study. What would God tell me about Himself if I were to ask Him long enough and intense enough? I put all caution aside. To me, it was a one-way trip. For better or worse, nothing else mattered but this painting.

I re-built Golgatha before me in a preliminary series of images that formed out of my pencil drawings. The plan of perspectives designed for this painting would put me at the very place where He was crucified and among those who lifted Him up where I would be in a position to look directly into His eyes. Those elements and more were the focus of my mind and heart.

Several months of continual work passed, and in the late evening on October 1975, I was meditating on my sketches when something unusual pricked my mind and broke my concentration. Believing that I was only getting tired, I closed my eyes to rest them a moment when I saw remarkable things forming in my field of vision as though I were watching a fireworks display. I opened my eyes and I saw nothing in the room. I started to worry. The imagery changed rapidly into dark, incomprehensible forms and shapes, and I had no control over it! That was completely outside anything I had ever experienced. My anxiety became rising fear. I was on my feet frightened and completely bewildered! I was in the presence of something far more stronger than I that I could not see or touch. This *force*, whatever it was, had great power, and it was set against me! For hours it tore at my mind, abdomen, and soul with terrifying might. I felt like a leaf being ripped to shreds in a raging tornado! I put up all my strength to resist it by forming a single word in my heart and mind saying, no! That was all I could do, but I engaged all the strength, will and determination I possessed. The event was *absolute!* I had no idea how it would end.

Dawn came. My torment lessened slightly. I took my drawings of Golgatha outside and burned them. I was ashamed of what I had done. I was filled with anxiety and wracked with unbelievable tension, but I went to work that day with my brother. I desperately tried to convince myself that this awful power was from my imagination and that normality would come back if I kept myself busy doing ordinary things. We worked that day putting shingles on a roof. I spent that day on my knees silently begging God to forgive me as I drove nails into wood. That brought up a frightening thought of me driving nails into Christ that day on Golgotha. I transcended time at that moment, and I was on Golgotha with Him as though centuries had been overcame. Every sin I had ever committed paraded before me like ugly monstrosities. I trembled with shame, fear, anguish, disgust, and regret. There were so many. I was completely abased. I wanted to crawl in a hole and hide.

We went home late that day from work, but I could hardly stay there for even a moment. My ordeal suddenly came back with full intensity. With extreme alarm, I believed that God had not forgiven me! I left the house immediately, but I had no idea where to go or what to do. In a panic, I stopped my jeep a few blocks away and got out. I felt an immense force pulling my spirit toward a *dark realm*. The whole darkened sky was its mouth. I erupted in tears. I was completely heartbroken. There was no more fight left in me. I could only cry. I had never cried so deeply as that, not ever in my life, or since then.

At once, I was overcome by a much Superior Force which brought peace to me at the blink of an eye! It stopped everything instantly. I was filled with love from a Heavenly Being and a great calm settled upon me. My heart fixed upon the Savior, the Lord Jesus Christ. I knew it was He! Only He could have such commanding power!

Constantly thanking God for forgiveness, I drove home where I tumbled onto a couch utterly exhausted. I could hardly move, but I wanted to jump with gladness! Laying there with hot water streaming from my eyes, I was being cleansed. I was in a Heavenly place though I was in the same room as before. I could feel a hand above me moving from my head to my feet expelling impurities from my body. I could feel its magnificent power! I could hardly stop thanking God in Heaven for everything happening that day. I closed my eyes and in my field of vision came the word, "Morman." It subdued all of my faculties and held my attention spellbound. Above it was a white bird with wings. I knew what it meant. I was in the presence of God. I eased off the couch and onto the floor with my face down, I put my arms forward and clasped my hands together in complete supplication.

He spoke. "Thy body is a temple of the Lord. Keep it holy." The voice was slight, yet it pierced me through. I heard it not with my ears, but with my very bones. I was up off the floor and on the couch again. Again, I lay there with eyes streaming water when another wonderful thing occurred. Just like I was a new-born babe, a Being of Noble Majesty lifted me up into His bosom. I saw with *spiritual eyes*, and I heard with *spiritual ears*. Those loving arms enclosed me with the uttermost simplicity of all human existence. Words are impossible. Timelessness met briefly with mortality trapping for an instant the magnificence of creation in between. It was utter peace, utter calm, utter unity. For an instant, I knew all things past, present and future, and I was enlightened to origins, unity, and purpose though not a word was spoken.

Oh, the limitations of a mortal being having an eternal experience while possessing such a pitiful memory! Yet in the years following my wonderful presence in that eternal place, all would be re-affirmed to me time and time again as I prayed, as I fasted, as I studied the teachings, obeyed His Law, tended my duties, learned the doctrines, heeded the Prophets, and read the Scriptures of the Church of Jesus Christ of Latter Day Saints. There is no end to the knowledge of God that we can attain here on earth as we mature spiritually through the Spirit. He is here to help us every step of the way. The meaning of the universe is contained in our power to love, and it is His Love that guides us forward into it.

I felt total oneness with that Being of Noble Majesty. That

Love cannot be described, only felt. I was home; I belonged there. I am a fundamental element to the whole of creation. I am a child of God. I know those things with certainty. All things are given to those who ask. This is inclusive to everyone who has the heart. I knew also that I wouldn't be staying in that majestic place much longer; I had great things yet to accomplish as life would come to offer me. I had a purpose to fulfill, a contribution that must be completed. Onward thence, I would go from off that couch to finish my trials and assignments on earth which had been given me so long ago. Like a butterfly emerging from a cocoon, I prepared for flight into an enlightened spiritual world.

About J. Paul Foreman

Paul is retired. His email address is: paulfore@xmission.com if you wish to contact him.

GOD IS LOVE

Tim Hill, North Carolina

I will share this for as long as I live and as long as someone will listen. It changed my life and continues to this day.

Many years ago, maybe fifteen or more, I was accustomed to meditation and prayer every night. I was not religious by any means, and I did not attend every church service. Much of my relationship with God developed outside of the traditional church service. There are many more things I could share that would help bring you to a point of this experience, but to save time, I will just start here.

Every evening and for many years now, I look forward more than anything, to that time of prayer. To a time when I feel I am connecting and communicating directly with God. Many of my prayers were much like anyone else, asking for the things I felt I needed in my life, and that of family and friends, co-workers, and the world. But I began to realize a deeper need that wasn't so evident.

For years, as many do, I spent time asking for things or situations from someone I didn't even know. God was my security blanket or band-aid. I imagined if this God loved me as much as I have been taught to believe He did, then didn't He also long and even ache for me to know Him and not just what He could do for me? I experienced this later in life with my biological father, always there to provide money and buy me things, but I never knew him. So I made an effort to listen and to become attuned to that "voice" within. My mom explained it to me when I was a kid, and I will never forget it. "Mom, how do you know when you hear God's voice?" Her honest reply was "It's that little voice in your head that tells you not to do something that you shouldn't." Simple answer and sufficient for probably a seven-year-old at the time. I later realized she was really speaking about consciousness. And that was the God-consciousness I would hear when I was about to do something wrong, or some would call the "mind of Christ," unlike my own.

So this particular evening I laid in bed praying, listening, and trying to shut off my brain with all its thoughts and ramblings, until it was still, so that I might hear that voice. I remember so many nights feeling what I call the presence of God, that tingly, electrical feeling you get is all I can use to describe it. Many, many mornings that is the same feeling that would wake me up and not the alarm clock. Even now as I type, I am aware of His presence, but not always. I am laughing remembering that I would often say "God, I have everything I need, I want to hear from you, I want to know what you're thinking, what's on your mind, if I never was given any other blessing, even if you took away the breath in my body, I still have everything, YOU...and because YOU created all things, and all things exist in YOU, if I have YOU, what else is there?"

I don't remember falling asleep; I don't remember a specific moment when things changed, but at some point just being caught in this feeling of His presence, I found myself in another world, another place. A place where time didn't exist, where there was nothing physical to be seen or experienced. The only way I can describe it visually, was space without stars, dark, but full of light because before me and all around me were beings of light. I suppose you can call them angels, but that is a very elementary description of what I was seeing. Some people would say I had an out-of-body experience. More progressive Christians would say I was having an open vision. All I know is that it was the most real experience I have ever had to this day.

I didn't have a body and couldn't see myself. It was as if my mind or consciousness was existing somewhere else. I remember feeling like I was being held up or supported by two of these angels, but I couldn't see them.

There was a tremendous, beautiful white light in the center of my view. It was pure. I don't know how I knew this, but I just knew it. And I realized that this was God. I didn't see a man in a long, flowing robe, or with long hair or a beard, just pure white glorious light. All around Him were billions, even trillions of angels that extended for what seemed like millions and millions of miles. I felt so far away, but I felt so close at the same time. It was as if time and distance didn't exist. Hard to explain or convey with the words I have in my vocabulary. I could write a book on this one experience and all the things I have learned since because of it.

The angels all were light; there were no features that were recognizable, or distinguishable. I could not see a difference between male and female, black or white, American or European, there were no differences. They all had somewhat of a bluish indigo color in the center and other colors, smoky, even, but brilliant. I was absolutely fascinated and overwhelmed by what I was seeing. Then I became aware of what I was feeling.

I can't even begin to describe what I was feeling, but only what I know because of it. I was completely and totally saturated with love. Every molecule of my being or body or whatever you want to call it was permeated. His love is so powerful it literally touches every single molecule, atom, electron. I realized in that moment here on earth in this life, we are poorly equipped for the expression of this great love. Here, we get glimpses of love, through the nice things we do, the things we say, the tears we shed. We can only attempt to express this through our acts and words. But in Heaven (if this is where I was), love is not expressed, it simply JUST IS!!!

I remembered scriptures that describe God as being love, God **IS** love. His love is so pure it's as if it's tangible, like you touch and really truly see it. This feeling that everything about me was permeated is the same feeling I get now when I say I feel His presence. It's like every molecule just lights up, and you have this electrical feeling radiating over your body. It's like everything inside you starts to vibrate. I would imagine it's like the behavior of two tuning forks. If you strike one and another is within "range," the other one starts to vibrate and resonate with the other on its own. I felt totally connected with Him, like being submerged in warm water, but not only do you feel its effects on the outside on your skin, but also within. I guess you could say I felt like what a sponge would feel like if submerged and completely saturated.

Here in this life, love is so often mistaken for many other things, and many other things are mistaken for love. We do things in an attempt to express it, but fail many times. There is no greater love than that of God, even a mother's love for her child pales in comparison. The reason this is so is because we are limited in our ability to express it, to show others what it is. I think of a person born with no sight or hearing. I would imagine the only expression of love he or she could comprehend would be through touch, and one day if he/she was able to hear and see, and someone said, "I love you," even with tears running down his/her face, he/she would still not be able to comprehend what was being communicated. Often times our frames of reference of what we perceive is love, is distorted and corrupt and therefore, so is our expression of it.

Another remarkable thing is that I was communicating with these angels, but not with spoken words. We didn't even have vocal cords. That's flesh, and nothing of flesh could withstand His glory. I understood it, remembering again, that if you saw the face of God, you'd die, not being able to withstand it. There was so much warmth there.

In Heaven everything is visible. Here we communicate with body language, with the spoken language, with writing, with music. In Heaven everything is before you, there is no need

to question, no need to discern or figure out something. No
language barriers. You get tremendous amounts of revelation
knowledge by seeing. Imagine if you were blind, and someone
was describing a bird to you. Having never seen one, you'd probably have some crazy image in your mind about what a bird
looked like. But if you could actually see it, immediately you'd
know, no description needed. I now understand the importance
and advice of the scriptures to "not look upon sin" because you
literally take it into your being. Our eyes are truly the windows
to our souls. Likewise with our ears, what we choose to listen
to, ends up residing in our spirits. Like computer programming,
what goes in comes out, even if it's a defect, and sometimes it
shows up in the most unusual or unexpected places and may not
show up for months or even years.

In Heaven you truly are transparent because you are a reflection of Him. I remember formulating the question in my mind
why all the angels were the color they were. I received my immediate answer then and continue to receive it to this day. The
angels were literally a reflection of the pure white light. This
is how God taught me about the light spectrum and how you
could split pure white light up with a prism to see all the colors
of the rainbow.

Days later I asked for more information, more answers to
what I experienced and God caused me to think about a prism
and taught me a simple principle. God has many, many characteristics, and it is our purpose and should be our goal to line up
just so with Him, to reflect all the many colors/characteristics
of Himself. Because when you line up a prism just right with
a ray of white light, all the colors become visible (well most,
indigo isn't visible to the naked eye.) The true nature of the
light is revealed and expressed. It's the same with God. When
we become attuned to Him, lining up with His ways, His true
nature is revealed through us.

I am saving the best for last.

One other aspect of this experience was much more powerful than what I was seeing or feeling. It was what I was hearing.
There was such beautiful music. The most beautiful music I
have or most likely ever will hear. All these millions of angels
were praising Him, in complete adoration and worship. But
what was even more amazing was that again, this music was not
being sung with their mouths, it was simply emanating from
their inner most part. In this life on earth, you would say it was
coming from their hearts. I was so humbled and moved by this.
The only way I could describe it so that you might comprehend
it, is to ask you to imagine the whole world, all of creation, every
living thing, from the biggest mammal to a one cell organism,
even the ocean and winds, singing in perfect, absolute perfect
harmony. To this day, I wonder what would happen if everyone
on earth decided to at the very same moment, to sing the same
song, or even hum. I can't imagine what that would do.

I realized so much and had so much revelation that I can't
begin to touch on here, but one thing that I knew without any
doubt was that the music is what kept the angels lifted up. The
vibration of this sound was what kept them suspended and cir-
cling around Him. They were compelled to worship and praise,
and it was as if they had no control of this music that emanated
from their inner most part.

I remember the story of the woman that had an issue of blood
in the Bible and how she struggled to touch the hem of Jesus'
garment. He spoke about how "virtue" went out of Him. Being
in God's presence like that, you lose control, and this music/
praise just comes out of you. I wish I could explain it better.
This part of the experience led me to the study of Cymatics,
which proves that vibration does in fact have the ability to cause
physical matter to transcend gravity although there was nothing
physical in this place. What I was hearing, I have learned since,
is what some have called "the music of heaven" or the "music of
the spheres."

There is a man I haven't met personally but who is a minister that speaks of this very same thing in a way that confirmed to me so beautifully that he also has experienced this "music of heaven." Cymatics describes the principle of "order out of chaos." When physical matter such as sand is exposed to vibration the grains of sand seem to jump around in mad disarray, but as the vibration continues, the sand takes on an intricate geometric pattern, many of which are found throughout nature and in the design of our bodies, the veins of a leaf and so on, and may change according to the frequency and amplitude. Order is established. It makes perfect sense.

Although I knew it was next to impossible, if the angels were to ever stop praising and just one, even one, had the beginnings of a thought to praise Him and sing, all the other millions and millions would instantly join in. Even thoughts are visible in Heaven. I think about all the evenings I sat on our back porch growing up and listening to the crickets and frogs, sometimes, even the whippoorwills. If one started to sing, they all did, like a mighty chorus instantly turned on by the voice of just one. I am amazed even to this day at the evidence that surrounds us that speak of God and Heaven. As above, so below, on earth as it is in Heaven.

I could say so much more. But I think this gives you an idea of why I have such compassion and interest in studying and reading so many things. Like I said, everything in some way for me, is an effort to understand and know who God is and who I am in Him. What better way to that than through His creation, from the simplest things to the most complex. There is TRUTH everywhere, if you seek it, you shall find. Knock and it shall be opened.

I think our experiences are shaped by the limitations that traditional teachings put on us. I realized after this, how extremely important it was for each person to have their own personal relationship with God. We don't have relationships with our parents through our brothers and sisters, neither should we attempt to have a relationship with God through our pastors, our Christian friends, etc. God teaches us in the way we individually can understand. Certainly we can glean wisdom and understanding through others, but He is the source of Truth.

At the same time, I learned that even though I have been taught indirectly and directly to shun other religious systems of belief or practices, there is still truth to be discovered and embraced. The basic fundamental truth, I have discovered for my own life, is that no matter where you go or what you do when you search for God you will find Him. He exists in the person you work with, the flowers that spring up along the roadside, in the wind that brings the rain and the same wind that destroys. He is revealed in the complex research that is being conducted about DNA, to the vastness of the galaxy we look upon at night. I hear Him in the angry voice of a politician and the sound of a violin as the bow moves across its strings. He is indeed everywhere and in all things.

The road narrows when in the past we traveled down many, many paths, leading us to different conclusions, ideas and beliefs, and what we are finding is that they all end up pointing in the same direction. So I am compelled, driven even, to discover, to search, and to continue on this journey that has been and continues to be one of magnificent and awe inspiring adventure. Perhaps this sheds some light on what fuels my fascination and my intrigue.

He provided a scripture that comes close to what I witnessed, wanting some confirmation shortly thereafter, I asked for it. He said, "Open your Bible" and this is what I found.

Revelations 5:11-13 "Then I looked and I heard the voice of many angels around the throne, the living creatures, and the elders; and the number of them was ten thousand times ten thousand, and thousands of thousands, saying with a loud voice:

Worthy is the Lamb who was slain to receive power and riches and wisdom, and strength and honor and glory and blessing! And every creature which is in heaven and on the earth and under the earth and such as are in the sea, all that are in them, I heard saying: Blessing and honor and glory and power, be to Him who sits on the throne, and to the Lamb forever and ever!" (New King James Version)

I am reluctant to share this experience with most for many reasons. Sometimes there is fear of being judged or misunderstood, and other times because I am afraid people will focus on the experience itself rather than the deep truths revealed through it and ultimately a greater revelation of God. If there is one single thing I want people to know from this experience, it is this: Seek Him in all things, great and small. Acknowledge Him in all things. Search for the God of your understanding and being, however you perceive him or her or it to be. Take time out to listen to that inner voice, the one that you think is yourself, the internal dialogue that takes place in your head. When I was a child I asked my mother who God was and her honest reply was, "That voice in your head that tells you when you are about to do something wrong, and the same voice that assures you that everything is going to be ok."

We MUST seek Him for ourselves. Whoever, or whatever you call God, the Supreme Force, the Great I Am, whoever or whatever you perceive as God, you must seek Him for yourself. That voice has never left me, I just stopped listening for awhile. This experience made that voice real, and just because someone else hasn't had the same experience, doesn't mean they can't experience God in a very real and life-changing way right this very minute.

An example of this recently was on my way home from work, and I stopped at an intersection and while waiting for the light to change I noticed along the curb some trash and debris, but in the middle was a bright yellow flower growing through

Seek Him in all things, great + small.

the cracks of the asphalt. I suppose I was beating myself up over something that day or week, and God spoke very clearly to me that "even among the trash there is beauty, even among the most dire situations, I am there." So when I am feeling regret over past mistakes and choices, or perhaps when I step into a place of judgment toward another, I am reminded of this truth, He is there. He has always been there and always will be. We simply have to listen and observe. He shows up everywhere, but only if we are looking for Him.

About Tim Hill:

Tim is a Healthcare Revenue Cycle Consultant and he lives in North Carolina. He would welcome all inquiries to share experiences. For more information, please see his website at: www.timnc1.com. His email address is: timnc1@gmail.com

IMMACULEE ILIBAGIZA SURVIVOR, RWANDAN HOLOCAUST

Immaculee Ilibagiza

I read the story of a young woman named Immaculee Ilibagiza in a book she wrote with Steve Erwin called, *Left To Tell: Discovering God Amidst the Rwandan Holocaust*, Hay House, 2006. Her true story had a very powerful effect upon me and I suppose, upon anyone who has read it. I want to tell you a little about this amazing woman, her spiritually transformative experiences, and why I feel her inspiring story should continue to be brought to world attention.

In 1994, Rwanda, a small country in South Africa where Immaculee lived with her family, was shattered by a horrific genocide that killed nearly one million people in 100 days. Its citizens were divided into two tribes, the Tutsis and the Hutus. I need not go into the historical details of the politics involved, suffice it to say, the leaders in charge of the government declared that all Hutus were the elitists while the Tutsis were considered the inferior ones. The objective was to eliminate all the Tutsis from the country by organizing all the Hutus to slaughter them, many of whom were their neighbors and friends! The killing methods are too horrendous to describe here.

Immaculee, a Tutsi, fled her home to take refuge in a pastor's home, and for 91 days, she and seven other women lived in a tiny bathroom, so small only a toilet could fit in there. The door to the bathroom was hidden by a wardrobe closet. The pastor gave them food and water only when he felt it was safe to push aside the wardrobe closet. Sometimes it was days before they ate or drank anything. The women had to be very quiet as often times the Hutus would search the pastor's house looking for Tutsis.

It is hard to imagine what it was like for Immaculee and seven other women cramped against each other to survive against all odds. Immaculee spent most of her time praying and had many Divine Moments that transformed her life forever. I wholeheartedly recommend that you read her book to learn more of the many Divine Moments she had. However, I would like to mention one in particular. One night she had a vivid dream in which Jesus stood before her. He reassured her that He would never leave her. He told her that He would be her family now because her family was with Him now. She learned later that her family had been brutally slaughtered while she was in hiding.

She kept a strong vigil day and night praying and asked God what her purpose might be if she would survive this ordeal. She writes, *"He'll wait until our eyes and hearts are open to Him, and then when we're ready, He will plant our feet on the path that's best for us...but it's up to us to do the walking."*

The fact that she survived this horrendous genocide is hard to contemplate, yet, it points in the direction of the Divine as her Source - her reliance upon someone greater than herself to survive this ordeal. Wayne Dyer writes in the foreword to her book, *Left To Tell, "she found her destiny - to tell her tale and to be an agent for ushering in a new spiritual consciousness, and a story of a love for God that was so strong that hatred and revenge were forced to dissolve in its presence."*

About Immaculee Ilibagiza:

Immaculee studied electronic and mechanical engineering in Rwanda. After emigrating to the United States in 1998, she began working at the United Nations. Presently, she is a full-time speaker and writer. In 2007 she established the *Left To Tell Charitable Fund*, which helps support Rwandan orphans. She received the Mahatma Gandhi International Award for Reconciliation and Peace 2007. Additional information can be found at her website: www.lefttotell.com

IN THE TWINKLING OF AN EYE

T. G. Langston, Florida

After finally getting the strength to leave an unhappy twenty-three year marriage of domestic violence, I thought I'd be happy. I began a career in hypnotherapy, and I loved it! I was helping people for the first time in my life, yet there was a big hole within me missing - I didn't know what. Helping others had opened my mind to infinite possibilities. And so I began my search. For what, I didn't know.

I read several books a week, attended seminars, retreats, and began meditating. After a year of finding nothing, I finally made a decision to go to the mountains and find what I was looking for. I was tired of searching and finding nothing. The day before I left, a friend I hadn't talked to in three years stopped by. He brought me a book and tapes, all on "A Course in Miracles." I listened to the tapes on the eleven-hour drive to Tennessee. The tapes spoke about God, Jesus, and the Holy Spirit - humorously, which I loved. By the time I got to my cabin, I knew I had found what I was looking for...God.

What a blow! Although it felt right, I was pissed and fighting it all the way. I still couldn't even say the word "God" out loud! I didn't want to become some born-again Christian fanatic. I literally cried for three days. This was NOT what I was searching for, but at last, acceptance came. Now at least, I knew what it was I was to search for! That God guy!

I put my heart into it for months. The "Course in Miracles" spoke about 'the peace of God' often, and I knew this is what I wanted for myself. Peace. Peace of mind. I knew nothing about peace. But finally something caught my eye..."Seek ye first the Kingdom of God." What an eye opener! It is fascinating looking back to how all the pieces fell into place. There was no obstacle to bar my way. People came into my life for whatever I was needing. Steps were given to me internally. I knew what to do and when to do it. It was amazing and felt wonderful!

I began disciplining myself, searching for this Kingdom of God. I wanted nothing else. On January 1, 1993, I began a daily ritual of studying "A Course in Miracles" and meditating. The desire to "Seek ye first the Kingdom of God" was unlike anything I had ever experienced. Boring meditations were now replaced with a deep peace within. I chose thoughts of God and peace to replace my usual thoughts throughout the day. Things that irritated me were surrendered with my willingness to look at everything differently.

On March 1, 1993, this was a day that would forever be implanted in my mind. A day that changed every thought, every idea, every belief I ever had. This was a day that would change my life forever.

I awoke early that morning to attend to my daily rituals. As I finished my discipline, I felt so peaceful! The phone rang. It was a friend of mine that was irritating me with her nagging, "I needed to do this or that." This conversation had drained all sense of any peace I had prior to the call. I laid my head on my table and cried and cried, sobbing deep from within my soul, as I realized I could be completely fragmented with a ten-minute phone call. It didn't make sense. I prayed for an answer through my tears. I was so willing to see this friend differently. To see whatever it was that God wanted me to see, instead of this separation I was feeling. And in the 'twinkling of an eye', for the next several hours, my whole senseless world was transformed into pure white and light. There was nothing left of the world I knew. There was no world! Everywhere was only white and millions of small golden suns, extending everywhere and forever like an eternity mirror.

The quiet that surrounded me from within and outside of me was like nothing in this world I had ever experienced. There were no thoughts or sounds inside my mind. The quiet was so magnificent. It was hard for me to distinguish which was the more beautiful - the peace and quiet within or the peace outside of me in its truest form. I was in awe. I sat there looking at what was so unbelievably believable. It was definitely the Peace of God and the Kingdom of Heaven, all rolled into one. It was like I had never left, but at the same time, it was a place I truly forgot existed.

It was obvious that God was everywhere and everything! Everything was known and not seen. I understood that nothing really matters, and that everything is the same. Everything is light. There is nothing else. God is in everything we see. I realized peace is here now within each one of us, waiting on us to be willing to see that extension of peace is all there is to truly give. I felt no love in the sense of love as I knew it. I realized later I didn't know what love is. It is not a feeling or thought or even something to give or receive. Love is who we are!! And when we are who we are, which is love, there is nothing else, nothing to give, nothing to receive. Love is only to recognize in ourselves and in each other.

I realize that to be happy, I had to be myself. I didn't have to pretend any longer - pretend to be happy, pretend to be spiritual, pretend to be someone I'm not. I've learned that acceptance is the greatest gift that I can give to myself and to others. It is the closest form of love there is. I've learned to be who I am, do what I love, and everything falls into place. I was led to further healing from my domestic violence experiences and now work in the field of domestic violence as a counselor, working with victims of domestic violence. It's my passion, and I love it. The hole I searched for has been filled, with wholeness. ACCEPTANCE

About T. G. Langston

T.G.'s email address is Leteegee@gmail.com if you would like to contact her.

TRUE AUTHENTICITY

Julie Lapham, PhD, North Carolina

To begin at the beginning for me requires a brief introduction to the setting within which I arrived on this planet. Born in Danbury Palace, during wartime, surrounded by midwives, Nan (my mom's mom), the family matriarch, provided me a framework for life. Nan was creative, an accomplished violinist, used the Ouija board, sang songs, read the Bible, owned a series of green grocery stores and encouraged me to experience. Neighbors, who lived at the end of our street in a caravan, on a farm, were gypsies, who let me ride their horses, eat their food, sing their songs, and dance their dances.

And so I feel I've been prepared, given permission perhaps to experience differences. Coincidences, intuitive thoughts, visions, meditations seem commonplace to me. Perhaps, and even more importantly I tend to seek them out. I migrated to this country at age twenty and began work in polymer chemistry. I loved this creative science and was awarded a patent or two. But at age twenty-six I had an accident in the lab; a glass desiccator shattered as I was removing the lid and a piece of broken glass sliced my wrist almost to the bone severing the nerve and artery whilst leaving the tendon hanging by a thread.

An important intuitive thought occurred to me as blood gushed like a geyser. The telephone was located at the opposite end of the lab from where I was standing. We employees had been lectured with frequency regarding lab emergencies. "Go to the telephone." But I didn't. Instead, I turned and exited the door, only to collapse in a pool of blood in the hallway. (Apparently, had I attempted to reach the telephone I would have collapsed and probably died as I was alone in the lab at the time of the accident.)

I felt people jostling me, calling my name. My vision was blurred. Something was being placed over my mouth. I heard a voice telling me to relax, breathe natural and that I was being taken to the hospital. I remembered the journey to the emergency room vaguely, hearing sounds, then not, seeing blurred surroundings, then not.

I remembered being placed on the operating room table. Then suddenly I was on the ceiling looking down on myself with visual and audio clarity. I watched medical personnel cut my clothes off me, call for blood matching and a fibrillation unit.

Then I was in the sky surrounded by the deepest blue I had ever seen. In the distance was this brilliant light the size of the sun, yet white, like I had never seen before. The light and I were moving towards each other, slowly. Eventually I could see within the light, blurred though. There were mountains and valleys, rivers, trees, animals, and people.

Then, for some reason unbeknown to me, I began to turn slowly, away from the light, and my eyes fell on the universe; planets, stars, galaxies, and eventually earth. A silver ribbon, like a loose cord, seemed to connect me with earth.

The next thing I remember was waking up in the recovery room. I looked towards my injured hand bandaged to the fingertips, wiggled those fingertips then went back to sleep. Later that evening I awoke, said hello to family and friends who had gathered, feasted on a stale peanut butter and jelly sandwich rescued from the nurses' station, said a few words, and then returned to sleep again.

The following day I was visited by the surgeon and recounted my experiences. He commented that it was not unusual for people to recount similar stories after experiencing such a trauma. Instantly I felt relief and excitement. So I'm not alone in my experience. Well then, where did I go, and how do I get back there?

Languaging the experiences were, and still are, particularly difficult. Not so much the description of my remembrances but rather the relationship to my feelings.

Fifteen years went by before I spoke of them again. In 1987, at the invitation of a pastoral counselor whom I had studied with, I was invited to record my experiences for a local hospital. Of course it was still much easier to describe the details of the accident than it was to describe the changes in my being.

I lost any fear of death I may have had. I truly feel my experience of that light was the experience of a portal. Meeting life in the moment, trusting events as they unfold, rather than planning or forcing my hand is becoming easier.

It wasn't as though there were sudden changes in my behaviors but rather I felt as though I had experienced a huge opening on a continuing journey- a pivotal experience. I became aware the universe had plentiful gifts to offer and all I had to do was to be open to whatever came along.

I met recently with a friend who asked how did I plan my life, how did I go about setting my goals. I didn't. I simply show up, pay attention, tell the truth and stay in the moment, unattached to outcomes. I feel as though I'm in a dingy, without oars, on a river experiencing pools of tranquility, rushes of torrents, and heights of waterfalls. In other words, I'm just along for the ride; grateful for all that comes to me including difficult experiences.

As a truth teller, not everyone really wants to hear. Oftentimes I am at odds with friends who ask questions. Eventually, with enough time, all seems to have its place but at the time it can be painful and separation does occur for a while.

I must admit a distinctive and immediate change in my

behavior was my inability to kill even the smallest of creatures, scooping up ants and taking them to the garden. Gratitude abounds for fruits and vegetables as well as meats who had given their lives for my sustenance.

Gradually my interest in the field of science waned and I began to focus more on accessing this other world I had been privileged to witness. Studying and practicing meditation, facilitating Holotropic Breathwork sessions has provided me with opportunities to witness others accessing this other world.

So, what is this other world, this other place I experienced? Well, for me it is the universal omnipotent wisdom or God or nature. For me it is the place of unconditional love, compassion, forgiveness; the place of true authenticity, peace, at oneness.

I feel content, wanting for nothing, satisfied with every moment of every day even though I may have encountered judgment, jealousy, or criticism. I am content in the knowledge I have brought my full weight of authenticity to hear, see, feel, smell, taste, and touch. It isn't about how long I live in this world; it is about how authentic I live in each moment.

My studies, and I have never stopped studying, have shifted from science to subjects such as meditation techniques, contemplative practices and indigenous wisdoms. I remember when I was much younger being attracted to a television series about comparative religions and noting that the world's religions were far more similar than different. Maybe that's why I became an interfaith minister. It's not that I reject religions per se; just the rules and regulations mankind has imposed upon them over the years.

I could easily describe that incredible light that I witnessed as the face of God. I feel privileged to have witnessed it and still, to this day, tear as I remember it - as though I had been standing on hallowed ground.

I feel safe in this universe. It is friendly. Maybe it wasn't my fear of death that was lifted from my shoulders but fear itself. Am I able to experience that light since the accident? Yes, but infrequently. Sometimes in meditation, when I least expect it, there it is…fleeting. As soon as I pay it attention, it disappears as though it is playful, which is probably why I classify myself as a spiritual rather than a religious person.

Doesn't everything have a spirit? After my experience of "death" I feel as though I have a relationship with everything in the universe, not just sentient beings but also the paper I'm writing on. And so I find myself treating everything with care, unconditional love if you will. I waste little, live frugally, give away my possessions if they haven't been used in the previous year.

This is what studying indigenous wisdoms have shown me - to walk with the universe, grateful for all that comes my way. Aho!

About Julie Lapham, PhD

In addition to being a management consultant, Julie Lapham teaches meditation techniques and contemplative practices and facilitates Holotropic Breathwork.™ Dr. Lapham can be reached at her email address: JnLapham@gmail.com

THE CASE OF HAISLEY LONG

Montreal, Quebec, Canada

In August of 1991, I received a phone call from Haisley Long, a Canadian who had heard that I was doing research on near-death-like experiences. He told me he had a very powerful, life-transforming experience and wanted to tell me about it. He was very insistent that he was not close to death at the time, nor suffering serious illness or physical trauma. In fact, he was sitting in the living room watching television and got up from the couch when his experience occurred. Naturally, I was very interested in hearing what he had to say because not only was I researching this particular type of experience, but I also had a near-death-like experience. We had something in common. We spoke on the phone for over two hours expressing the similarities of both our experiences. At that time, very little information was available about near-death-like experiences, so when two of those experiencers have the opportunity to talk to one another, it is a very special time. I listened to Haisley open up from the depths of his soul as he told me what happened to him and what he learned from his experience.

Basically, Haisley told me that the room lit up and he was suddenly "standing on the outskirts of heaven and walking into it." At that time, I was organizing an International Association of Near-Death Studies, Inc. (IANDS) Midwest Regional Conference on near-death-like experiences to be held in October, 1991 in Columbus, Ohio. I invited Haisley to attend that conference and asked him to please write out his experience for my research study. He promised to do that for me, and he kept his promise. I met him in person at the IANDS conference in Columbus, and he gave me a nine page typed compact version of his experience which also included the knowledge he received during his transcendent experience. He titled this document "The Meaning of Life" which I still have.

To the amazement of many biblical scholars, Haisley returned from his experience with spiritual understanding of the Bible even though he never read the Bible before. He lived a life of service to others through the unconditional love of the Light that he so generously offered to others.

Haisley has since passed on, but I know he would be very happy to know that his "service" for God is still being carried out through the work of others who have been touched by his legacy. Because Haisley died before I could get his permission to publish the story he gave me, PMH Atwater gave me her permission to publish the account Haisley gave to her which appeared in her book, *Beyond the Light*. This is his story.

"I wondered how I was able to withstand this. It was like standing in front of a huge star and being amazed at the power a star can pump out, then having the star go supernova and the power jump incredibly, but you're not fried. It was total ecstasy. More and more waves came. You just cry and cry and cry, while waves wash you and clean you and remove what little pieces of humanity are left stuck to you, so that when you go into heaven you are as perfect as the environment you are in. I became aware that there was someone standing next to me - Jesus. When I looked at Jesus, I saw myself. How can this be more me than I am myself? It was like looking at a big mirror. So I reached out to try and touch it, and I did. The word that exploded in my mind was *expansion*, and I started to fuse, to blend and become part of the Awareness of Consciousness Himself, Jesus.

I absorbed all the information, all at once. It was as though Life took the little sentence, "What is beginning and end?" and fused it into my brain. At first, I didn't realize how huge this phenomenon was. All the information in the world lies between beginning and end. When I absorbed that little question it was months, and even years, before I began to realize that one step in between those questions branches off into three weeks of speech. It was an incredible experience. It was not necessary to ask a lot of questions while I was there. The answers to all my questions were given to me and locked into my head. Before this experience, I had no interest and paid no attention to biblical matters whatsoever. For myself, it took a trip to Heaven and to come into contact with Life directly, going through the gates of heaven, traveling at the speed of thought through Life's presence, and coming into contact with God in His natural state before I tuned into biblical matters."

Haisley's life was transformed in the ways that are so striking with near-death experiencers and others who have had mystical illuminations. These life-changing experiences speak highly of the love, power, and wisdom of the mystical raptures that so many individuals feel compelled to share with others. Haisley was one of those gifted individuals.

DANCING WITH LIFE AND DEATH

Sharon Lund, Ph.D. California

We are born into this world pure, loving, whole, innocent, and beautiful. Yet in a matter of days, weeks, months, years, or decades, we may be shattered from neglect, abuse, or judgment from others or ourselves.

I remember the circumstances that shattered me as a child. From the age of 3 to 12, I was raped by my grandfather. Every time he raped me, an angel by the name of Laura appeared before me. I could see her; yet, I could see through her. She wore a long pink gown, and had sparkling blue eyes and long blonde hair. Love flowed from her as she lifted me out of my body. She took me to places I enjoyed, such as the zoo and the park, and sometimes we'd play dolls together. Laura taught me how to communicate with the various kingdoms-plant, animal, mineral, spirit- and told me we are all connected. She also showed me how to use energy and later taught me the importance of forgiveness.

My parents didn't know I was being raped, because my grandfather told me, *"If you tell anyone I will kill your mommy."*

When I told my mom about the various things Laura taught me, she believed me and understood, because she herself could see Spirits. She encouraged me to listen to Laura, learn from her, and welcome her into my life. What my mom didn't realize was why Laura came to me - because I was being raped.

Due to my abuse, I grew up with low-self-esteem and in 1983 married my second husband, Bill, who was verbally abusive toward me. In his eyes and words I was fat, ugly, stupid, worthless, would never amount to anything, couldn't do anything right, and the list went on and on. I became anorexic and divorced him within six months of our marriage. Unfortunately, anorexia took a toll on my life. I found I could no longer take care of my nine-year-old daughter, Jeaneen. I sent her to Hawaii to live with her grandparents and her father. I knew she would be taken care of and loved.

While Jeaneen was in Hawaii, my mind was tormented with intense feelings and thoughts of my grandfather's and husband's abuse. I thought that the only way to end my suffering and ease my pain was to kill myself. I swallowed a bottle of pills and then felt angry because I couldn't keep them down.

A few days later, I went to the bathroom and put a bright shiny razor on my left wrist. As I leaned against the bathtub I said my final prayer, "God, please forgive me for what I'm about to do, but I have to end this pain and suffering. If there is anything I need to know before I kill myself, let me know now."

Immediately the entire bathroom filled with the most beautiful, radiant white light, brighter than anything I had seen on this Earth plane. I felt warmth and love from this Light. My body became calm, and I felt a deep sense of inner peace and love surge through me. Then telepathically I heard, *"My child, it's not your time to die. Get yourself into the hospital, and when you return, you will become a healer, teach around the world and write books."*

None of that made sense to me because I had never done it before. However, I knew I had received a message from Infinite Spirit/God. I called my doctor and was hospitalized for three months. While in the hospital, two Spirit Beings, Semitar and Vira Cocha, came to me and became my teachers and guides. When I was released from the hospital, I had healing abilities - I became a clear channel for Infinite Spirit to work through me. I could see what was wrong with people's bodies, I could see past lives, and also future events. I felt comfortable as a healer working in the AIDS and cancer communities. I also taught mind-body-spirit healing techniques. I felt blessed to assist people to prepare for their transitions and be with them at their bedsides as they departed from their physical bodies.

I only held onto my ability to see the future for a year - I didn't like the responsibility that came with it, even though my Spirit Guides taught me how to handle the negativity. In 1986, I discovered I was infected with HIV/AIDS. I saw my ex-husband, Bill, on a Dan Rather AIDS special, "AIDS HITS HOME," saying he was infected with the disease. I called Bill, and he denied it was him, but I heard in meditation it was him and I needed to be tested.

My test came back positive for HIV. Bill called me before he died from AIDS complications and told me it was him on the AIDS special, and he was infected with HIV when he married me in 1983. Instead of becoming a victim, I allowed the virus to empower me. I found a new life purpose which allowed me to travel around the world teaching people about women and HIV/AIDS, alternative therapies (mind-body-spirit), and spirituality.

From 1996-97, I was in the hospital due to AIDS complications - PCP (Pneumocystis carinii pneumonia) and MAC/MAI (Mycobacterium avium complex). I weighed only 86 pounds. Nothing stayed in my body. The stench of vomit and diarrhea enveloped me and permeated my surroundings. I had fever over 103 degrees and then chills cold as ice.

March 16, 1997, my doctor called my family and told them I probably would not make it through the weekend. When my daughter, Jeaneen arrived she stood at the doorway in shock looking at me. Then she ran to me crying "Mommy, I love you." She asked, "Mom, can I crawl into bed with you and hold you in my arms? I'll try not to move or hurt you." I welcomed her to join me. The warmth of her body next to mine and her hand and arm placed on my chest made me feel safe and loved.

"I love you!" she said, and I felt my shoulder get moist from her tears. No words can describe the rich love we share for one another. I fell asleep in her arms. The next morning Jeaneen asked, "Mom, if you don't mind, I'd like to drive back to your house and take a shower. I'll be right back. Do you want anything from home?" I smiled and said, "Just you." I watched as she slowly walked out into the corridor.

My body trembled, and I became weaker. All of a sudden, my Spirit lifted out of my body and hovered over it. I saw my dead form lying below. I immediately felt healed, more alive, and more free than ever before. Warm love and inner peace cascaded through me, coming from within.

After my Spirit floated over my body for a short time, two Spirit Beings, one male and one female, appeared before me. They were dressed in long white gowns. They looked to be physical, yet I could see through them. The Spirit beings reached out and took my hand. Telepathically, they told me they wanted to show me a review of my life.

In an instant, I was taken to different scenes and events in my lifetime with numerous people and situations from around the world. As I had a bird's-eye view looking down and witnessing the scenes, telepathically the Spirit Beings said, *"Look at the difference you have made in their lives."* After I had seen numerous events and some people I had forgotten, and the impact I had made on so many lives, the Spirit Beings took me away.

I felt myself upright and horizontally move into and through a bright Tunnel of Light. I noticed gray figures like people on each side of the tunnel attempting to reach out and touch me. Swiftly, I passed unfamiliar faces looking at me. I wanted to cry out, "Where are my brothers, Tommy and Raymond? Where are my friends and loved ones who have gone before me?" Yet, I remained silent.

At what seemed to be the end of the Tunnel there appeared, once again, the most immense, beautiful, warm, brilliant, radiant, loving Light shining upon me and enveloping me. It was the same Light I saw when I attempted suicide. I was awed by the beauty, peace, and serenity. Telepathically, from the Light of God, I heard, *"My child, unlike the time before, this time you have a choice. You can come with me or you can return. Before you make your decision, I want to show you one more thing."*

Instantaneously, I relived - not reviewed, but *relived* - my life with Jeaneen. I felt her in my womb; I felt the sensation of her first kick within me; I rubbed my tummy, sang to her and told her how much I loved her before she was even born. Then, I relived her actual birth and felt her tiny lips suck on my breasts. I listened to her gurgles and coos. I smelled the wonderful scent of my baby from her first bath. I relived numerous experiences and special times with Jeaneen throughout her 20 years. There was laughter, playfulness, tears, as well as the challenges we had shared together through our life journey. There were moments when we were not only mother and daughter, but friends, companions, spiritual teachers, and so much more to one another. We felt blessed to be together.

A spark of Light then hit me, and once again I appeared before the Light of God. Telepathically, I was asked, *"My child, what is your decision?"* The intense love, healing, and peace I felt in the Light of Infinite Spirit was so profound. Yet silently, *I thought, I cannot leave Jeaneen. Not yet!* I expressed in sincere love, "I have to return to my daughter."

Immediately and without warning, I found myself back in my body in the hospital bed. My deteriorated form still looked like a skeleton; however, I was alive! Tears of joy streamed down my cheeks. For the next hour, my entire Being glowed with love and light. I could see burst of Light go into every cell, sparkling and vibrating with energy. The healing power of Infinite Spirit was restoring me cell by cell. The sensation felt like effervescent bubbles. It was as if I were being newly created with life, strength, and energy. The intense surge and vibrant life force running through me was so strong I knew before long I would be back in my Earthly home, healthy!

A few days later in meditation, I asked why I didn't see

Tommy and Raymond, and I was told, *"My child, if you saw the one you call Tommy, your decision might have been harder."*

The next day Tommy appeared to me as he had in the past. He said, *"Sharon, you do not have to die to be with me. I am always with you, and I love you."*

Jeaneen's love brought me back to life. She is my hero! In a matter of days I was home and in the loving care and hands of Jeaneen and my sister, Joyce. A doctor and family were amazed as they saw a miracle happen before their eyes.

After my near-death experience, I was guided in meditation to continue to do my public teaching but also write books. I have been blessed to author *Sacred Living, Sacred Dying: A Guide to Embracing Life and Death*, as well as *The Integrated Being: Techniques to Heal Your Mind-Body-Spirit*. I was also Divinely guided to produce the documentary *Dying to LIVE: NDE*, which won the 2010 Silver Lei Award from the Honolulu International Film Festival.

My life is not mine. I am now committed to be Divinely Guided to do the work that Infinite Spirit desires of me. When I'm in this space, everything flows to me with ease and grace. Through my near-death experiences, I've been able to embrace and understand deep within my heart and soul that we are all connected. There is no separation, and we can communicate with all the kingdoms. Love is all there really is, and the spirit realm (angels and spirit guides) are eager to work with us. We all have a purpose, and the Divinity resides within everyone and everything. There is no death, therefore no need to fear it, and Infinite Spirit/God truly is all loving.

I embrace all of my past challenges and see them as sacred blessings because they have healed me, brought me to self-discovery, and helped me live my life purpose with love and passion. What a blessing life and so-called death has been! Embrace the whole process!

About Sharon Lund, Ph.D.

Sharon Lund, Ph.D. has danced with life and death - she has had three near-death experiences. As an author, international speaker, New Thought Minister, and award winning documentary producer, she has inspired and offered hope to audiences throughout the United States, Canada, Europe, Japan and Russia. She has spoken at the White House, appeared on: *The Oprah Winfrey Show, 48 Hours, Eye on America,* and *CNN,* and was featured in *"O" The Oprah Magazine.*

Sharon is the author of *There is More…18 Near-Death Experiences; Sacred Living, Sacred Dying: A Guide to Embracing Life and Death* (award winning); and *The Integrated Being: Techniques to Heal Your Mind-Body-Spirit.* She is also the producer of the award winning documentary *Dying to LIVE: NDE,* and co-producer of *The Mustang Man.*

To contact Sharon Lund, Ph.D., please visit her website at www.SharonLund.com and www.SacredLife.com

MIRACLES

Mary Ellen "Angel Scribe", Oregon

You are not alone in your quest for miracles and a greater understanding of them. There are as many definitions of miracles as there are people, but the Dictionary defines them as: 1: an extraordinary event taken as a sign of the supernatural power of God, 2: an extremely outstanding or unusual event, thing, or accomplishment. The word miracle is derived from Latin miraculum "a wonder," from mirari "to wonder."

One thing is for sure, we all wonder how to have more because miracles are amazing moments in life! When miracles are present, life flows much smoother. They add beauty, color and depth to our spiritual nature. It is my deepest desire to teach you how to become a Miracle Magnet, so that miracles happen not just once but daily for you. As the author of two book on miracles, *"Expect Miracles"* and *"A Christmas Filled with Miracles"* I may have heard more miracles than most humans, but I never tire of their wonder, blessings and magic!

One recurring theme is the people who experience a miracle often know it, and they shyly add that they have miracles happen to them all the time. What is their magic? How can you also live in the world of miracles? Possibly a new way to view miracles is to look at them from many different angles. Many people think a miracle happens only to others. Or that a miracle is a dramatic event, such as someone hanging off a cliff and in need of a helicopter to miraculously fly over for a rescue. Begin to realize miracles are subtle and often are disguised by our daily vernacular.

What you think of as a random occurrence, a coincidence may indeed be God/the Angels or Spirit working overtime to show you how important you are to the large scheme of the universe. Miracles are in every waking breath, and once we recognize how they continuously inundate our lives, the more miracles we are able to manifest.

Many of us think of miracles with such awe. When you watch a TV show and see a miracle you know it with every cell of your body. Living through your own miracles is not quite so obvious unless you start to pay attention. The following is one of the most astounding miracles that ever took place in my presence!

It all started with Stinging Nettle Tea! In my twenties the oddest and most dramatic experience took place. Once I share this miracle with you, you will see immediately it is one, but originally neither did Della, my new friend, or I see it that way. It was not until twenty plus years had passed, and I was writing inspiring stories for my Angels and Miracles Good-news-letter that it suddenly dawned on me that what took place was a colossal miracle!

To confirm it, I telephoned Della, and she said that she had also not shared the event with others. She felt dumbfounded and questioned the experience too. Today, with greater wisdom, and more knowledge of miracles, the experience can definitely be recognized as a miracle! It is typical of most miracles. Dreams, Divine timing, and an unexpected result were the key ingredients to create a desired outcome for someone else's prayers.

Twenty years ago I was working in Mercia's Health Food Store, in Duncan, British Columbia, Canada and met Della, a beautiful and kind Cowichan's First Nation young woman. (American Indian.) I asked her if she had any stinging nettle to plant in my yard for its healing qualities, and she broke into genuine joyful laughter. "Stinging nettle is a nasty weed that grows all over our reservation. We are trying to get rid of it, not plant it in our yard!" she said.

We became friends, soul sisters in the love that we both had for herbs and their medicinal qualities and our desire to help others. Shortly after we met, I had a dream about Della. I dreamt that she phoned me. It is important for you to know that Della was very poor at this time in her life. She had no phone, three small children, and no car.

The dream unnerved me, so I got dressed and drove over to the Cowichan Reservation to see if she needed something. This was totally out of character for me. I did not dream and then think it was real, but this dream had an odd left-over feeling when I woke up, an urgency. I found her old wooden house on a dirt road in the Reservation and knocked on it's unpainted door. She opened it with a look of surprise. She was plainly agitated over something. Della was upset because her much loved Minister of their First Nation Shaker Church had been found outside his home in a coma. Because of Della's healing skills, several of the tribal members had suggested over and over that she go and visit him. Here was her dilemma. No car and no idea what to do when she went to see him. She was feeling helpless and frustrated. So when I mysteriously landed on her porch first thing in the morning, she knew this was a sign from Spirit that she was meant to go to him.

We drove over to Della's friend, Doris' home and picked her up because she always goes with Della as a witness and a helper in accordance with their beliefs. We arrived at the hospital not knowing what to find, or what we were doing there, or what we were supposed to do! Della had such confidence that I went with her into the hospital, not sure of what I would see, and definitely not what I had ever expected to find.

The entire second floor of the hospital corridor outside of her Minister's room was full of his family members and friends. Nearly one hundred First Nation people silently sat in chairs or stood on both sides of the hall. It was eerie because no one was talking, just sitting in silence, waiting.

Della and I entered the hospital room of the dying man. I was shocked how young and good looking he was. He looked to be in his late thirties. The room was also like the hallways with about thirty concerned and upset people of many different First Nations in the room, sitting all along the wall, in chairs, silently in this tiny room. A few stood and they all stared at me. I thought, "Gosh, why am I here, the only white person?" It was a privilege, and it was unsettling. No one talked to me; they just looked at me wondering why I was there too.

I was honored to be trusted among them in their time of grief. Della walked over to a family member of the handsome Minister in the coma and asked him if we may stay and help. She told him that my dream had brought me to her and that we were here on some higher Divine reason.

The elder let us approach the man lying so still in the bed, deep in a coma. Della ran her fingers over his head and found a large lump. We had taken a weekend reflexology class, and she did a gentle manipulation of his head; then she showed a respected Native healer how to do it, and he did. Others in the room were sending prayers in their many languages. This is the God's truth-we knew the dying man was in a coma, and in reflexology, a coma is connected to the brain, and to the big toe, so I pulled back the sheets at the bottom of the bed and hit the brain point on his big toe three times with my boney thumb. What happened next caught us totally off guard! HE SPRANG TO LIFE! HE SAT STRAIGHT UP IN BED! It was such a surprise because he was yelling, yelling loudly, "HI, HI, HI!" One time for each time I had pushed on his big toe!

Della said he was saying in his own language, STOP! STOP! STOP! So with big, bugged eyes and a rapid beating heart, I stopped. The room immediately filled with his friends rushing in upon hearing his voice. I can't remember what happened next, but we knew we were not needed and left. Della and I did not talk on the way out of the hospital.

I lost contact with Della, and after twenty years, located her and phoned to get her side of the story. She said she had not shared this day of her life with others, as she was just as startled. Della talked fast like a river that had been dammed up and burst loose, letting the words she had held in for so long spill out. Della was later informed by his family members that he remained fully alert after we left. He mumbled something about a stake. So his friends who had been sitting so quietly in the corridor scurried around the hospital looking for a steak for him.

But it turned out he had fallen on a stake, off his back porch and hit his head. The fall had given him epileptic seizures, and the doctors felt there was nothing to do for him. This is why all his loved ones sat so quietly in the hospital. They were stunned that this handsome, dynamic man who they loved so deeply was dying with no explanation before them. Della said that after we left the hospital, he remained fully alert through the day and late into the night.

He talked to his son from his heart, apologizing for not being there for him, and told him he loved him. He told his wife he loved her. He laughed, told jokes, and shared with his many friends. Then, just as unexplainable, he died the next morning. Della and I saw this experience as baffling; we never realized it was a miracle. Basically, waking folks from a near-death state was not in our repertoire as two young mothers in our twenties.

Dreams are often precursors of miracles, such as my dream that Della needed me, and the dream literally drove me to her home. Prayers are often a key ingredient to miracles. Della had been praying that she could be of some assistance to Gilman's family. My arrival was the answer to her prayer. What about the prayers of all the folks who loved their Minister in the hospital? Della's and my unexpected presence allowed him the time to say his final good-byes and express his love to his family.

This is how angels work through us. Della and I both have

the intention in our hearts to be of service to others. The last day of the Minister's life, we were obviously used as a Divine vehicle for many people's prayers and as angelic helpers. This is how a miracle magnet's life works. When you ask to be of service, when your heart holds the desire to let God/Angels/Spirit work miracles through you, don't be surprised when they do!

Imagine God in Heaven receiving billions upon billions of worthy prayers a day. How do you think they come to pass? Out of all the miracles that have crossed my computer screen, one thing is evident-humans are the hands, the feet, the voice that comes to other's rescue, to answer their prayers. Imagine God saying, "Today is a busy day; I have twenty-eight billion prayers to answer today, who is going to help me?"

Once you wake up in the morning and let your intention be known that you want to be a miracle magnet, imagine God/Angels'/Spirits' reaction. "Whew, finally, someone is offering to help with our work load!"

Once you become a vehicle for miracles, you will always be a vehicle for them! Be careful what you ask for. You may be walking or driving down the street, and the next thing you feel is a strong pull in your heart center area to spontaneously turn to the right, and there you encounter a person or situation that needs your help.

This true story of the mysterious connections that greet us in our lives and unfold into miracles, still, after a quarter of a century, leaves my brain in a whirl of confusion. The Divine timing is baffling! It is now twenty-five years after this amazing morning, and Della and I are still friends, cemented in humor and herbs. We are soul sisters in the love that we both have for herbs and their medicinal qualities and our desire to help others continues. She is a respected healer in the Cowichan tribe, and I grew up to be an author on miracles. It appears we had a date with Destiny twenty-five years ago!

the intention to be of service to others

About Mary Ellen "Angel Scribe"

Mary Ellen "Angel Scribe" is the International author of *Expect Miracles* and *A Christmas Filled With Miracles*, *Pet Tips 'n' Tales* newspaper columnist, and an award-winning photojournalist. Her popular Angels and Miracles E-newsletter is filled with inspiration, humor, and beautiful photography to uplift readers' hearts and souls. Recently, she transformed her warm and fuzzy pet newspaper column into an E-newsletter. To date her work has been featured in fourteen books. Join her "Angels and Miracles and Pet E-newsletters" at: www.AngelScribe.com or contact her at: AngelScribe@msn.com

MESSAGES FROM THE COSMIC RAINBOW: A RAINBOW BODY EXPERIENCE

W. H. McDonald Jr. California

One night in bed, I began sobbing, overwhelmed with a sense of loss at having to return to the physical me. My body felt heavy, while just moments ago I had been a rainbow of light, free of all restrictions. My journey in the rainbow seemed to have encompassed thousands of centuries, an eternity really. But when I glanced at my clock, I saw that only a little more than an hour had passed. In truth, for what had happened to me, "time" was totally meaningless. My wife, Carol rolled over and asked me what was wrong. I had great difficulty explaining, yet this was the most enlightening spiritual encounter of my lifetime.

The evening had begun normally enough. I had a long meditation and was feeling peaceful and relaxed as I went upstairs to bed. As I lay there, I turned to gaze at a photograph of my guru, Paramahansa Yogananda, smiling at me from my bedside table. I was particularly focused on his eyes when all of a sudden my whole attention seemed to be sucked into him.

While my physical body remained in my bed, the inner me was soaring faster than light, faster than thought through a vast heavenly universe, inside of and - at the same time - part of a streaming rainbow of beautiful colors. I couldn't see myself, but I knew I was color, too, and I was not alone. We were a traveling rainbow of souls, and there was no separation from anything around us, not from the colors or the music we heard. We were one with everything we saw, heard, felt, sensed, believed, and thought.

We passed slower moving colors, even colors that were blasting along at almost incomprehensible speeds. To give you an example, think of the old television series *Star Trek* and the multihued lightning streaks of warp drive. Our velocity was far greater than that. At the same time, we were accompanied by lush harmonic music, all-encompassing, not just around us but inside us as well. This was the music of the universe, and it propelled us lovingly along on our journey.

There were never any negative feelings, no fears, no anger, no worry. I was at peace with everything and happy beyond what I had ever known happiness to be. The bliss wrapped its presence around me as if I were in a rainbow cocoon of joy. And just as the colors, the music, and the joy were part of us, so was an incredible love that bathed and engulfed us. It seemed to me I felt loved in ways no one in a body had ever been loved. It was if I were love, and love was the universe, and everything that surrounded us traveling souls was made of love and reflected love. There were no boundaries, no borders, no separation, and no judgment.

As we flowed along, I learned something about who they were, and who I was, and the purpose of what was happening. It turned out that I had always been a member of this "family," and they had always been one with me although I was unsure how that worked exactly, or what it signified. I was also told we'd been gathered into a group because we had a mission, and again I struggled to understand the meaning.

I was with my rainbow family for what seemed to be an ageless amount of time, but then time didn't exist in that universe of colors and music. I saw and felt things that have no words or ways to convey back in our material world although as I was in the experience I understood everything. I know the details remain with me, stored within my higher self. I came away with the following impressions and beliefs:

! *No one is ever truly alone.*

! *All of us have a spiritual family looking after us and helping us to progress.*

! You are given information that when needed, you can evolve enough to recall and use.

! All of us have a mission, a purpose.

! Love is everything. Nothing else matters.

! Life on earth is the real dream universe.

I did not want to return to my flesh-and-bone body lying on my bed in the material world. Longing for my escape to continue, it seemed to me I was being asked to return to prison. Still, I felt a release of energy, and I began to slowly slide down until I found myself slipping into my body.

Later, as Carol and I talked, I struggled to fill her in. What I had experienced was real, but why it happened and how, I was unable to explain. Plus, there was no way she or anyone could fully comprehend the myriad emotions at work in all the various levels of my being. I was already lonely for my other family with whom I had just been reunited and then abruptly had to leave, but I was also joyful and blissful.

My journey wasn't a dream, and I was never asleep. In fact, I was more fully awake and conscious than I had ever been. I still reflect on this supernatural voyage as a turning point in my life. I know now that I am never alone, and that unseen forces and energies are at work in our lives helping us. This is what has come to pass for me, and I believe strongly this is true for others as well. I believe some people have chosen to keep these kinds of experiences to themselves to avoid being judged as strange or insane. Others may have allowed their own minds to convince them that it was all just a dream and not real.

Significant and life-changing would all be understatements to what transpired this one night. In the truest sense, it was a spiritual journey of my soul. All my notions about reality and the purpose of life were shattered as I crossed from my physical world into a consciousness of light. I was cosmically altered. A part of me now realizes what we call life is just a dream, and the only reality is love.

About W. H. McDonald Jr.

William is an Author, Minister, International Motivational Speaker, Veteran Advocate, Poet, Artist, and Film Consultant. His website is: www.vietnamexp.com

MY EXPERIENCE

Tim O'Reilly, New Jersey

I saw this huge rock coming toward my head. I said to myself, "This rock is going to hit me." It was 1962, and I was ten years old, living in Queens, New York where I grew up. My friends and I stopped at an empty lot; actually it was a huge pit, about 100 feet wide with swampy water and weeds at the bottom. We were throwing rocks from the top of the rim into the water. I decided to walk across the water on some boards that were placed over old tires. The water was about a foot deep.

I was about halfway across the pit when another group of boys showed up on the other side. Then the both groups started throwing rocks at each other. I was caught up in the middle; I began to run to my side of the pit. I was about five feet from dry land when I looked up and saw one of my friends at the top of the rim, about thirty feet away, holding a huge rock with both hands over his head. He let it go. Just before it hit me, I turned my head to my right. I don't remember the impact, but I was knocked out and fell into the water, face down.

I remember, I was still standing surrounded by total darkness. I still had my mind, yet my body felt transparent. I could feel my arms and fingers, but I could not see anything. My arms were outstretched to either side, and I heard a buzzing sound. I wasn't afraid, and I didn't have any feelings of love, although I remember being calm. And I didn't see any light at all. Then I thought the buzzing sound reminded me of a TV movie, called "Rodan," about a dinosaur bird that sent an electric charge from it's beak that buzzed to destroy cities in Japan.

Then the next thing I know, I am swaying back and forth and slowly sinking down. It felt like my legs were melting below my knees. I believe my spirit was going back into my physical body. I didn't feel myself going back into my body, but the next thing I remember, I am walking home with a couple friends bleeding from the back of my head.

I do believe I experienced the "spiritual form." The strangest thing was, I still had my mind, and I did not miss a beat. My physical body was in the water unconscious, and my mind was the same one I had in my physical body, yet I wasn't in my body. I believe my spirit ejected when I was hit by the rock that was about the size of my skull.

My parents were not home when I arrived at my family's apartment. My grandfather who we called, "Pop Pop," was home, and he called a neighbor who drove us to the hospital where I received several stitches. I didn't give the experience much thought at all. I don't remember telling anyone about my experience.

Twenty years later, I was enrolled in the School of Visual Arts in Manhattan and had to complete a short film for my thesis project. I started working on a script based on a short story, but I wasn't into it one hundred percent.

I had read Raymond Moody's book, *Life After Life* some six years earlier, and I was very intrigued with the subject of near-death experiences although I never connected my experience with them. One day I thought about doing a near-death experience documentary. The next morning when I woke up, I decided, that's it, a near-death experience documentary. It was as if a "light" went on (no pun intended); it was a very strong feeling, and it felt good, and I was into it one hundred and ten percent. The purpose for the documentary would be to help people who are bereaved and to use it in colleges for its' educational value. Basically, to create a "healing" documentary, that was my goal.

I started the research by reading more books on the near-death experience, and it was then, that I realized I had, I believed at that time, a beginning of a near-death experience. And it was then that I started telling people about my experience. Yes, some people didn't believe me or maybe they thought I was crazy, but I *knew* the experience was real. You can tell the difference between a dream and a spiritual experience; there is a *knowing*, that cannot be denied.

I began the project by searching for people to interview. It seemed very seamless. I had no problem finding the people I interviewed. I remember people telling me, what a great job I did selecting people to interview. I did not select anyone. The people who I interviewed were the ones that were available and probably were meant to be in the documentary.

I remember one of the interviewee's telling me that I understood what he had gone through. I think, because of my own near-death-like experience, they felt comfortable talking to me about their near-death experience, and because of that, I believe that is why they came across so well in the documentary.

During the making of the documentary, I learned a major lesson about listening to our intuition when I attempted to interview a medical doctor. All the other people who I interviewed, I had no problem coordinating and setting up the interview. When I located the medical doctor, it was very difficult to set up a time. I realize doctors are very busy, and I was having a very hard time getting a crew of two people together which never happened. That was the first sign, and I missed it. So I proceeded to go ahead with the interview with a shorthanded crew.

Five minutes into the interview, our main lamp blows out, the second sign. I used the same lamp in the other people's homes, no problem. The doctor was "sitting on the fence," answering my questions about the near-death experience and leaning toward a skeptic opinion. I am not discounting a skeptic, but for this healing documentary, it was not needed. I firmly believe my angels or my spiritual guides were not going to let that happen.

The third and final sign was five minutes later after our main lamp goes out, his office and the entire office outside his office consisting of four desks loses power. I decided to call it a "wrap" at that point. The doctor's footage ended up as they say, "on the editing room floor" never used in the documentary.

After the documentary was complete, I started to have this feeling of not being attached to the documentary, separate from it, as if my "ego" had no business being attached to it. I still have that feeling today. Yes, my name is on it, and it is still my job to make it available to Hospices and the general public, but I feel separate from it. I remember saying, "I feel like it was my job to show up with the camera and do the interviews and everything else would be taken care of and it was, as long as I stayed true to my intuition."

I believe that one of the reasons I had my near-death-like experience was to make the documentary, "Round Trip: The Near-Death Experience." My experience laid dormant all those years until when it was needed. It provided me with understanding, openness and compassion needed to create this powerful healing documentary.

During the making of the documentary and since then, I have grown tremendously spiritual and will continue to grow and learn. I have become over the years less judgmental and much more open and compassionate toward people, animals, and all living things. I have realized that we are all connected somehow, and that everything happens for a reason which is for a "bigger plan," something we cannot comprehend at this level.

The main lesson I learned from my own experience and the documentary is that when our physical body dies, our mind/spirit does not. I believe we are spiritual beings existing in human form on earth to learn lessons of love, forgiveness and whatever we need to learn as individuals.

About a year after the documentary was completed, one of my family members lost his mother. He watched "Round Trip" and it made him feel better. I believed it affirmed his faith that his mother's spirit never died. That made me feel very good because I felt like I accomplished what I believed was one of my jobs on earth to do.

About Tim O'Reilly

Tim produced the DVD, "Round Trip: The Near-Death Experience coded for "all regions" meaning it can be played worldwide in English, Spanish and French subtitles. It is available on Amazon.com

THE BRIGHT LIGHT

Terry Orlando, New York

The following experience is taken from some of the answers on my research questionnaire that Terry submitted to me with her permission to publish them.

Q. Describe what you were doing at the time of your experience.

A. "I was sleeping during the first part of my experience, then awake during the other part of my experience. I had a dream that a battle was taking place between good and evil."

Q. Did you see a light? If so, who or what did you perceive the light to be?

A. "The dream was frightening, yet it only consisted of darkness with flashes of light like lightening. The darkness in the dream was replaced by a brilliant white light. I was now awake lying in bed with my eyes closed. I perceived the light to be an entity of love. The light seemed loving and peaceful. I opened my eyes and the light was in the room and so brilliant that I couldn't see any details of the room. I remember holding my hands in front of my face and couldn't see them; the light was too bright but not harsh on my eyes. When I closed my eyes, the light faded slowly away."

Q. Did you hear any sounds during your experience?

A. "I heard the light speaking through telepathy, not audible, telling me to read the Bible and some of my answers would be there."

Q. Did this light have any immediate effect upon you? If so, describe.

A. "I immediately had knowledge about the natural world, of how everything worked together - like going to sleep not knowing about mechanics and waking up knowing in detail how all engines work. I knew there was a God, and I had a joy and peace unlike anything I had ever felt and desired. I no longer had any desire to do anything harmful to myself such as smoking or to harm others."

Q. Did this experience seem real or dream-like or a hallucination?

A. "The experience was REAL."

Q. Did you experience a sense of oneness or unity with everyone and everything?

A. "I experienced a unity with everything and understood everything - like I expanded into everything."

Q. What was the most relevant and meaningful part of your experience?

A. "Love is more important than material goods. The unseen is just as real as the seen."

Q. Did this experience increase or decrease your spiritual or religious beliefs or practices in any way? If so, in what way?

A. "I had an increase in spiritual beliefs. I was an atheist prior to the experience."

Q. Do you feel more, less, or still the same in areas of compassion, love and acceptance of others?

A. " I have the same compassion, love, and acceptance but a sadness for the ignorance that people have when they hurt each other and the environment. At first, my joy and happiness was all encompassing, and I could not feel darkness, now I have a sadness for the darkness, but I also know how wonderful the world would be without darkness. I now believe that life after death will experience the total love that is not possible on the earth."

Q. Do you feel more, less, or still the same in your desire to help others?

A. "I want to help others more and seek ways to do that professionally and in general."

Q. Did you talk about this experience with anyone? How did people react?

A. "At first I didn't tell many people about the experience and now tell only people I feel are ready to hear it. My husband, at the time of my experience, divorced me -not because I saw a light but because of how it changed me. He used to say, "You are not the same person I married.""

Q. Did this experience lessen your fear of death?

A. "I don't fear death of the body. I only fear leaving my family."

Q. Is solitude more important to you following your experience?

A. "I love solitude. People spend a lot of time conversing over things that I don't feel are important. I'd rather watch a sunset."

Q. Following your experience, do you have more, less or still the same feelings of an inner sense of Spirit or of the God of your understanding?

A. "Spiritual matters are my first desire in life; second is being with my family."

Q. Following your experience, are you more accepting of all people's different religions or less tolerant?

A. "I am tolerant of all religions, I just wish there weren't any religions; they seem to be one way people separate themselves from others."

Q. Do you personally have a sense of mission or purpose to fulfill upon your return to physical consciousness?

A. "My purpose is to be more loving and forgiving."

Q. Do you view life and humanity's purpose on earth any differently now?

A. "Yes, our human purpose is to develop those qualities that follow us after the body dies."

Q. In retrospect, do you think this experience happened for a reason or to help you in some way?

A. "I believe the experience happened at that point in my life because of the prayers of others for me of which I was not aware at the time."

Q. What is the single most important bit of wisdom you wish to tell others who have not had a transcendent type of experience?

A. "Go beyond the five senses; seek and you shall find; ask

and the door will be opened to you, and be sincere."

About Terry Orlando

Terry is a nurse and lives in New York and may be contacted at: torland1@optonline.net

MORE REAL THAN ANYTHING

Christopher Matt, Connecticut

In 1975 I was working the midnight to 8:00 a.m. shift in a bank's data processing center. When morning came, I left to head home as usual, driving my VW Beetle. I was extremely tired and was literally fighting to stay awake. As I was driving over a long bridge that brings you to our shoreline town, I must have closed my eyes for one or two seconds, and the next thing I know, the car had veered and struck the guardrail.

All of a sudden, the car is rolling over and over and over, and I am watching this person from about three or four feet above, and I notice that the person is me! How strange. I am feeling the most intense calm, peaceful feeling as this scene unfolds, and time seemed to no longer exist; in fact, I was thinking when is this rolling going to stop. It seemed to take forever. But two things are forever ingrained in my memory. Our consciousness is not tied to our body/brain. I know this because I was outside my body watching it get tossed around. Also, outside the body, consciousness lives in such pure peace and calmness and love that we cannot even imagine what it is like.

The following experience took place approximately six months after the VW Beetle rollover described earlier. I was twenty-one at the time.

In the months after the rollover, I developed a compulsive interest in all things spiritual, read voraciously, visited churches of all denominations, began a daily meditation program, etc. During this particular time period, I was also experiencing a lot of stress and dissatisfaction in my life. A year earlier, I had relocated to southern New Jersey with my family after having lived up to that time two-hundred and fifty miles away in

Connecticut. I had no friends in the new town, and a job I hated, etc. These were not particularly calm or contented times for me. By mentioning these things, I am trying to set some context for the events that follow.

During a particularly stressful period, I remember turning to meditation as I had been doing daily for some time. I was home alone in my room. I remember feeling desperate to receive some kind of answer from God or whatever higher force it is that intersects with humanity from time to time because I think I needed a reason to continue on with my life, which I felt was becoming too difficult. Maybe I was suffering from depression. Anyway, I'm sitting in the chair in my room, doing the meditation thing. After a while, I am going deeper within, and the next thing I know I am above at ceiling level looking down at the individual in the chair, basically looking at the top of the head, and how the hair looks from above, now novel. I had never seen my head from that angle before.

Now some kind of momentum, or motion is happening. I feel like I am being propelled forward at a very fast rate of speed. I don't remember anything 'visual' during this propulsion, just velocity, speed, and a sense of breaking through the ether, almost like you see space vehicles breaking through the earth's atmosphere. At some point, a most incredible light becomes present. It is not normal light; it is an all-consuming 'living' light-presence/personage, and it just radiates all things and all love in it.

Words cannot adequately describe its characteristics because it is not something seen in this normal plane of existence. And the light kind of spoke, and the main thing I can remember it saying to me personally was, "See, there is no reason to be afraid. Everything will be whole/good/wonderful." They were not the actual words used, but just understanding. I realized that this Divine Light is God. It is incredibly evident; it is known to you as soon as you are in its presence. There is no doubt. You want to be in that presence forever and never leave.

Now the next thing, and it is very important to note that this is not really sequential because there was not a sense of sequence, more a sense of timelessness, like time as we're used to it did not exist there. Anyway, there's this human/spirit presence (male) with me, and he's showing me something, almost like a book. All of a sudden my entire life up to that point is displayed to me in incredible detail holographic-like, every moment, second by second is shown to me, and I see and feel the emotions of all the people I interact with. It is incredible because I had forgotten maybe 95% of these interactions, and they go all the way back to first consciousness at maybe two or three years old and extend all the way to the present. The detail is incredible, and it all takes place in maybe five seconds it seems. Yet it is incredibly detailed so how can it be so detailed? Again, time does not exist there. And I remember seeing all these interactions that I had with people and almost all were very, very good and loving, and I felt kind of proud of myself for that.

At some point now, I am with this human/spirit presence, and he wants to show me how all knowledge is available here, and he opens something, and I see all the centuries accumulated knowledge and information in incredible detail from the beginning of time onward. It covers every category of knowledge; history, science, art, architecture, religion, medicine, mathematics. I am absorbing it all very easily, and it is limitless, and the human/spirit presence says to me, "See, this knowledge is available to you when you come here." The knowledge continued to flow and then there is some sort of transition I noticed. I was then shown FUTURE events and technologies, and peoples and progressions of humanity. The human/spirit presence (an elderly male presence) says to me, "Now this part of what I am showing you, you will not retain when you go back." That was very true. There is nothing of that phase that I can remember; only that I was shown events and people from the future.

Now during these experiences, I cannot emphasize enough

the overriding feeling of love and total peace. It is wonderful and cannot be described adequately, at least by me. You just know it is everything. You also know that existence is about two things- love of others and the attainment of knowledge. That's what I came away with.

I do not remember how I arrived back in the room from which I had begun this journey, but I remember being told that all I had experienced will be available to me when I return, so "do not fear." I returned, and I felt I had been gone maybe thirty minutes. It could have been more; it could have been less. I was in such an exhilarated state of mind for weeks to come. I think my mother thought I was crazy. I said to her, "Mom, let's take a walk around the block, I have to tell you something." I tried to describe to her what I had experienced, and that the meaning of life is all about love and knowledge. She kept reverting the conversation back to religion and Catholicism (which I was brought up in.)

Let me tell you it's kind of hard dropping down to the level of religion after you have experienced something like I had just lived through. We're walking around the neighborhood, and the colors were incredible. I looked at flowers and bushes and they were just pulsating with life. I commented on how incredibly alive they were, almost as if they were breathing. The sense of love permeated everything, and the world was not the same. It was alive and beautiful and growing and expanding toward that Light. I remained in this frame of mind for weeks, and I had such a sense of compassion for others, and a realization that love is the only thing that really matters.

I often think of this experience, and I have no doubt that it was real. It was vastly more real than anything we experience here. Hope this conveys some sense of what I experienced. It has been thirty years, but its impact on me has remained.

the love of others the attainment of k

Questions and Christopher's answers to
my research questionnaire:

Q. Do you feel more, less, or still the same in your desire to help others:

A. "I am a hospice volunteer these days."

Q. Did this experience lessen your fear of death?

A. "Absolutely. This is why I bring up my experience with people, to help them understand that this life is just a passing experience. There is much more!"

Q. Do you have a greater desire to read, study, share, or discuss matters of a spiritual nature following your experience?

A. "Absolutely. I read voraciously since then-spiritual books, quantum physics, cutting edge psychology, etc."

Q. Do you view life and humanity's purpose on earth any differently now?

A. "Yes, we are here to learn as much as possible and to love each other."

Q. In retrospect, do you think this experience happened for a reason or to help you in some way?

A. "Yes. It awakened me and gave me strength enough to continue the journey."

Q. What is the single most important bit of wisdom you wish to tell others who have not had a transcendent type of experience?

A. "There is a lot more to reality than meets the eye. The

perception we have on a day to day basis is very limited. After we pass to the next life, our perception will be a thousand times magnified, no limitations."

About Christopher Matt

Christopher Matt is a Systems Programmer. If you would like to contact him, his contact information is: Christopher matt@sbcglobal.net

MY TRANSFORMATIVE EXPERIENCES

Mark Pitstick, M.A., D.C., Ohio

Throughout my life, I've been blessed with a number of transformative experiences that have greatly guided, instructed, and comforted me. In 1958 at the age of five, my parents showed me a beautiful sunset, and I told them "it reminded me of God." I wasn't told about this until I attended theology school many years later. My parents knew of no teaching at home or our church that would cause me to associate God with a sunset. Maybe I retained some memory of our Source from before this incarnation.

While sitting in church at age eleven, the minister was talking about hell as a place of fiery torment for eternity. As he went on, a calm, clear voice inside my head gently spoke: "They have that one a little mixed up, Mark. God has no need for such a place in His plan of salvation for all." I looked around to see if anyone else had heard the voice, but they were all looking straight ahead. As I recalled that experience, it felt like a sacred moment, a vibration in the center of my chest that I revered.

At age twelve, I was sitting by myself reading the obituary of a prominent man who had just died. As I looked up, light refracted through our beveled glass windows, and I went into a deep reverie. A calm loving voice or thought said, "You too will die someday, Mark. What will you do with your life in the meantime? Will you leave this world a better place or will you just take up space?" These and other experiences have motivated me to study soul and afterlife issues.

In 1974, I awakened in the middle of the night and saw a vision on the ceiling. A huge golden central orb had many tiny dots connected to it by golden threads. As I wondered what it all meant, a wise voice or thought said: "This is how life is. The central sphere represents God."

Further, the voice continued: "The infinite numbers of golden dots are like the many souls in the universe. Some of them realize Oneness and are in or on the central sphere. Some are very close but don't fully realize their inseparability from Spirit. Others believe they are quite distant from God. Of those, some paths are straight and simple while others appear tortuous and complicated."

The teaching concluded, "The good news is that, viewed from a sufficiently enlightened perspective, the entire assemblage is seen as One. A perimeter can be drawn around even the most distant dots, revealing the unified nature of all life as love and light." This miraculous vision reminded me of my higher self and led to an exploration of meditation, yoga, and other spiritual paths.

In 1994 on the night before I finished my first book, *Radiant Wellness*, I felt a profound peace as though I had finally arrived after many years of praying, searching and working. I had originally planned to become a medical doctor (M.D.) but a series of events guided me to become a doctor of chiropractic (D.C.) That night, I deeply felt that these life changes had occurred for good reason and worked out for the best.

Early the next morning, I started to complete the last few hours of work on the manuscript. Just as I had done many times, I turned on the computer and monitor that usually showed a black screen followed by computer codes and prompts. That morning, however, the monitor immediately showed a vivid display of royal gold and maroon squares.

These colored squares each contained the same two letters. I rubbed my eyes and pinched myself to make sure I wasn't dreaming. The letters were D.C.! This miracle still inspires me to practice advanced chiropractic and help people enjoy the many benefits of holistic health care.

In 1997, I had a multi-sensory experience of the Source during a long yoga and meditation session. While silently repeating the mantra OM, a louder and deeper chorus of that sound spontaneously resounded within and all around me. I smelled an unknown but wonderful fragrance although it was the middle of winter and all windows and doors were shut. Even though my eyes were shut, I saw a radiant golden-white light in my mind's eye. Then I felt what seemed to be Divine love, acceptance, and understanding. This glimpse of the Beloved was so overwhelmingly beautiful that tears welled up in my eyes. Next, I felt a vibration throughout my body that was both tingling and euphoric.

It seemed that information and energy were being transmitted to me. The power and splendor were so great that after just a few minutes, I felt I couldn't handle the current. I murmured aloud, "Oh my God!" and started laughing, and then the experience was over. But that sweet memory helps carry me through life's challenges and reminds me I'm always Home, no matter what the external circumstances.

One teaching from that event is that I was not prepared to directly experience Divine frequencies for very long. That level of power blew my mind's circuit breakers; my nervous system wasn't strong enough to handle the current. This experience motivates me to live as healthy and balanced a life as possible, so I can increasingly sustain that energy level.

Once we see the Light - even a little bit - we increasing realize that energy, love, intelligence, and bliss are the totality of life. Knowing this allows us to participate in all of life's experiences fully, no matter what is going on around us. Spiritual enlightenment helps us remember that we chose this brief earth-walk for the exquisite opportunities for service, adventure, growth, and enjoyment. We then can increasingly surf through all of life - the good and bad, happy and sad with power, courage, trust, joy, purpose and passion.

About Mark Pitstick, M.A., D.C.

Dr. Pitstick helps others know and show their magnificence in body, mind and spirit. A frequent radio and TV guest, Dr. Pitstick authored *"Radiant Wellness"* and *"Soul Proof"* and produced the documentary film *"Soul Proof."* His "Radiant Wellness Centers" use natural, advanced and holistic approaches to help others heal and fine-tune themselves.

More information about Dr. Pitstick and his work can be found at the following websites: Center@radiant101.com, www.soulproof.com, and www.radiant101.com

BLISS

Harvey Rhodes, DDS Texas

Up until the spring of 1989, I thought I was quite unique in having had a near-death experience without being near-death. However, I found out that several people have had similar experiences. Due to my natural inclinations and my scientific training, I am more skeptical than most. Unless this happened to me, not once but twice, I probably wouldn't believe it.

In the summer of 1964, I was in perfect health. I was in athletic shape as to fat and muscle mass, cardiovascular system. I had a routine medical check up once a year. This statement is to emphasize that I was not near-death! Something was disturbing me in my personal relationships, and I cannot remember what it was.

Approximately 5:30 p.m. on a summer work day, I arrived home, I greeted my wife and son, then for some unknown reason, I decided to go to our bedroom and lie down. This room faced west and even though the blinds were down and the drapes partly drawn, it was well lighted by the sun. I lay on my back, probably thinking of this problem. I became aware of total blackness. Then this white light appeared in the distance and started coming closer. I was concerned with eye damage (it was becoming very bright) but even up close it didn't hurt my eyes.

As it approached, all apprehension left and the indescribable feeling, (bliss, at home feeling, peace, security; all are inadequate descriptions) completely enveloped me. The light took on <u>no</u> figure or shape, It stopped just past arms length. The communication began and I was "told" everything would be alright, <u>that nothing in this world mattered anyway</u>.

I questioned, "Nothing really mattered?" Answer, "No."

The desire to be <u>in</u> the light kept growing, but the light retreated when I started toward it. There was a firm communication that this was <u>not</u> to be. I reached out my arm to touch the light, and it retreated further, just out of arms reach. At this point, I decided to move my arm slowly toward the light and then as the light did not move, I would move rapidly toward it. This I did, I "awoke" and found my left hand stretched out toward the ceiling, However, the memory of "bliss" was very strong. If I could be positive that death would unite me with the light, I would have left this world in an instant.

The next day upon arriving home, I greeted my wife and son and immediately went to the bedroom, lay down, and waited. Then the same darkness came, and the light appeared some distance off. I could not control myself. I started toward it as fast as I could. Immediately I "awoke" to find the room same as the day before.

What I learned from this last episode was that although there was no communication that I was not ready to become <u>one</u> with the light.

As I mentioned earlier, I do not know what was troubling me, but it must have worked out and maybe the reason was the encounter with the light. To this day I cannot remember the problem.

As to the after effects, I felt I had a very privileged experience. My life did not change, good or bad. The feeling remains to this day that it is to a much better place we will go when we qualify to become one with the light. The one thing which does not seem right was the idea expressed emphatically that nothing in this life matters, at least as far as the human race is concerned. Perhaps, this happens to be one of the things we are not meant to understand.

The experience did not make me more religious but more spiritual. No matter what your religious beliefs are, we are going to the same place. For the people who have not had such an experience, I feel for because all doubt is removed!!

Incidentally, I have no concern with being thought of as strange and have been reciting my experience ever since it happened. Perhaps this is the intended purpose of the experience!!

About Harvey Rhodes, DDS

Dr. Rhodes is a dentist in Houston, Texas.

PEACE AND LOVE

Russell " Wishes to remain anonymous

His account is documented in the question and answers from my research questionnaire

Q. Describe what you were doing at the time of your experience?

A. "Laying on my side in my bed."

Q. Did you experience a feeling of lifting out of your body or something other?

A. "I felt a spirit-like energy entering me from my head down to my stomach."

Q. Did you see or sense any other beings or entities present during your experience?

A. "Yes, inside me. It is hard to explain to someone who never experienced this. I did not see anything. It was sensed. It was like an invisible force coming down into my body. The best I could describe it was a sensation-like spirit which felt electric or magnetic. It felt like every cell was being cleansed as it moved down me. There was an emotional component where I not only sensed its presence physically, but I could feel it emotionally and it felt very emotional in a good way. It is so hard to put the feeling into words."

Q. Did time or space seem altered to you in any way?

A. "My consciousness felt like it was held in a very awake state. I was already more awake from feeling all the sensations of energy moving down my body, but there was a point where I was not paying attention to that any longer. My consciousness felt held, very aware, and super awake but empty of any thought. My eyes were wide open. I guess that the closest word that would fit would be a trance. It felt like my consciousness was locked in a position very awake and aware with no thoughts of anything."

Q. Did this experience seem real or dream-like or a hallucination?

A. "No, very real. Very, very, very real."

Q. During your experience were you given an understanding of the meaning and purpose of life?

A. "The message that I received was that God wanted to use me for His purpose which had to do with bringing peace. I wish I could remember what was communicated exactly. There were no words, but the communication definitely had some components. God wanted to use me, and it was to bring peace and love. It was a calling very similar to the St. Francis prayer."

Q. Following your experience, do you consider yourself to be more spiritual than religious? If so, how would you explain this to others?

A. "Due to the nature of my experience (in thought I had asked, I wonder what is true in that book, the Bible and what is not?) Three seconds after I had that thought I had the experience. I have always been open-minded to spiritual stuff from any religion as long as it preached goodness, peace, etc. I guess I still am, but I am very interested now in learning about Jesus and His message much, much more than in the past. I also like Native American Spirituality."

Q. Do you feel more, less, or still the same in areas of compassion, love and acceptance of others?

A. "Much, much more, but dislike and hate still creep in sometimes when I come across someone who I don't like. I believe we are all children of a living God, and so I try to love even those I really do not like. I am not perfect, and I believe God asks me to try. My experience was an ending to this end. To be used by God to bring peace and love. So I try."

Q. Do you feel more, less, or still the same in your desire to help others?

A. "Much more and to fashion my life around helping others."

Q. Did you talk about this experience with anyone? How did people respond?

A. "I was very afraid of telling anyone. All responded good, but I know that the experience is 100% subjective, and I have to accept that people are not going to understand or be skeptical. I don't know how I would have responded if someone else had told me this prior to me having the experience. I would have perhaps been skeptical too which really hurts me in a way. I really wish I could have everyone with me in the experience to erase any doubts in their minds. My mind is more open to the experiences of others than before I had the experience myself."

Q. Do you have a better sense of self-acceptance following your experience?

A. " Yes, that I am a child of God just as everyone else is."

Q. Have you lost interest in materialism and competition to achieve a higher standard of living?

A. "That was lost to a good degree before I had the experience. It just lost a good deal more. I am still human, and still like material comforts, but I do not take ascertaining these things to be the aim of my life. Fellowship and peace and love between people, salvation and reconciliation are more important to me. I am still human and I know I need God in helping me to see what is important and what is not."

Q. Do you feel this experience is sacred or holy in some way?

A. "Absolutely in every way. I have thought backward and forwards about the experience and about what could have caused it besides God. I am someone who abused mostly alcohol and marijuana as a teen. As part of my recovery, I tried to walk with God or have God in my life. I had suffered from major depression on and off while not resorting to the bottle or drugs. The kind of depressions where you wish every day that your life would end. I was taking prescribed Depakote for depression when I had the experience. After I had the experience, I read books trying to find others who have had the same and read about scientists who believe that experiences such as mine can be contributed to neuron firing in parts of the brain. I thought maybe it was Depakote. The thing I wouldn't be able to get over is how a drug for depression could follow your thoughts and then three seconds after questioning what was true or not in the Bible, I have this experience. I am really still open to any scientific explanations to what I experienced. I really wish it was not such a subjective thing, so that others could have experienced what I experienced."

Q. Following your experience, do you have more, less or still the same feelings of an inner sense of Spirit or of the God of your understanding?

A. "I feel the same except the 100% conviction that God is very real and watching us and loves us."

Q. Do you have a greater desire to read, study, share, or discuss matters of a spiritual nature following your experience?

A. "Oh yes. In the experience I received, God wants to use me to bring peace. I did not get explicit instructions on how to go about that. So I read. I also reasoned that if God spoke to me He probably spoke to others, and I am very curious to know what communication they received. Perhaps I can learn from them, and I will have a better understanding of what it is God wants me to do in my walk with Him."

Q. Following your experience, are you more accepting of all people's different religious beliefs or less tolerant?

A. "Before I had my experience I was contemplating conflict between people of different religions and races; if people could learn to live in peace with one another. I have to reason again that if God came to me while I was contemplating these things, then there must be something there. That first and foremost, God wants us to live in every way shape and form at peace with one another and that is more important than differences between religions. My leaning is to learn more about Christ. I am not sure exactly why I have a pull in that direction."

Q. In retrospect, do you think this experience happened for a reason or to help you in some way?

A. "Well, before my experience, I would become very depressed, and I would see things as having no purpose. I don't believe that anymore."

Q. What is the single most important bit of wisdom you wish to tell others who have not had a transcendent type of experience?

A. "To keep an open mind to spiritual things and to try to have a relationship with God in your life."

LOVE

Virginia L. Senders, Ph.D. Massachusetts

On December 15, 1972, I had a transformative spiritual experience. Its effects have totally transformed my life and continue to this day. To tell you all about it would require a compete autobiography, which is more than you want.

In its external manifestation, it was totally different from the classical near-death experience we are all familiar with. Then forty-nine years old and a professor of Psychology at Framingham State College, MA, I was attending a Christmas party at the Seminary of the Oblates of Mary Immaculate ("the OMI's") in Natick, Mass., where several of my students at Framingham were seminarians. (They took their religious courses at the seminary and their secular ones at Framingham.) My husband was with me while my teen-aged sons were off elsewhere doing their own things. I had been feeling very good since the semester had been interesting and rewarding and was coming to a happy conclusion. I had looked forward to this party (unusual for me; I am generally not a "party person.")

And I did enjoy this party! I nursed a glass of wine and joined a group of my students in chatting and caroling. My husband, John, went off and found himself a chess game. I looked around as I sang and sipped and noted several things that made this party different - a number of men and women in religious garb, and unusual number of people with physical handicaps, a very fat girl in a shiny green dress who recited a parody on "The Night Before Christmas" to much applause, a troop of Brazilian Indians who sang carols in their own language. At some point during the singing, I turned to the seminarian who was my host and said, "You guys have something very special here." The student (knowing that I considered myself an atheist) replied, **"It's God."** I opened my mouth to make a smart-ass reply, and instead, I blurted out: "Y'know David, you just could be right!" And then, amazed, I said to myself, "Now <u>what</u> did you mean by <u>that</u> ??!! In answer to myself, a series of things happened in my head: I remembered the words of some religious songs I had been listening to, one of which asked me to "come take the chance of new life in a land so fair and free" and added "without the risk, life isn't worth the pain, the sorrow and the strife that every man (sic) must know until the end." And more. This was music from the Weston Priory. The words seemed to speak individually and uniquely to me. So perhaps I had already "taken the chance," but still, <u>what is God</u>?? I reviewed all my college philosophy courses (in 1 minute) and said, "No, not that," and then a part of me asked, **"Well, what is it that these guys have here?"** And the answer came back (from where? Some other lobe of my brain, I guess!) and it said, **"Love!"**

While externally I looked normal, sipped wine, and sang carols, inside my head a dialog began. "You mean, this wonderful experience that I'm having, Love, is what other people mean when they use the word 'God'? "Ya, but to say 'God is love' doesn't mean anything if you don't believe in God. But when you're having an almost ecstatic experience of joy and communion and affection and attunement - this love - this transportation out of myself - this experience of LOVE - this is what they mean when they talk of God. I believe in that - that it exists - because <u>I'm having that experience right now</u>. And if LOVE IS GOD there is so much more to be included!

My mind raced through Love's endless meanings and variations - not limited to personal ones nor to emotions or feelings. Old Christian teachings came back to me with new meaning, new value, new passion. I was flooded. I was almost, but not quite, in a trance when it came time to go home. I had never seen anything more beautiful than the sleety streets that night, reflecting the colored lights on houses and yards, and I knew that somehow this beauty was a part of the whole of LOVE.

The weekend was a fine time for incubation. On Monday, alone at home with the vacuum cleaner (a perfect instrument for meditation), the in-head dialog began again, asking about Jesus. Q. "If Love is God, who, what - is Jesus?" A. "Jesus is the embodiment of Love - you know - the Incarnation." When I said that word, the whole of my childhood religion came back to me, but in an adult form - a form that was not in conflict with any science, or with any psychological, sociological learnings that had shaped me over my adult years. By Monday night, I called my parents and told them that I was once again a Christian or trying to be. Their joy and appreciation was palpable over the telephone wires. Love flowed.

In the weeks to come, I changed and changed. So much that I wish I could tell you! One son said, "This is the most disorganized Christmas we've ever had - and the best!" When I taught my General Psych students about emotions, we started, this time with LOVE instead of my traditional FEAR AND ANGER. My childhood friend, Bobby, by then a Sacred Heart nun, was thrilled when she heard my story and became my instructor in Scripture and in Church History. For a while, I went to church at The Oblates every Sunday. Of course I didn't need to go to church, but by that time I had learned that "the communion of saints" included people (dead or alive) who had been touched by love and wanted to live in its spirit, and I wanted to be part of it, so I wanted to go to a good church where I could be with them. The Seminary was a good place to find it. My students welcomed me and so did the priest in charge.

So much has happened since those years! The next year, John and I went to Toronto for a sort-of sabbatical. I taught at Scarborough College of the U. of Toronto. I have to quote one student. She said, "We love you! Because you love us! Somehow you radiate your love to us!" I knew that was true, but I was surprised to find that they actually "got it."

Not everything was smooth sailing. My husband thought I was psychotic, or maybe that was just his excuse for wanting a divorce and freedom. I came back to Framingham and stayed at the college (now University) until I took an early retirement. I did that so that I could find new ways of serving and more learning. I could have of course, have volunteered to wash dishes at a local settlement house, but I still craved fun and adventure, so I went to Nicaragua and studied Spanish and learned about Central American politics and economics, then came home to write and lecture about it. Over the years, I have made five more trips to Nicaragua, and also one to Guatemala, and one to Cuba. I also joined the Sirius Community - an outgrowth of the Findhorn Community for those familiar with the latter. The focus at Sirius was on sustainability - a way of practicing Love in accordance with natural cycles.

I am now living in a fine retirement community and at 87, am still learning and growing. I'm an active member of a UCC church, a student of NDEs and OBEs, integrating scripture study, new age, politics and activism, learning and sometimes teaching in the Learning in Retirement Program and, I hope, seeking new forms of loving. I have wished I were a classic NDE experiencer, but I guess I had to do it my own way. Did my experience that December night some 38 years ago have a profound and continuing effect on my life? You bet it did!

About Virginia L. Senders, Ph.D.

Dr. Senders is Emeritus Professor of Psychology, and artist (painter.) She has written a book, *Measurement & Statistics, A Basic Text Emphasizing Behavioral Science Applications*, NY. Oxford, 1958. Her email address is: ginnysen@crocker.com

MY GUARDIAN ANGELS

Shirene Sethi, India

I have a beautiful baby girl, and there are times when I question myself if we are being fair in bringing these precious innocent angels into this crazy, tormented world. With "bomb blasts" becoming a commonality, innocent lives lost in the name of Allah, churches being destroyed in the name of whichever other God. Is this what we are now reduced to, political warfare? Terrorists using bombs, destroying churches, places of worship, all in their perceived notion of religion? So what can we do? Stop having children? Lock yourself indoors? Stop living? …NAH!! No way!!

Experience has taught me that for every nasty terrorist out there, there exists their counterparts, the guardian angels. These people who, with their acts of kindness, generosity and big hearts, make you believe that there IS a God, and He will win the war!! I have been blessed and protected several times in my life. There have been so many instances when these angels, disguised as humans, have stepped forward and bailed me out. These have left a powerful impact in my life. While the occasions have been many, I share with you some experiences that have made me believe that GOOD EXISTS!

The first incident took place in the busy area of Delhi. I was rushing as usual, trying to ensure that I didn't miss the company bus to work. I made it in time, however, when I boarded, I realized to my horror that I had lost my husband's very expensive phone. I hunted frantically through my bag, checked the floor of the bus but no luck. That's when it struck me that I must have dropped it in the market. I stopped the bus and got off.

I decided to retrace my steps back home in wild hope that

I would find it. I reached back home extremely disappointed. Clinging onto every bit of last hope, I dialed the cell phone number from my landline. I was shocked when a man picked up the phone. He said, "Madam, I am a salesman. I found your phone next to the grocery story in the market. I will wait for you right here. You can come and collect it." Holding my breath, I ran into the market again, and there he was, a very simple looking, middle-aged man carrying a big black bag of some product that he was trying to sell. He must have seen the worried look on my face because he suddenly smiled at me very reassuringly. I walked up to him and he handed my phone back to me. I thanked him profusely and asked him how I could repay him. He just smiled and said, "Madam, it's okay, thank you." With that, he turned and walked away and did not turn back even once. I was left speechless. An expensive mobile phone returned to me in this day and age? God bless that Indian angel!

The second incident took place in the airport of Bangalore. Just before we went inside the airport, my husband, Dushyant, stopped at an ATM to take some cash out. He must have taken out about RS. 4500.00. He handed me his wallet, my bags, etc. while he went to look for a trolley for our luggage. We then proceeded to enter the airport and then went on to wait for our flight back to Delhi.

Feeling thirsty, I requested Dushyant to get me some coffee. He asked me for his wallet. I hunted for it but just could not find it. I then realized that I must have dropped it somewhere, probably when I was struggling with all the bags. That wallet had the cash, all his ATM cards as well as his credit cards. I was mortified! Suddenly, my phone rang. A lady was calling. She informed me that she had found this wallet outside Bangalore airport. The only source of identification was my business card that Dushyant carried in his wallet. This stranger made an STD call to my Delhi number to inform me that she had found his wallet.

I told her that we were inside the airport and begged her

to wait outside. She told me not to worry and to take my time. Dushyant had to ask for special permission to get outside the airport again, and there she was - a lady. She was wearing a torn overcoat, obviously not from a well to do family. Dushyant took out RS.500 and insisted that she take it. She refused saying, in Hindi, "Sir, why would you pay me for doing the right thing?" He pushed the money into her hands and said, "Madam, we don't have the time to take you out for a thank you dinner, so please have dinner on us. Take this small token of thanks. By taking it you will be helping us to do the right thing!" She smiled and reluctantly, took the money. A wallet loaded with cash and credit cards returned in tact! God bless that Indian angel!

The third incident took place at the Singapore airport. Dushyant and I had gone there to celebrate our fourth year anniversary. With it being our first trip together abroad, we had gone a little berserk with the shopping. We had four suitcases among the two of us. When we got the baggage weighed, well no surprises there, the baggage was severely overweight. We had two choices - pay the $550 or throw out some stuff. We did not have that much money left, so the two of us opened our suitcases right there at the airport, and we were at our wits end wondering what to do.

Just then a gentleman, a Canadian Indian, walked up to us. His name was Ashish. Apparently he had lost his luggage while in transit from Vancouver to Singapore. He was now on his way to Delhi to meet up with family. Without blinking an eyelid, he said that as he had no baggage of his own, he could take on some of our luggage as his own. We were shocked. In this day and age, to offer to take on a stranger's baggage at an international airport - well, we just could not believe our luck. With him taking on a suitcase, there was no question of extra baggage. We thanked him profusely. On reaching Delhi, he gave us the luggage tag, wished us all the best and walked away! God bless that Canadian Indian angel!

The fourth incident happened with my husband. This was a month before we were going to get married. He had to go to Chicago, USA for work. He was so excited about setting up our new home after marriage that he bought a whole lot of home decorations like crystal vases, paintings, etc. Naturally his baggage was overweight. The custom officers would not allow him to go through unless he paid the overweight baggage amount or threw some stuff away.

Dushyant looked at them and said most sincerely, "Look, I am getting married next month. All this is for my wife, for our new home. Please tell me what can I do?" The personnel along with the air hostesses who were standing nearby all got excited when they heard he was about to get married. One air hostess asked him, "Will it be a typical Indian monsoon wedding?" Dushyant laughed and replied that it would be. All four air hostesses promptly took over Dushyant's baggage and checked it as their own. God bless those four American angels!

The fifth incident took place in Australia. I had gone there for work. I was on my way back from work when I stopped at a Seven Eleven store. It was quite late at night. Being the end of the month, I had just $10 in my wallet and desperately needed to buy some groceries. The store in charge was a Muslim, a Pakistani. When he saw me, he dropped everything and asked me if I were Indian or Pakistani. I smiled and said that I was an Indian and was here in Sydney, Australia for work. He came forward and shook my hand proudly and said, "It is wonderful to see such a powerful young Indian woman. May Allah be with you and may you be even more successful.

He of course, had no idea what I did or what I was there for. I thanked him. He then went on to say that he had visited India many years ago and that it was such a beautiful place. He also asked me to visit Pakistan sometime. I told him I would try. We chatted for some time, and I then went on to pick up a couple of groceries. When I went to the checkout counter, he added a box of chocolates to the bags and told me that on no account would he accept money from me. I was his Indian sister! He said that I had made his day by chatting with him. I was the closest that he had come to being back home! I shook his hands and thanked him for his generosity. Promising to meet him again, I went on my way. God bless my Pakistani angel!

So many incidents, all heart-warming. Perfect strangers going that extra mile to keep another stranger happy. Strangers who are not bound by any silly political or religious reason. They live for other human beings and make no distinction by caste, color, religion, sex. They are those angels who make me walk out of my house every day, allow me to tell my daughter that the world is good. So to all the people out there I say, "Step out! Let's kill those cowardly terrorists with kindness! Keep on living! God bless you all!

About Shirene Sethi

Shirene Sethi is a trainer and content developer specializing in communications and behavioral trainings and lives in Gurgaon, Haryana, India. Shirene has this to say: "I freelance as a trainer and content developer. This gives me more time to be at home for my children. Besides my four-year-old daughter, Sairah Vivian, I also have a one-year-old baby boy, Ranveer Mikhail. I truly believe in miracles. My life has been full of them!" She can be contacted at: shirene_sethi@hotmail.com

MY SPIRITUAL JOURNEY
BEGINS WITH DEATH

Tiffany Snow, U.S.A.

"Stars!" I shouted through the thunder to the appaloosa pacing behind the chain link fence. "Stars! You are always the one getting into trouble! In the middle of a storm trying to find fresh grass!" As I let the chain of the tractor shed down with one hand, I steadied myself against a wooden structure pole with the other. The horse bolted up the pasture, as the finger of God bolted down. That stormy day on my horse ranch in Tennessee, standing in the pouring rain with my arms outstretched, I was struck dead by a bolt of lightning and a bright light burst around me with a deafening roar.

My muscles instantly contorted this way and that-reminiscent of the wild gyrations of John Travolta in "Saturday Night Fever." I was doing an uncontrollable electrical dance. There was an instant of terrible pain, and then I felt no pain and actually gained clarity of thought. In that split second, I turned around and tried to push my chest against the corner of the parked truck, remembering that electrical shocks often stop the heart. Then, my eyesight narrowed, and I felt my body slowly slide down the bumper onto the wet earth, and all went black.

The next thing I knew, I found myself standing on nothing, way up in the universe, and there were distant colorful planets all around me. As I lifted my arm, I could see misty pinpoints of stars through it, and when I moved it back and forth, it made the stars look wiggly, like a reflection on water. I felt dizzy. I had a sense of being able to see not just in front of me, but all around me at the same time. Floating just a few feet from me, I saw a man with a spirit body just like mine (no wings), though he was short and had slanted eyes. He spoke to me with a voice that I heard inside my own head, saying, "Don't be afraid, it's ok."

On the other side of me, another spirit person nodded approvingly at me. All the while, we were moving with great speed toward a great ellipsed ball of spinning light; it was brilliantly white in the middle and yellowish on the outside edges. The closer we got to it, the more I felt overwhelming Love; it seemed so warm and comforting, it encompassed my very being…like the security of a favorite grandfather's arms gently wrapped around a child on his lap. How wonderful I felt!

We stopped. The bright light was still far from me. I wanted to go on; I felt like a magnet, irresistibly drawn. The desire to "blend" had grown stronger the closer we got. I knew this place was the heavenly throne of God himself! Why had we stopped? As I stood there confused, yearning toward the Greatness beyond my reach, a glowing luminousness appeared in front of me. Gold and white sparkles came together in a glowing spiritual body, a giant image in the shape of a man with broad shoulders. A Divine Presence was here!

A gentle voice called out from this realm of golden sparkles massed brilliantly in front of me. "What have you learned?" he asked, in a nondiscriminatory and non-accusing way. The voice was so soft and tender, yet the presence of Divine authority was there; I knew without a doubt that it was the voice of God's own son, the very-much alive Jesus Christ.

Then all of a sudden, life events unfolded before my very eyes! Key moments where I showed anger to people, and also where I had showed love, appeared like scenes out of a movie. I could feel the anger and hurt of the other person whenever I had been mean; and I also felt the anger as it rippled through to others. I had never before faced the horrid deepness of my own sin. Then, where I showed love to people, I felt that too and how much further that rippled out from person to person, as a warm pulse triggering cause and effect in all things that were wonderful and blessed. I had never before experienced such joy!

Then the presence of Christ said, "The flesh is the test of the spirit...love each other." Words of wisdom imparted to me! I felt overwhelmed with love and so privileged. The spirit on my right then talked inside my head again and answered many questions on my mind. He also taught me details about many wonderful and sacred things. A seed was planted within me; a groundwork had been laid. And I knew that God wanted me to share this information later on and would give me the ability to understand it. In fact, many things "I didn't know I knew" end up being in the pages of the books that I am asked to write, and what a joy they have turned out to be - to love and share with so many people in this way and to be loved back!

While I floated there before the consciousness of Christ, the very presence of Jesus, the spirit then told me something that I didn't at all understand: "Welcome to the world of healers," he said. This was a shock - I had no idea what that meant. I had never believed in such a thing! The church I had been with believed healing had died out in the first century with the Apostles, and also that near-death experiences were only reactions to a dying brain. What could this welcome mean?

At this point, Christ went back into formless sparkles and faded away, and the stars and space behind his glowing features were visible once again. Such effervescent beauty and colors twinkled around me, like being in the midst of a sparkling aurora borealis. So many shapes of heavenly bodies transfixed in the cosmos, all unique and necessary, all untold distances away. Yet they felt so close that it seemed I could reach out and pluck them out of the sky and carry them home cupped in my hands.

The spirit went on and continued to teach me even more. He pointed out different stars, planets, distant colorful swirling lights of all kinds and gave names for all of them. He continued to fill me up and give me answers to thousands of questions that I never had questions for! Reams of information seemed to be exploding in my brain, like an empty library suddenly being realized! Details flooded my being about many wonderful and sacred things. I wondered: were these things newly learned or just somehow remembered? Everything somehow felt familiar in the Oneness of it all. I also became aware of thousands of others around me, observing, encouraging and fully loving and accepting me. I saw two children excitedly talking with each other about coming back to earth and what their new purposes would be. We live more than once. And I remembered that I had forgotten that! And I realized that in many things, I had chosen tradition and pleasing others in how I viewed myself, others, and God.

The spirit who was talking to me did not offer his name, and I did not ask. I wanted to be careful to show homage only to the True God, not to anyone else. And I wanted to stay! I wanted to join myself with God's swirling life force, his essence, the core of heaven, was just beyond! But, I wasn't allowed to go any further. No! I wanted to go to God! I wanted to feel more Love! "Why can't I be with you now Father? Please, Abba, Please!"

I listened as hard as I could listen, waiting for the words of God. Then just on the outside of my understanding, I faintly heard voices singing the most beautiful melody I had ever heard in my entire life. I absolutely knew that these were the blessed voices of angels, and those joined with God and came from his swirling brilliant presence, the core of heaven. There were no musical instruments, but instead, each voice lent itself as one in perfect harmony and variations in pitch and melody, flowing and moving perfectly together as easily as a flight of winged birds.

I knew it was praise for The Father, but I just couldn't make out the words the Angels were saying. If only I could step forward just a bit more...but I was rooted in place. I felt so sad. Then all at once, words started resonating throughout my entire body as if I was standing in front of a huge amplifier at a concert stadium. It was the voice of God. It was not a hearing through my ears, but throughout my entire being. "If you love me, heal my children, help them remember who they are."

Free will. What would I do? Yes, I would participate, I would offer. How could I not? How could I say no to God?" I knew I would be totally loved and approved of either way, but I knew I would be missing out on an opportunity to expand the ripple effect of love. I needed to go back to the earth. I also wanted to make a "better movie" of my life. So there and then, I vowed to be a vessel to do only his will, I would go back.

I absolutely gave myself to him. I wanted desperately to show how much I loved him and to share the reality of his existence with others! His will, not my own, I promised, would govern the rest of my life. If he could use this broken piece of clay from the earth, it was all his. I totally dedicated myself and surrendered all desires. Instantly, I felt a child-like sense of wonderment as a warm flood of bliss and peace overpowered me, and a warm tingling sensation filled me, like warm liquid honey flowing from the top of my head down to my very toes! What was happening to me? It was the baptism of the Holy Spirit, an anointing more commonly experienced on earth that I was experiencing here in heaven. At that moment I knew that I would have abundant help with the work. For his children, I would be an instrument of opportunity for teaching and healing. They would be shown the true identity of a powerful loving God who loves them and desires to be an active participant in their lives. Clearly, I had a mission.

I was shown by Father that in the future I would be speaking to thousands of people at a time on spiritual things, not religious - and great healings would be happening. And the gifts of God would be poured out just for the asking, and great manifestations of signs and wonders would be occurring within the audience itself, and the Spirit of God would move all to love and remembrance of who they are, who one another is, and who Father is! All this would be occurring as the darkness in the world got darker; for the light would become brighter too. And love would win. This time is now.

Then I felt myself sinking as if falling through a bed. I was being pulled back. I was leaving Heaven. Instantly, all my emotions welled up inside-remorse and joy, grief and exhilaration.

With that, I woke up, my husband shaking me by the shoulders. Somehow my physical body was now lying on the front seat of the truck although I had left it outside in the mud. I knew clearly this was God's hand in helping the physical body to survive. Three hours had passed since I had left the house to go to the tractor shed. The storm had moved on, though later we observed that there was evidence of at least three other strikes on the pasture besides the one that had struck me. We saw the spots blasted on the earth. I had been under one of those blasts.

At the emergency room, I was hooked up with wires and given tests to check my heart. A thorough exam revealed that it had not been damaged. But, my eyes and ears were affected very badly, as was my sense of balance. I couldn't see very well, or hear much at all. I felt dizzy but keenly calm and aware of the reality of the experience. The only piece of jewelry I had been wearing at the time was a single diamond earring. A brown burn mark now encircled the gold stud where it went through my ear. My skin tingled all over and was extremely sensitive to the touch, especially on my arms and in my hands. It hurt to wear clothes.

The doctors told me that I had been very lucky; the doctor said that often an arm or leg gets blown off during a strike (was he kidding?) People often die (and don't come back - yes, I knew that). They reasoned that because I was holding the chain with one hand and the wet wooden pole with the other, the current had passed through me, instead of grounding in my body. I knew they wouldn't believe me if I told them it had been a Divine strike, that God offered this as a wake-up call, and that I had been before the presence of God (and oh, by the way, Jesus spoke to me!). They would have kept me a lot longer than they did and probably in a little white jacket in a locked padded room to boot!

I spent a few days in bed, oscillating between a wild mixture of extreme happiness and unbelievable sadness. The emotions ran deeper than any I had ever felt. I was glad for the experience, but I was experiencing such homesickness! I kept re-living the event over and over in my mind, every detail emblazoned into my brain. I was determined that even if I forgot my own name, I would never forget this. I tried painting what I had seen - oil paints on canvas. The colors, no matter how I mixed them, were not brilliant enough. Nothing could capture what I had seen. Then I was confused. What did it all mean? I was losing the clarity. I prayed constantly to God to help me hear and feel him even though I was back in a physical body. I was afraid I would forget everything and all would be lost.

After a few days, I was back to my chores, including putting salve on Star's skin infection. For six weeks I had smoothed on the medicine the vet had given me, but still the red blisters kept spreading and killing the hair all around his girth. Now I had run out of medicine, so I just rubbed his belly lightly around the outside of the infection because he had grown used to the attention. I noticed that my hands were getting very hot. I thought it must be bacteria from the infection, and when I washed my hands under cold water it went away. I didn't think anything of it.

The next day, I walked up to rub his belly again, reminding myself to get new salve soon and noticed that all the blisters had turned white and some were falling off. I once more rubbed around the infection, and my hands turned hot once more. The next day when I went out, all the blisters had fallen off, and there was evidence of new hair growing back. I thought this was mere coincidence. The medicine must have finally worked. I didn't correspond it to what I had been told.

The next week, I took my cat in to be spayed. The vet said it would take 10 days for the stitches to completely heal. On the first day, she didn't want anything to do with me. But the second day, she was in my lap as much as possible. She just would not leave me alone - even yowling for me if I left the room! Every time I would rub her and pet her, I found that my hands would heat up again. On the third day, she tried pulling the stitches out with her teeth. On the morning of the fourth day, I decided to look at what was going on, and found that the skin had healed so well that the stitches were puckering her skin up tight. I found myself embarrassed to take her back to the vet. What would he say? So I carefully cut the threads and pulled them out myself through skin that bore no surgical scar. Now I began to understand what was happening. I could heal animals.

Then, I wondered, will this work on me? The very next day, I made connection in prayer to God, and as I gave free will for healing, I was mentally transported to heaven, and saw myself standing before God once more as in the near-death experience. I saw myself lifting a body up in my arms towards God, and the body was me. In real life, I placed my hands hot on my forehead and on various parts of my body. Then, I made an appointment with the doctor. A previous mammogram had shown a lump in my breast, which they had recommended further action on, but I had put off. A former doctor had told me I had fibroid cysts in my uterus which could only be removed through surgery. Also, I had a torn rotator cuff in my shoulder which had prevented me from sleeping well for the past six months.

I anxiously awaited the test results. The mammogram showed the lump was gone, the diagnostic ultrasound showed clear, the fibroid cysts had disappeared. Also, I could sleep at night without any pain; my rotator cuff was healed.

Hesitantly, I started sharing this new gift with my friends, and that's when I ran into trouble. I found that I was taking the pain of their ailment onto myself. If they had a migraine,

I would get a migraine. If they had stomach pain, I would get stomach pain. That scared me. I found myself afraid to use the gift. Maybe I was using it wrong? Why would God give me a gift that would harm me to use it? I felt I wouldn't last very long in this work. And yet, I knew in my heart that God wouldn't give me something that would be unsafe for me to use. What was I missing?

I thought I might find answers if I watched the healing ministries on TV. For the first time in my life, I wondered if they could actually be legitimate. I had never believed in this sort of thing. I had always felt it must be fake, simply a show display to raise money and give people false hope. Now I wanted desperately to talk to one of the healers. Did they feel sick afterward? Had they each been told, "Welcome to the world of healers? In some way? Was I part of this same group? What did God want me to understand? There was no way to contact anyone. I knew somehow I would be guided to the answers that I needed about how to expand upon the gift and how and where.

A friend told me about a group of people in town that offered hands-on healing so I thought I would go talk to them. I went through the training classes of Usui Reiki. As soon as I made the decision to become trained, any pain from doing any healing disappeared, and I felt energized and euphoric after the healings. It wasn't the Reiki that made it disappear; it was the decision to openly follow-through on what I had promised to God. The Big Guy has always used healing and miraculous signs and wonders in all parts of the earth in all cultures in all periods of time. It doesn't matter the training or technique - it matters Whom you are making connection to and choosing to be an opportunity for that Love to transform and manifest. And it is up to the person who is receiving that healing to use free will to participate in welcoming it or not. God is big on free will. But he offers opportunity to all regardless of boundaries, cultures, or era.

When God gives his people a commission or Divine gift,

he does not do it without a specific purpose. So many times I had been absolutely shattered, yet he had still held me gently in the palm of his hands. There had also been many times we had walked together hand-in-hand, and many times I had turned away from him, hid my face in shame or in anger, and withdrew my hand from his. Yet, his arm was still outstretched, and he still loved me…I was astonished. Unbelievable! And now, he gave me a real purpose, along with a job where I would be working in direct communion with him everyday. He wasn't tired of me yet! I would also be making friends and helping people from all walks of life, social standing, color, and religious or spiritual background. I would get to be the nurse's assistant to the Great Physician. I would get to see the miracles as he reached out to tell his children he is not only real and cares about them, but also has the power to manifest and transform our struggles. He desires us to have no distraction from the joyful, abundant, healthy and loving lives he created us to have, and from fulfilling the dreams and purposes placed within our hearts.

So why the lightning strike and near-death experience? We all have defining moments, and this was mine. I was a most stubborn child in clinging to what I thought I knew. I had been so resistant, having "blinders" on and putting "God in a box," then only an empirical, first-hand experience would open me up. I had a purpose now, and I did not have to suffer in silence or ignore my plight. I could be strong again because his strength was in me. Everything was made anew! By Free Will I had died to self at the foot of heaven and upon the earth, and he had resurrected me up again. I was a new person. He opened me up! I vowed I would never allow myself to be closed down again.

Now, my entire life is an adventure and an aware spirit journey! I get to see cancer disappear, brain tumors shrink and go away, blind eyes see, and deaf ears hear. I get to be there when the arthritis melts away and chronic disease abates. I get to be there to see the addictions leave without side-effects, and I get to help bring peace, calmness and joy to lives of mental depression and hopelessness. I get to see infertile couples experience the joy of carrying a child in their bellies and in their arms. I meet people from all over the world and get to be there everyday when incredible things happen, and form friendships that are deep and moving. Along the way, this wider connection to God has led to other interventions of Spirit, such as miraculous long-distance healing, medical intuition, locating missing children, helping on crime scenes, visions and prophecies. Through this Oneness of connection, nothing is impossible! I praise God continually as I enjoy every day, every moment, and every experience I have! I am always amazed how he brings his kids together, to learn to love one another and help each other. It totally humbles me to be involved in this kind of work. For this is not about me, he wants each of us to remember who we are, to be the mystic, and to transform darkness into light.

The point is this: You don't have to be struck by lightning or have a near-death experience to open up, change your life, appreciate each other, or to have a special connection with God. Love is the key to everything. Remember, the life-review you have will be about the love you showed or didn't show. It's all about love!

When I was before the Ultimate, I wished only to love and be responsible to him. But what he wanted was for me to be responsible and love everyone else. So, we prove our love by loving everybody else! And, it has opened me to surrender in faith to whatever God needs from me, and he has continued my enlightenment. Since July of 2005 I have been experiencing the Holy Stigmata, the five wounds of Christ. Stigmata is the spontaneous manifestation of bloody wounds on a person's hands, feet, brow, side or back, similar to the wounds of the crucified Jesus. People may know what it is by having seen statues or pictures of long-ago Catholic saints such as St. Francis of Assisi or the recently canonized Padre Pio. But to a growing number of people worldwide, it is part of their everyday reality - a place where the supernatural fully exists within the modern world. That place is where I live every day.

I am not a saint, nor perfect, nor was I a Catholic when the stigmata began. My every thought was *not* focused on receiving such a gift, nor did I even know much about it until it actually happened to me. The wounds open spontaneously about once a month and lasts for 3 to 9 days. Part of that experience comes with new visions and information for the important time of shift we are living in, which is then written down and shared. We have even been given prayers called "Divine Decrees" that are here to help the world participate in this transformation of our lives and global events with Angelic help. And the healings that are occurring since that connection are even more miraculous!

My brokenness has led me to a mending of the very highest kind, and everything in my life has changed in alignment to fulfilling that purpose. I stood up for love and everything not of love shifted out of my life. To that end, after many years I am now re-married to a loving and spiritual partner who hears God clearly for himself and follows through on the mission placed in his heart besides supporting me in mine. I am blessed to have healed thousands of people and see miracle upon miracle.

So even when I didn't know what to ask for in my most broken of times, the Big Guy gave me my life's work. And I am happier than I have ever been before! Whatever periods of brokenness in my life I had to go through, whatever lessons I needed to learn to get to this place in my spiritual journey, I can release and be glad for it! Now, I am making a better "movie" for when I come before the presence again, and I'm sharing the gifts our Father freely gives us. I am thankful everyday that when I was stubborn and striking out, God stepped in and struck me down! Truly, the best thing that happened in my life was almost losing it. Being dead healed my life; and now it heals others. I'm glad to be back.

About Tiffany Snow

Tiffany carries the 5 marks of the Holy stigmata, and is a documented miracle healer, award-winning author, near-death experiencer, and public speaker. Her latest book: *God's Workbook - Shifting into the Light* is available on Amazon.com. Distant healing, deliverances, classes, live teleconferences and more articles are offered through the websites.

www.tiffanysnow.com is focused on Miracle Healing, Holy Stigmata and Blessed Tiffany

www.thefourthhealing.com is focused on Deliverance, "Becoming the Mystic Classes," Ordination and Father Billy Clark

www.lovewins.net is focused on Prophecy, The Divine Decrees (prayers given through the Holy Stigmata for the end times and the shift into timelessness)

Blog: www.godslovealwayswins.blog.spot.com

Office phone: 800-535-5474 Email: thefourthhealing@yahoo.com

MY JOURNEY

Vernon M. Sylvest, M.D. Virginia

As a child growing up as the son of a Methodist minister, I saw a lot of tragedy coming to my father's office. I also witnessed my parent's concern about safety and the future. My religious upbringing was a mixture of love and fear. Jesus loved me but hell was always a possibility if I didn't do or think right. I later laid spirituality aside as irrelevant to my life journey. My family and culture determined what was right, not so much to be saved but to be right and liked. Success was the answer.

I did have a curiosity about it all. Why was there so much misery? This stimulated my interest in science. I felt there must be some unknown, that if discovered, could possibly answer that question. Since we are bodies, I felt the study of the body, its anatomy, its chemistry, its physiology, might lead to answers. Religion hadn't. The study of the mind through traditional psychology didn't. I read my father's psychology books as a teenager. He had a master's degree in psychology as well as a Ph.D. in theology. Later, I also studied psychiatry in medical school. There was no answer to be found. Only more confusion and questions. I ultimately pursued pathology. This, I felt, was the science of medicine, but I found no answers, only more questions.

I gave up the search and tried to make myself happy. I finished first in my class in medical school, went through one of the best pathology residencies in the country, and became a successful, respected pathologist in my community. I found a smart, attractive woman to commit to me and become my wife. We had three darling daughters. We had a house in the right part of town, etc. But we, my wife and I, were not happy. We blamed each other.

I thought it would take a woman, the right one, to make me happy. My wife felt the need to leave the relationship for her own self-discovery. It is difficult for an unhappy husband to make his wife happy. Because she wanted to go back to school and get masters degrees in business and international business, she let the children stay with me. My feeling was, "thank goodness." They were a source of joy for me. That is not to say she was not a good mother. During medical school and my residency she was a very active stay-at-home mom.

I thought I was free now to go out and find the right woman to make me happy. I did, I thought, but it only lasted six months. Then I discovered I did not know how to breakup. Plus, I felt guilty over the failed marriage and lost family. I felt sad for my girls because they didn't have a mom at home.

Then it happened. In one day, I went from perfect health to acutely and then chronically ill with excruciatingly painful inflammatory disease known as Ritter's disease. In my workup it was determined that I have a genetic marker for the disease and in the form of HLA-B27, an abnormal tissue antigen. I was told by my rheumatologist that it was incurable, but hopefully, medicine would control it. I searched the literature which confirmed his opinion. Medicine did not control it. At first, I had to crawl to go to the bathroom, but I improved enough to hobble back to work and continue my life of manipulating my relationships, so I wouldn't feel guilty and could be happy. Still, spirituality was not part of my life. I belonged to a church for social and P.R. purposes and also, for my daughters' cultural education.

After four and one-half years of severe chronic pain and unresolved relationships, the emotions could no longer be repressed. The depression was severe enough that I finally surrendered. If I were to remain alive, there would have to be another way. I surrendered to that possibility. The only thing left was spirituality. My prayer life began in earnest. What I later recognized as significant synchronicities began to happen that led me to information that was enlightening. I developed an avidity to study spirituality and became open to all sources. Synchronicities led me to scientific information on the frontier of a new understanding of the relationship of the body to energy fields, including the source of that energy and to the most recent mathematical developments and experiments in quantum physics that point to the illusionary nature of what we call reality.

One of the most profound synchronicities was my discovery of the Shroud of Turin. About six months after my surrender, I went to Duke Medical Center for one last reach for a conventional medical cure for my condition. Shortly after my admission, I watched a local TV program in which Dr. Alan Whanger described the research that had been done on the Shroud of Turin. I was amazed by the findings and the conclusion that the forty scientists involved in the study had reached. I researched the research, subsequently including the more recent carbon dating. My conclusion then and now is that it was valid evidence of the crucifixion and resurrection of Jesus.

This made Jesus and his life real to me. I felt his love. I felt loved. I also realized that he loved my ex-wife and everyone else. I began to experience the energy of forgiveness. Within three months of my discovery of the Shroud of Turin and within nine months of my surrender, I was completely well - no more symptoms or signs of Ritter's disease. No more pain. I found peace and happiness. I ultimately discovered that it is possible to be married and happy at the same time. A couple of years after my healing, I met Anne. We have been married 24 years and are still happy. What a blessing! What a miracle!

After my healing, as I progressed in my spiritual journey, I experienced obvious guidance from Jesus. I heard his voice when I was wide awake praying out loud for an answer to a question. He said to me, "I have shown you - with the life that I lived and the teachings that I left." He led me to the teachings and confirmed the answers I discovered. Those teachings included ancient forms as well as more recent forms such as "A Course in Miracles" and "The Aquarian Gospel of Jesus the Christ." He spoke to me in dreams. I learned to meditate and got answers and sometimes unexpected guidance.

Jesus took the fear out of Christianity for me as he led me to a correct understanding of his life and teachings. The resurrection demonstrated the power of unconditional love and that sacrifice is not the will of God. I understood that forgiveness occurs in a willingness to emotionally let it be as if it had not happened. In that process, I experienced my own "resurrection." He also led me to discover that truth can be found in the world's many religions. I had valuable experiences with Sai Baba. We are led on a journey of self-discovery and Self-discovery. In that process, I have discovered that happiness is not found in accomplishments or in the opinion of others. It is already present in each of us. Releasing the blocks to our awareness of its presence is part of the journey, and because of who we are and the help we have, the journey will be completed.

About Vernon M. Sylvest, M.D.

My dear friend, Dr. Sylvest recently retired after 36 years in the practice of pathology in order to devote his fulltime attention to sharing the information that led to his own healing. His first book, *The Formula: Who Gets Sick; Who Gets Well; Who is Unhappy; Who is Happy and Why*, is now in its third printing and his second book, *The End of Fear*, will soon be published. Interest in his work has led to lecture tours across the country and abroad.

Currently, he is developing the Healing Waters Lodge in Head Waters, Virginia. The site was previously owned by Elisabeth Kubler-Ross M.D. and before her, by Raymond Moody M.D. Dr. Moody researched the near-death experience and brought much public attention to his work in his best-selling book, *Life After Life*. Dr. Kubler-Ross studied the dying process, and shared her discoveries in her book, *On Death and Dying*. Her work helped to establish and refine the hospice system in this country.

Dr. Sylvest is now the present owner of this site and is presenting programs at Healing Waters Lodge which focuses on studying *life* to enhance the *living* process. He is presenting programs based on his experience in his work with the whole person, including Spirit, mind and body to bring all aspects of a person into perfect alignment for a healthy, long, productive, and happy life. Dr. Sylvest has served on the Board of Directors of the American Holistic Medical Association among other prestigious medical societies.

For more information about Dr. Sylvest and the wonderful work he is doing, please refer to the following internet sites:

www.healingwaterslodge.com www.vmsylvestmd.com

Email: vmspc@mindspring.com

MY PRAYER

Tiffany Tsou, Illinois

Authors Note: Tiffany contacted me for my research study and while her English is not proficient because it is her second language, I wanted to include her story exactly as she wrote it in the letter she wrote to me.

Dear Nancy, By a chance, I read your book *"Hear His Voice."* I cried. Even though I have not finished your book, but I know where your heart goes. I don't have an extraordinary out-of-body experience like your. But your experience explained what I have experienced. And I have hart time finding people to share. Many thought I have be visited by demonic things. My father suggested that I visit a doctor. I has been searching for an answer ever since that encounter in January 2002. And I am so glad I meet you.

I realized that God has prepared a way for me ever since I was a little girl. As far as I remember, I'll go to church on Sunday morning by myself to worship God. I grew up in a foreign country where we worship Buddha, and my family are not Christian. So for me to go to church instead of temple is kind of unusual. But I didn't know that. In January, 2002, I experience a light during a prayer. I believe that was God. The light of God answers my questions. I never know why God wants me to ask Him questions. He should know my heart. Why didn't He just give me the answers. There is a long story leading to all these events. And not until years later, I realize why God wants me to do certain things. It's a true blessing. I cherish His Love every day.

I giggles when you talk about the love of animals. I thought I was the only crazy person who pray and talk to them. Thanks

God for you. We feel the same way. Through grace of God, He teaches me to play violin last year. Now I play at nursing home. I love to share the Love of God to them through music. And I agree to share with residents my story. Yes. I learned without taking lessons cause Jesus is my violin teacher.

There are so many events tied together to make a new event. So I asked God to help me write this email. I'll try my best to convert my experience to you. I wish I could just transfer all the thoughts to you at once. English is my second language. So bear with me.

I was coming home late that night. And I was debating where I should accept a job offer or not. I was working as an accountant at University. And I love my job. So I didn't think of leaving. But I received offers from the University Library. And that was the third times they asked me for the same position. So I now if I refuse the third times the folks from the Library will probably give up asking. Not knowing what to do, I asked God to help me.

It started like all other prayers. But this time was different. It's the Light. This Light was there as soon as I was about to close my eye. The Light was so bright it shined through my eye/head onto my bed while kneeling in front of my bed. I feel surprised and embarrassed. I said, "Oh, you have been waiting." So I asked about where I should go to the library. I didn't hear an actual human voices, but the Light answered my questions as soon as the question pop up in my head, and I obtained or understood the answer right away. It's kind like instantly know and why was I even ask. God wants me to go work for University Library. Even though that was not the answer I want to hear. But I said, "Well, okay." I don't recall how I ended the prayer exactly. But I know I always thank God.

So I left accounting and went to the Library in January 2002. I felt miserable when I went to the Library. My ego just could not give in. You see, I am a very strong minded person. If I want something, I'll get it. Coming to the United States and learning a new culture and language were all very hard. From a person speak broken English to finish my MS with CPA was no picnic, but I get it done because I wanted. So for me, doing something not what I want is hard, and I was not happy. Several months passed by, I prayed again for help. I asked God why He made me feeling miserable. I was doing what He wanted me to do. And I was not happy. God didn't answer me this time. So I said to him, "Whatever I do, I do it for you." After the three times I said, "Whatever I do, I do it for you." My thinking and attitude changed after that. The rest stories are blessings after another blessings. The people I met become best friends. They still help me to grow spiritually this day.

God did bring me back to accounting department later on in November 2005. Without the experience at Library, I wouldn't be able to take my current job, since it requires a higher degree of accounting skills. But that was another story. It will be a very long story if I shared everything. People has been asked to write a book about my experience. But I don't speak English that well, so I don't feel like writing anything. If you could use my experience to Glorify God, that would be just fine.

After the experience with the Light, I was always try to find someone who shared the same experience. But most people I spoke to didn't understand what I was talking about. And I have to be careful not to confused with God and demonic things. So I don't talk about this very much.

Here is a song God sang to me while I was walking to work one morning in June 2008. It came in Chinese. I translated into English for you. Hope you able to see it. This is the song inspired me to play violin. And God taught me other songs after this one. My mother was so surprised and thought I took from somebody, since it is so unusual for me to write any piece of music or songs. As she knows me very well, I have no music talent.

There is a God. A perfect God. God loves the world. Blessings given.

There is a God. Holy true God. The love He gives Never will change.

There is a God. Gentle and kind. Mercy from Him. Forgive my sins.

There is a God. Wisdom of Father. Open my eyes. Leading my way.

May Peace and Love be with you,

Tiffany

A VISIT FROM HEAVEN

Josie Varga, New Jersey

Transformative learning leads the learner to an inner knowing rather than a belief. In other words, it changes who you are as a person. It expands your consciousness to a new reality, and if you are lucky enough to have such an experience, there's no turning back.

My life changed forever the night my husband's friend, Rich, who died in the World Trade Center attacks, came to me in a vivid dream. I saw myself going down this long hallway. I had no idea where I was, yet there seemed to be a force pushing me forward as I eventually made my way through a doorway at the end. I walked into this room seeing a bunch of desks and windows. Although I say "walked," it was more like I glided as I don't remember my feet touching the ground. I actually felt myself moving. It was as though my soul was out wandering while my body remained in a deep sleep. Suddenly, Rich appeared before me, wearing glasses and smiling reassuringly, as he telepathically communicated, "Josie, thank you for mentioning me in your book." (I mention Rich in the epilogue of my first book, *Footprints in the Sand: A Disabled Woman's Inspiring Journey to Happiness*.)

Ironically, I had never met Rich. I had only spoken to him on the phone and knew him through pictures yet I had no doubt that this was my husband's friend standing before me. I looked up at him squinting as there seemed to be a density or fog about us. I don't know why but I said, "Rich, you have to give me proof that this is really you?" He looked at me with a comforting glance and walked over to a desk picking up a cell phone containing a picture of him, his wife and son.

He then said, "Boston is O.K." The next thing I knew, I was going through a window and found myself on the street looking up at a pickup truck. In the bed of this pickup truck was Rich standing behind his wife and son. He looked at me motioning for me to give his family the message. I don't remember anything much after that except for waking up panting and sweating in a sitting position feeling like something had just hit me in my chest.

Nothing like this had ever happened to me before, and I was left feeling scared and confused. Though I could not understand what just happened, I was certain that I had to get this message to his wife. It was about 8:00 a.m., and my husband was already at work. I rushed to call John telling him what happened. His response was nothing that I didn't expect. "You've got to be kidding me," he yelled. "You want me to call Rich's wife who just lost her husband and tell her that he said "Boston is O.K." He was convinced that I had lost my senses.

I persisted telling him that I was certain the experience had been real. It had been unlike anything that I had ever experienced. As I would later find out, I had just experienced a form of O.B.E. (out-of-body experience) known as astral travel. When this occurs, the soul leaves the physical body to travel in its astral body to other dimensions or realms of reality. My husband listened reluctantly but finally agreed to forward an e-mail written by me explaining what had occurred to Rich's sister-in-law. He would ask her to forward the e-mail to Rich's wife only if she felt it was appropriate.

Shortly after, we were on vacation when my husband received a response from Rich's sister-in-law on his BlackBerry. She explained that her sister had a brother in Boston and was considering moving there. But having purchased their home just before her husband's untimely death, she felt guilty. My husband read this message to himself but did not grasp what the message meant until he read the e-mail aloud to me.

We both looked at each other in complete shock. I never even met his wife let alone know that she had a brother in Boston. Now, it all made perfect sense to me. His words, "Boston is O.K." was meant to let his wife know that she need not feel guilty about moving. He was telling her that it was alright with him.

At first, I honestly did not know what to think. So a deceased friend had given me a message in my dreams that had actually been validated. What did this mean? I had no doubt that I had visited with Rich's spirit and that he was alive and well; my ego self had difficulty processing this information. Yet while my unconditioned self or spirit believed what I had experienced was perhaps more real than anything I had witnessed on this earth, my ego self was afraid and doubtful. After all I reasoned, if Rich is dead and if he did, in fact, communicate with me, then not only is it confirmation of the existence of an afterlife, but it must be possible for the dead to communicate with the living.

I did not realize it then but this would ultimately lead me on a spiritual journey which would later result in my writing *Visits from Heaven*, a book which contains many evidential afterlife communication accounts from around the world.

I was given a gift on this day. I no longer believe in life after death; I know. There's a big difference. I want to share my experience with anyone who will listen. I wish I could stand on the tallest mountain and yell, "Life never ends and love never dies." As I said, there's no turning back. My life will never be the same. I am truly blessed.

About Josie Varga

Josie Varga is also the author of *Visits to Heaven, Make Up Your Mind to be Happy, Visits from Heaven* and *Footprints in the Sand: A Disabled Woman's Inspiring Journey to Happiness*. Besides being a former communications consultant, she also served as the director of communications and editor for a trade association. As a speaker, Josie helps the bereaved by sharing her message that life never ends, and love never dies. She also teaches others to focus on the positive explaining why happiness is all a matter of how we think.

She has several other book projects in the works, including *God or Chance?*—an unparalleled book which provides mathematical and scientific statistics (based on the Anthropic Principle) answering the question: Was the universe the result of chance or was God or some other Supreme Being responsible? In addition to her book writing, she has completed several treatments for reality television including a television series for her book, *Visits from Heaven*. A creative thinker, Josie is the holder of two patents. For more information about the author, please visit her website: www.josievarga.com.

DIVINE ORDER

Dawn Wanzo, Ohio

In 1985, I had a very vivid dream of seeing someone very special to me killed in a car wreck. The next morning, I awoke feeling very disturbed and concerned for her well-being. When I saw her later that day, I told her about the dream of the car accident but I didn't tell her that in the dream she had died. One week later, she was in a terrible car accident and was killed. Her name was Lisa. When I saw her car at the junkyard, it looked exactly the way it had appeared in my dream.

Little did I know at the time that this life-shaking event would be a turning point in my life that would land me on my spiritual path. Lisa and I were very close, so her death was a major shock to my life. I spent fifteen years blocking out Lisa's death by playing, writing, and recording music, until April 27, 2000, when Lisa began visiting me in very vivid dreams.

Very soon after that she would communicate with me during waking hours. She would validate herself in many amazing ways to build my belief in her existence. I quickly learned to meditate so that I could become more aware of spirit energy and communicate with her more often. She would teach me over time how to develop my senses to the inner realms.

One particular time during meditation, I saw her sitting at a round table where she asked me to join her. As we sat together, she shared with me all the things I needed to know to help me have the closure from her death.

I then noticed on the table a plate that had steak cut into little cubes, a baked potato, and corn which had been shaved off the cob. There was also a champagne glass filled with water. I asked, "Why the food? You don't need it anymore where you are." She told me it would be a validation that I was actually with her in another realm. That same day, when I came home, my sister was in the kitchen preparing a plate for me. I found this very odd since it was something she never did. I noticed she had on the plate steak cut into cubes, a baked potato, and corn shaved from the cob. I was so surprised and asked her, "Why did you prepare this combination of food, and why are you making my plate in the first place?" She said she didn't know why, she just felt like it. As I sat down at the table, she placed a champagne glass filled with water next to my plate.

This experience really strengthened my belief and proved to me that I really was with Lisa in another realm and that there is life beyond this physical world. As time passed, and with many more amazing experiences, I wanted nothing more than to help others to realize that we are still connected with our loved ones in spirit, and that there is no separation. I wanted others to be able to have the closure that they needed to move forward in their lives, so they wouldn't have to spend so many years stuck suffering over losing someone as I had done.

So one night, I meditated with so much appreciation for the ability to communicate with Lisa and to finally have the closure I wished for back in 1985. I saw a huge bright Light in front of me. This Light felt so loving and understanding of me. It did not feel male or female, but I was aware that it had consciousness. I was able to communicate with the Light telepathically, and as I was drawn closer into the Light, I was able to see and be told why I had to suffer in 1985 and that Lisa's death and our connection was in Divine order. I felt so emotional from this blissful moment in the Light. Although I was aware that tears were falling from my face, I knew my consciousness was in another realm. I had so much honor and gratitude as I was in the presence of this Light, and I told the Light I wanted to help others feel what I feel and know and what I know about the Afterlife. I thanked the Light for my spiritual awakening and awareness and repeated again that all I wanted to do was help others. The Light communicated very powerfully, "Very well Child."

The very next day while I was at work, spirits began communicating with me, wanting me to give messages to their loved ones here in the physical world. I was all over the college campus where I work, delivering validating messages to people I had to either stop or track down around the campus. It was like a gate had opened up, and spirits came pouring through. That day was March 7, 2003 when I realized my purpose as a Spiritual Medium and when I also started my public work.

I have had moments either meditating or just in alpha state when I would see myself going through a tunnel toward the Light and seeing my loved ones in the Light, then being pulled back before I could get any closer. Before falling asleep, I often see a tunnel that I travel through at a fast rate of speed or seeing glimpses of the universe that is so beautiful I want to cry, but realize that I am not in a physical body.

Once while walking in a parking lot to my car after leaving the hospital from visiting a friend there, I saw myself as if I was outside of my body viewing from above, like looking down at myself even though my physical self was aware of walking to my car. I was aware of me putting the key in the door to unlock it; at the same time, I was watching myself from outside of my physical body.

There was another time when I was feeling really tired and went to lie down. Suddenly, I was traveling through a dark tunnel following my deceased grandmother. In the tunnel, I could hear noises that sounded like metal hitting against metal. I ended up in a room with six to seven men sitting around a table. They looked very serious and never spoke a word to me, except telepathically. In the room, I noticed there were monitors of some sort above and around their table. I wanted so bad to see my life review, but I was told I could not see my review at this time and was pushed into another place, where I found myself in what felt like a place in the universe where the colors were so beautiful and the feelings were of such bliss.

What I have learned from my experiences is that there is an Afterlife, and that I am infinite and eternal. I know that I exist in many realms, and my consciousness is of many levels and is one with Divine Light. Even though I had to suffer in 1985 after losing Lisa in a car accident, I truly know that it was in Divine order for this event to occur for me to be who I am today and what I know beyond this physical world. Before the year of 2000, I never would have imagined my work as a Spiritual Medium and bringing to awareness that we are more than just a physical body and a personality in this lifetime. Before my spiritual awakening, I was a guitar player, a musician working toward my dream as a recording artist. Now, here I am.

About Dawn Wanzo

Dawn is a spiritual medium who does private sessions, phone or in person group sessions, workshops, speaking engagements. If you would like to contact Dawn, she can be reached at: wanzo14@yahoo.com Phone: 740-423-5957.

THE VIEW FROM THE CIRCLE BED

Barbara Harris Whitfield, Georgia

I was born with a deformity, a curvature in my lumbar spine called "scoliosis." In 1975, I underwent almost six hours of surgery to fuse the affected vertebrae. I awoke afterwards in a Stryker-frame circle bed. This strange bed looks like a Ferris wheel for one person. There are two big chrome hoops with a stretcher suspended in the middle. Unable to move, I remained in that bed for almost a month, and then I was placed in a full body cast from my armpits to my knees for six months.

About two days after surgery, complications set in, and I started to die. I remember waking up in the circle bed and seeing this huge belly. I had swollen up, and the swelling was pulling my incisions open and it hurt. I called for my nurse, and then I started screaming. People in white came rushing in. They hooked me up to all kinds of machinery, tubes, monitors, and bags.

I lost consciousness and later that night woke up in the hall outside my room. I floated back into the room and saw my body. I felt peaceful, more peaceful than I had ever been in this lifetime. Then I went into a tunnel where I was greeted and held by my grandmother who had been dead for fourteen years. Before this, I had never once thought about her surviving her death. I didn't believe in that. But now I knew I was with her. Her love enveloped me and together we relived all our memories of each other. I could see and feel all this through her eyes and her feelings of each moment too, and I know she experienced how her actions and her love had comforted me in my childhood.

Suddenly, I was back in my body, back in the circle bed. Two nurses were opening my drapes. The sunlight was startling. It hurt my eyes. I asked them to close the drapes. I tried to tell my nurses and then several doctors that I had left the bed. They told me that it was impossible and that I had been hallucinating.

About a week later, I again left my body in the circle bed. I was no longer on the critical list, but I was still debilitated and weak. I had been rotated forward onto my face. I was uncomfortable and fearful because the button to call the nurse had slipped off the bed, and no one was coming to rotate me back. Suddenly I left my body; I again went out into the darkness, only this time I was awake and could see it happening. Looking down and off to the right, I saw myself in a bubble - in the circle bed -crying. Then I looked up and to the left, and I saw my one-year-old self in another bubble - face down in my crib - and crying just as hard. I looked to the right and saw myself again in the circle bed, then to the left and saw myself as a baby. I looked back and forth about three more times, then I let go. I decided I did not want to be the thirty-two-year old Barbara anymore; I'd go to the baby.

As I moved away from my body in the circle bed, I felt as though I released myself from this lifetime. As I did, I became aware of an Energy or a Presence that was wrapping itself around me and going through me, permeating me, holding up every molecule of my being.

Even though I had been an atheist for years, I felt God's love. This love was holding me. It felt incredible. There are no words in the English language, or maybe in this reality, to explain the kind of love God emanates. God was *totally accepting* of everything we, God and I, reviewed in my life.

In every scene of my life review, I could feel again what I had felt at various times in my life. And I could feel *everything* that everyone else had felt as a consequence of my presence and my actions. Some of it felt good, and some of it felt awful. All of this translated into knowledge, and *I learned. Oh, how I learned!*

The information was flowing at an incredible speed that probably would have burned me up if it hadn't been for the extraordinary Energy holding me. The information came in, and then love neutralized my judgments against myself. In other words, throughout every scene, I viewed information flowing through me about my perceptions and feeling, and the perceptions and feelings of every person who had shared those scenes with me. No matter how I judged myself in each interaction, being held by God was the bigger interaction. God interjected love into everything, every feeling, every bit of information about absolutely everything that went on, so that everything was all right. There was no good or bad. There was only me and my loved ones from this life, trying to survive…just trying to *be*.

I realize now that without God holding me, I would not have had the strength to experience what I did. When it started, God and I were merging. We became one, so that I could see through God's eyes and feel through God's heart. Together, we witnessed how severely I had treated myself because that was the behavior shown and taught to me as a child. I realized that the only big mistake I had made in my thirty-two-years of life was that I had never learned to love myself.

God let me into God's experience of all this. I felt God's memories of these scenes through God's eyes. I could sense God's Divine intelligence, and it was astonishing. God loves us and wants us to wake up to our real selves to what is important. I realized that God wants us to know *that we only experience real pain if we die without living first*. And the way to live is to give love to ourselves and to others. It seems that we are here to learn to give and receive love, but only when we heal enough to be real can we understand and give and receive love the way love was meant to be.

When God holds us in our life reviews and we merge into One, we remember this feeling as being limitless. God is limitless. God's capacity to love is never-ending. God's love for us never changes, no matter how we are. God doesn't judge us either. During our life review, we judge ourselves by *feeling* the love we have created in others' lives. We also *feel the pain* we have caused in others' lives. This may be a kind of "Cosmic Equalizer."

I did not see an old man with a white beard who sits in judgment of us. I only felt limitless Divine love. And I feel that limitless love now, everyday in my life here on Earth because I was guided through incredible changes after my near-death-experiences. This Presence we call God is always here guiding us. It has been my partner through my journey so that I was able to go back to school and become a respiratory therapist. Then my patients told me about their experiences out-of-body. I wrote about this and was published, then asked to present at health-care conferences. My subject at the time was "The emotional needs of critical care patients." No one was talking about that back then.

Now I've written five books on these experiences and the after-effects. I'm in a second marriage that can contain all the changes and growth I've been through. My husband and I share a private practice helping people who were repeatedly traumatized as children (like I was) with individual and group psychotherapy.

About Barbara Harris Whitfield

Barbara and I consider ourselves "soul-sisters." She is considered an expert in the field of near-death experiences and is an author, therapist and researcher. The following books were written by Barbara: *Spiritual Awakenings*, Health Communications, Inc. Deerfield Beach, FL 1995; *The Power of Humility*, Health Communications, Inc. Deerfield Beach, FL 2006; *The Natural Soul*, Muse House Press, Atlanta, GA 2010.

Barbara has been a guest on major television talk shows, including *Larry King Live, Donahue, The Today Show, Oprah* and *Joan Rivers*. Her story and her research have appeared in magazines such as *Redbook, Woman's World, McCall's, Psychology Today*,

Maclean's, Common Boundary, and *Reader's Digest*.

For more information about Barbara and her work, please visit her website at: www.BarbaraWhitfield.com

GOD IS REAL

Anonymous

I had given birth to my son about a week prior to my experience. I was at home in my bedroom typing up a story about my childhood. My son was in his bassinet sleeping. I started feeling kind of odd, so I laid down on the bed. The next thing I knew I was standing in this large stone building. There was misty, smoky stuff in the air. The closest I have ever seen to compare this to was dry ice smoke. It was very, very quiet. I looked around and saw these huge stone pillars. They were made of light colored stone and were divided up in segments. I thought, "Where am I?" Behind me to my left someone said, "You are in the cathedral." When they spoke to me, I heard it in my head. As soon as they said that, I knew where I was, and I knew I had been there before.

I looked at my hands, and they were glowing from the inside out. They were still my hands, but they had gold specks floating in them. I could see through them! That's when I realized my entire body was also glowing in a soft yellowish whitish light from the inside out. I started walking through the cathedral. I came to some stairs and walked down them. At the bottom of the stairs was a large empty room. The misty smoky stuff was gone. At this time, I am not sure if the person was walking with me anymore. I walked through the room and noticed that there weren't any pillars either. Then I knew I had to stop. I turned and saw a man kneeling on the floor. He had on a brown rough looking hooded robe. He also had a belt that was made of gold cloth tied on the side. He had the hood on, and his arms were covering his face.

He asked me if I believed He was the Son of God. He spoke

to me in my head too. He never spoke out of His mouth. I answered in my head, "Yes." He asked if I believed He died for me. I said "Yes." Then I don't remember anything that He said. He kept talking to me, but I don't remember what He said. The next thing I remember is Him telling me, "Kim, you may pass." Then He started to glow from the inside out too. But His light was bright as a spotlight, and my light was like a lightning bugs' body. He also had goldish specks in His yellowish, whitish light. When I walked and His light blended with my light, I was in my body (I felt the bed beneath me), on the ceiling looking at my body. I thought, "She is so young." I was in the place with Him all at the same time. I was fully aware of being in all three places at once! I can't explain it.

Once I walked out of His light, I was just in the cathedral. I went up a few stairs. There was a rail on my right side. At the top of the stairs was a small platform. Once I was on the plat-form, a door opened toward me and outside was the brightest, most beautiful light I have ever seen. I often explain to people, imagine all the good feelings you have ever had in your entire life, ball them up and multiply them to the twenty-fifth power, and you still can't equal the love I felt in that LIGHT! I was thinking, "I'm going out there!" The Man behind me started laughing-not a mean laugh but a laugh like when you see kids doing something. He said, "Are you sure?" I said, "Yeah, I'm going out there!" Then I saw in my mind my kids walking home from school. My daughter was eight, and my son was six. I saw her pulling her brother up by his shirt and saying, "Boy, come on, you're always stopping to look at junk." Then I saw them at the door knocking. Then I saw my now ex-husband pull into the parking lot from work. I then saw him walk up to our apartment and ask the kids, "Where is your mother at? She is probably in there asleep." I could feel him getting mad.

I saw him open the door and yell, "Meal, you left the kids outside!!!!" I saw all three of them come up the stairs. I saw them walk into the bedroom. I could feel them when they found me. I could feel our new son in the bassinet cold, hungry and wet and crying. Then I was back in the cathedral with Him. The light outside started to dim and to my left I saw a street, complete with the yellow line in middle, unfold like a giant rug. The street unrolled in front of me and continued to my right. The Man behind me then said, "You have a long road to travel." Then I was back in my body on my bed.

Author's Note: I'm including some of the answers this individual reported on my research questionnaire:

Q. Did this light have any immediate impact upon you? If so, describe.

A. My entire life has changed. After it happened, I thought I was losing my mind. I started looking into different mental disorders. It was only after I finally told someone what happened, did I know that what I experienced was a spiritual experience and not a "mental" issue. So many things have changed. Most of the friends I had before this, left, as did my husband at the time. Some say I lost my "fire." I don't fear death. My thoughts on religion and people have drastically changed. I resigned as a correctional officer. I now work with the physically and mentally disabled. I do not cling to people anymore. I am not angry anymore.

Q. Did this experience seem real or dream-like or a hallucination? Explain.

A. No, it seemed real. More real than me sitting at this computer typing this.

Q. During your experience, were you given an understanding

of the meaning and purpose of life?

A. We are here to serve. Serve one another so that we can serve Him. I also realized that all roads lead back to God, regardless what you call Him.

Q. Did this experience increase or decrease your spiritual or religious beliefs or practices in any way?

A. I hardly ever go to Church anymore. My spirituality has drastically increased. I teach my children to learn from all religions. I don't believe there is only one true religion. I know that God is closer than the air I breathe. I don't have to go to a building to find Him. I do know that fellowship is important though. I just don't like when people think someone has to GO to church to find or believe in Him.

Q. Following your experience, do you consider yourself to be more spiritual than religious? If so, how would you explain this to others?

A. I am more spiritual than religious now. I tell people this and try to explain to them that I talk with God, not just pray, daily. Most don't understand, especially when I tell them that I rarely attend Church.

Q. Do you have a better sense of self-acceptance? Explain.

A. I love myself now. I even learned to laugh at myself.

Q. In retrospect, do you think this experience happened for a reason to help you in some way? Explain.

A. I sometimes question why He let me come back. Life can get hard. But then I will see something that makes me love my life, or a friend will call, and I can help them somehow. I worked in nursing homes while I went to college and there were times when someone would pass, and I could talk to them or their families. I hope I helped. I look at the people I work with now and know that I can make their lives happier, easier. Being sensitive to others feelings can become overwhelming, but I cannot see myself being the cold, uncaring, cruel, hateful person I was. Not saying I don't get angry anymore, but when I do, I try to look at things from the others perspective now.

Q. What is the single most important bit of wisdom you wish to tell others who have not had a transcendent type of experience?

A. I would tell them, and I do tell people that God is REAL. And on the other side is nothing but LOVE.

YEARNING FOR HIM TO LIVE THROUGH ME

Joyce Winkleman, Indianna

As a born again, spirit-filled believer with many years of char-
ismatic teachings of the scriptures, there was always something
else going on inside of me. The yearning of this Christ who lived
in me, I longed for Him to live His life through me. I wanted to
be an expression of Him. I had all the knowledge of Him, but
His character and nature somehow I knew had not been formed
in me yet. It didn't take me long to realize that this call within me
had to be pursued. I sensed the only way my longing and questions were going to be answered was through God alone.

I begged my husband for a small log cabin lodged in our
woods a few hundred feet from our home with double windows on each side. A table and chair, a Bible and journal, a bed
and rocking chair was all that was needed. All the children had
moved out by now, so my husband consented.

I remember my first day well and my prayer. "Who are you?
It's only you and me now. There is a longing inside of me to
know you deeply. You say that I know your voice, and I'm not
sure that I do; will you teach me?" I concluded my prayer with
a promise, that whatever He would teach me, I would obey and
simply trust Him, as a child, and apply that to my life. I also said
that I wanted to be a product of His molding hand, so that He
would live His life through me to this generation.

Because of my responsibilities in the home, I would allow
myself two hours in the cabin each morning. The pursuit for the
truth of who He was in me continued as I would walk up and
down our country road. I would not move forward until I sensed
an answer to this. I could not listen anymore to man's teaching.
I had come to the end and was willing to risk it all and begin a

new foundation with Him as my teacher alone.

A sense of love began to emerge during one of my talks. Love, that is who you are! This feeling of love felt good and seemed to push aside anything contrary to love. I couldn't stop thinking about His love. It had a personality. "Love is patient, is kind, is not jealous, does not brag, is not arrogant, does not act unbecomingly, does not seek its own, is not provoked, does not take into account a wrong suffered. It does not rejoice in unrighteousness, bears all things, believes all things, hopes all things, endures all things." I was taught these scriptures, and it was in my head but *the knowledge of it doesn't produce the change.*"

God was laying the foundation of love. He had answered my first question. We were on our way! Little did I realize He was going to take each negative characteristic in me, bring it to the surface through trials that would expose everything that was contrary to His nature. He had heard my cry over the years, but I had to be in a position to hear and work with Him.

He was going to expose the negative attitudes in me, so I could see the rotten fruit it produces. Always disharmony! While the roots were going to be pulled out, I had to stay very close to Him in prayer. As each ungodly characteristic was exposed and taken out through some sort of trial, I could see the damage that hate, unkindness, jealousy, boastings, impatience, selfishness, and anger does in our lives. God's ultimate goal for us is to be one with Him and each other. But how do we get there?

He is love, wow! All I have to do is love! Remembering the promise I made to Him that as He would give me instruction, I would obey. I dealt directly with Him as He enlightened the scriptures to me. Once I understood the characteristics of His love, enlightenment was not hard to distinguish. Enlightenment comes in purity, grace and everything that God is. Knowing God intimately helps us to be sensitive to enlightenment.

While under the microscope of God, His conviction was

never condemning. I learned His nature through His loving arms of correction. During the long months and years, as He was patiently loving me through my deliverance of my human-ness and the ego that lies deep within us, He was always loving and patient. Many times I deserved a scolding but He was always there with His love.

I was watching God in action and learning from Him as He dealt with me. I began to apply this to my life and in my dealings with other people. His grace was a major player in my life from now on. I remembered that only two years earlier, I had bought a small bottle of sweet oil. Each day I would anoint my heart that I might feel as He feels. My eyes were anointed to see through His eyes. My ears and lips and mind also.

I was beginning to know Him and sensing His character being formed in me. I began to see through His eyes. God's love for each person is powerful. He doesn't see as we do. We see the flaws and pass judgment. He doesn't! He looks on each person with hope and purpose. They are perfect and beautiful in His eyes. If we see man any other way, it is through our own eyes.

The divisions, ego, pride, self-righteousness breaks God's heart for it keeps us from Him and each other for the union He desires. It takes time to learn His voice. His voice is love and peace. It is everything that love is.

To think of the living God in us, and He living His life through us, we will take on His gentleness, the gentleness that could never do harm to anyone. The merciful, that remembers where they have been and can no longer find judgment with anyone. They leave the judgment in God's hands, and they only love, knowing His judgment is full of compassion.

We become peacemakers for that is who God is and where He is. Our opinions have no value anymore, only uniting and standing at His side in prayer, wanting only His purpose and plan for all men. We will know when His fullness is taking root in us for all destructive forces will have left us, and there is nothing left but love. We will work in harmony with God, man and nature. When we face opposition, we will remain poised. Arguing and debating is not His character. Peace will always be our objective. We will be willing to be misunderstood and lay down our opinions for the sake of peace. Where there is peace, there is God.

This is almost impossible for us to do for our ego and will is very strong. I could feel the resistance in me. How was He ever going to crucify my desire to be right? The great Master goes to work and lays His plan for me. He just wanted me to be willing as we worked together on this. I had to remain in prayer daily for the grace and sensitivities needed for the deliverance.

God allowed me to see a situation contrary to ninety-nine percent of the people around me. The desire to prove myself right or debate would nudge me inside. I noticed if I gave in to this, it would produce bad fruit. The respect and love for my neighbor was greater than my opinion.

I didn't arrive here overnight. God has kept me in this place for years, and sometimes the trials would escalate until the purging was complete. During this time of purging of my nature in exchange for His, I didn't read books or go on the internet for guidance or understanding. This was between God and me. My desire was only to be God's love.

In the years I was in my cabin two hours in the morning, His surgical work was being accomplished through my daily life. I was cooperating with God for the deliverance of my self-will or ego. Love had finally conquered the ego. I didn't have to bring a religious doctrine, just a listening and loving heart of hope. I was obsessing God's character and He was the player now. Much of the ego was gone, and following His sensitivities seemed natural. Although the world was going on around me, I felt untouchable, like an invisible protection.

I was moving in God. As He opened doors, I moved; when

they closed, the rebellions were gone. When the ego would try to assert itself for its own way, I could detect it now, for the ego or our self-will is only a waste of time, energy, money, and it will not produce harmony.

Sensing the oneness of character with Him, it was so natural to love. While the owners of a home traveled, I moved in and was responsible for two large dogs. During my morning and afternoon walks with the dogs, there was much opportunity for personal interaction with people, many from other countries and cultures. With the inhibitions removed, the fears gone, love was able to flow.

His eyes only saw perfection in everyone. His words were kind, loving, and without condemnation and judgment. The life and love He gave to the people I met, drew life and love from them, and unity was formed. We were in the experience of Christ without realizing what it was. The need for love and acceptance was being met in each of us, so there was no need to disturb the oneness through negative conversations that would break the unity.

I lived this way for three months and knew unity was possible when the ego and self-will is laid down. There was an article in the club house suggesting that there was a fountain of youth somewhere in the vicinity. I was experiencing the essence of the fountain we know as God.

I remembered that a few years earlier as I was pondering the Lord's prayer, He says we should pray for His kingdom to come to this earth and that His will would be done. Staying in my child-like faith and promise to Him of obedience to His word as it was enlightened to me, I asked Him about eternity, and I believed He was suggesting to me that His desire for us is to live it here and now. In the flashback of remembering my prayer, my heart leaped knowing His eternal kingdom was to be experienced here and now. I was touching it.

When I came back home from my three month trip, I kept the experience alive. He was in charge now, and the defenses and distresses were gone. I had learned to surrender each situation to Him. I would not argue with His providence and purpose anymore. I really believe when our will and character have been annihilated and replaced with His, that even the heavens are affected, and everything is working together for we have overcome the world and the flesh, and we have replaced it with His.

It's not about us anymore as we stand by His side for His purpose only. This can only be learned and taught by Him alone. We are in a new experience now and allowing Christ to live through us. This is different from knowing *about* Him. Many draw the line here and say if we are not part of a church, we will be deceived. But this is where you take the risk, the place of faith as you come as a child and dare to believe and take Him at His word. A place of complete surrender as He opens the scriptures to you. You will exceed your teachers as you grow and change in Him. Then you will begin to understand, "It is no longer I that liveth, but Christ in me."

About Joyce Winkleman

To contact Joyce Winkleman by email, her address is joyce. winkelman@att.net

AN ANGEL DURING THE HOLOCAUST

Esther Yehezkel, New York

During the Holocaust, my mother was a young woman with a small son. They were refugees in Russia having fled from the Nazi's in Poland. My mother did everything she could in order to feed both herself and her son, who went to bed each night with a small crust of bread under his pillow.

She had traded goods in the black market for some material. With this, she intended to get food from a nearby farm. When she reached the farm, the people were very kind. They fed her and filled her small sled with wonderful grains and vegetables. She was elated!

Suddenly a large sled with a horse appeared. The man in the sled had a fur covering his legs and ice hanging from his handle-bar moustache. "What are you doing here?" he asked. "Where do you live?" My mother couldn't believe her luck. He took her along with her small sled and food right to her door. It was only right to invite him in for some hot tea, but when she turned around to thank him and invite him in, he was gone. No trace of him could be found!

My mother is convinced he was her angel, and the answer to her prayer…and so do I.

DIVINE OUT-OF-BODY EXPERIENCE

Mark Ziegler, California

This occurred one night in early October, 1980, when I was thirty-five years old. I went to sleep in bed in my San Diego, California apartment after a typical evening following a typical day. What would occur while my body was asleep was the most atypical experience of my life.

It is easiest to relate from the perspective of the remembrances of the following morning. I remembered first being in a non-earthly setting, in an intense conversation with persons, about three in number, about a subject I could not recall afterwards. I also did not remember who they were nor what they looked like. But this was not in our Earth dimension, and they were not humans as we know them. And neither was I. I knew it was "too real" to be a dream, yet the particulars of the environment and the discussed subject were as if deliberately deleted from my memory.

What came next was very clearly remembered. Mental clarity and full wakefulness came quickly as a very uncomfortably intense light was shining in my eyes. I remember thinking "this is real!" as I was startled to full alertness. This light was seemingly far more disturbing and intensely bright than the light ophthalmologists had used to inspect my eye health in clinical visits. And worse, I seemed to be somehow drawing closer to it as the brightness intensified still more. In horror, I attempted to back-swim away from it, as I now realized that I was somehow floating toward this light that I could not shut out. With nothing to touch to brace my hands or feet against, I resigned myself to the conclusion that I was going to die from being burned up by this intense ball of energy that looked so much like our solar sun.

I remember that my main concern was to try to somehow shield my retinas from some of the horrible pain that would come from the blinding and burning. Had I been aware of leaving the body and seeing the Light from afar, I likely would have had time to realize it was to be joyful, as others experience. That didn't happen.

The next (of many) surprises, a moment later as I was drawn into this "sun," I entered some kind of goldenrod-colored aura around it, vision still intact. Not hot after all, it was instead a very pleasant warm feeling. Certainly a relief although I still had no idea of what was going on, nor where I was.

Inside this aura, I passed into...nothing. Nothing that I could afterwards remember seeing or hearing or touching, anyway. A void is all I could remember. But then it came to my awareness that I was not alone in there, and it felt as if I were being approached by some very powerful Other, a nonphysical personality that I could nevertheless mentally and undeniably sense. Perhaps the Spirit didn't move. Perhaps my awareness just opened to it gradually. Whoever this Spirit was, He/She/It was VERY happy to see me. At once I knew this Spirit knew me thoroughly well and loved me with an overwhelming, incomprehensible, unconditional love. Such love as I had believed could not be possible anywhere by anyone and by a Super spirit as I had believed could not exist. A Superspirit that gave no introduction (that I would later remember, anyway) but seemed to have an "I am that I am" attitude. And it was fine with me...just being there with that wonderful Spirit and experiencing caring as I had never known made me temporarily unconcerned with human theological questions. By now I felt more alive and alert than I had ever been as a human on Earth and realized that I wasn't now human, and this wasn't Earth. There was nothing physical there, and yet there was everything there, experienced as thought-intense thought, more real than any physical perception of a material reality. I somehow knew that this place inside this Light was outside of time, a place where only an eternal now existed. I realized that I was experiencing what "dead" humans do, yet it seemed humorous to realize that this was real living, and life on earth was death by comparison. What humans think is death is real life and vice versa. And this was pure joy that surpassed human comprehension.

Yet eventually, after how many moments I don't know, I did begin to conceptualize questions. And as quickly as I conceptualized them, the complete answers came to me fully, as if instantaneously telepathically downloaded. Each time, my reaction was as "of course, that's so simple and obviously true!" One question led to another, and another with the same result. And as the answers came and my understanding and comprehension grew, I could feel myself expanding as consciousness and becoming less and less like humans. Until, reflecting upon this, I asked this Spirit, this God, what the human existence I had just been experiencing was about.

This answer came differently. Instead of having the answer instantaneously imparted, my attention was directed away from this Being of Love and to my right. In the void, appeared a tiny dark dot. That it could be noticed in a void may indicate that it was not dark there although I remember no ongoing awareness of light as such. I do not recall having any bodily form there, astral or otherwise. This would be consistent with the formlessness there, and the dark dot may have been an imparted thought concept rather than anything visual even to a semi-material eye of some astral body form.

As I wondered why my attention was directed to this tiny dot, it began to elongate into a thin line. It lengthened at both ends simultaneously and eventually spread beyond the periphery of my awareness both left and right. It then expanded vertically until its height also was beyond the periphery of my perception. It seemed to have moved toward me or me toward it, and I was enveloped by it. At this point the formlessness was gone, and I was inside a well-lit and furnished room.

I was as if floating above the floor at the foot of a bed. Upon the bed lay a sleeping man, immobile and with a blanket pulled up to the neck. The face lay upon a pillow and facing sideways to the right. I apparently floated, not walked, around the right corner and up the right side of the bed. I stopped then and stared at the face of the man, wondering who it was and why I was here. Several moments went by before I recognized this as the physical form of the human I had been. I then began to see, while watching the face, the life and soul of this sleeping human as Enlightened Spirit saw it.

In sleep as in wakefulness, this human's conditioned consciousness was consumed with anxiety, stress, and worry. The body's brain was active, had dream thoughts different from my own, and was not aware of my mental presence. I experienced a growing mixed reaction of pity and revulsion, seeing this human's attitude of worry as totally unnecessary, counterproductive, and spiritually unaware. When I could no longer bear witnessing this, I quickly turned away from looking at this face to try to avert my attention from it.

After this, came my last memory of this unique and profound out-of-body experience. A sudden and terrible experience of a sudden fall, seemingly of about ten or twelve feet. The feeling of a sharp burst of adrenalin characteristic of falling dreams, but with a jarring impact, that caused my body to be momentarily impressed and depressed into the bed mattress. Simultaneous with this was a sensing of sudden, rapid mental devolution from a consciousness with understanding of the deepest meanings of all to a primitive creature of very minute awareness. I thought moments after this experience that it was like being a large mass of soft clay, thrown at a door, with only a small bit that passed through the keyhole remaining of my intelligence. That if I had just lost still another one or two percent of the knowledge I had acquired while outside of my brain, I might now be a squirrel or a reptile. But although I clearly remembered this glorious loving God and the thinking of questions and receiving answers, what they all were was...frustratingly gone. All excepting the asking about this human experience and being shown the unnecessary worry.

Why? Wouldn't I be a better person and more valuable to other humans if I remembered some of those answers? Was that the God of the Bible, or the spirit of Jesus? For awhile, I considered seeking hypnosis to attempt to remember. Then I remembered that all the memories of that conversation with souls at the beginning experience were deleted also, so there must be a good reason. Perhaps we have the temporary human primate experience to evolve spiritually and serve in some way that archangels cannot. Or perhaps our brains are inadequately wired for handling the bigger truths and have enough on the plate just contending with survival in the material and social worlds. I don't know. But I don't believe God wishes or expects humans to know all and doesn't want us to worry about it. Learning to be more like God in caring about others seems to be the purpose, not mental brilliance. I have been interviewing out-of-body experiencers since my own experience in 1980. In this and in reading hundreds of other accounts, I have found that among those who have experienced life reviews during divine OBEs (whether of the near-death type or others), the criteria for life evaluation seems consistently to be about the quality of regard for, and treatment of, other individuals. Individuals both of our own species and others.

Back to my return again imprisoned and encumbered in a solid, clunky body, I felt despair. I wanted to be back with the God of Love in the Light, where there was no worry and nothing to worry about. I was single and had no dependents who needed me here. Why was I sent back to this crude and cruel world?

Contact with higher consciousness was not quite over. As I lay there upon the bed and marveled that NOTHING that I had just experienced conformed to my yesterday's mental model of the real and possible, another seemingly telepathic "voice" inside my consciousness interrupted and interjected, "You knew it all the time." This was frustrating, and I protested this thought with, "I DIDN'T know this, and in recent years life has only made sense to me from a bio-evolutionary perspective! How else could I explain the coarseness of life?" Again it came, with great authority, "You knew it all the time."

As time elapsed after this experience, I came to believe that we have a greater aspect of our consciousness, a super-soul or over-soul or over-self (as some call it) that, while linked to us, lives a mental life apart in a dimension apart. This is not the God encountered in the Light but may have been the "me" that conversed with other souls at the beginning of the experience. A group decision to petition God for a Divine encounter for enlightenment may have been seen as a necessary step to dislodge my human mind from the strictly bio-evolutionary-model philosophical rut that I increasingly reasoned from. "You knew it all the time" may also have come from that source.

For about one month after this experience, several bizarre coincidental occurrences happened in my life. They primarily were of a pre-awareness of occurrences to come to pass within a period of minutes or up to twenty-four hours. They seemed as thoughts formed normally at the time they arose, and extraordinary only after a corresponding event occurred. They had no apparent benefit other than to keep me aware that cause and effect in the natural world includes more causes than conventional science recognizes.

What was that line I was drawn into? This question haunted me for years. Was it the Space/Time continuum of our physical universe? The continuum of all consciousness or of consciousness within biological evolution? It seemed a graphic representation out of place with the rest of that void and transcendent experience.

About twenty-five years later, I had an opportunity to speak with Dr. Raymond Moody about this issue. He was author of the mid-1970's best-selling book *"Life After Life,"* about near-death experiences. He had heard thousands of accounts with elements similar to mine. Yet he said he had not before heard of a line, such as I described. I was disappointed.

Less than one year later, I began reading the 1998 edition of the book "Lessons from the Light," by Dr. Kenneth Ring. In the first chapter, an individual named Craig describes his NDE experience. During the experience, he is shown a thin horizontal line that stretches to infinity. In the middle was a small area that was thicker than the rest. He was told that this area was his earthly life. The voice "seemed to be telling me that I existed in some form before this lifetime, and that I would continue to exist after it ended."

So finally, after twenty-six years, I was hearing and learning something more about the line. I didn't need it as verification for convincing myself of the legitimacy of my experience. I was convinced from the day it occurred, but I realized that others may receive it as such. And such experiences change the lives of all who believe their revelations of consciousness DOES NOT die; there IS a God of Love, and spirit realms, and our development, deeds and spiritual state are consequential far beyond biological deaths. Life here is rough, but it is a very short dot on an endless line. And Love will win out.

Divine spiritual contact may come when out-of-body, near-death, asleep or awake. It is especially likely when awake if a mood creates an intense emotion of disgust and revulsion for all that is cruel, corrupt, and unfair in this world. Seemingly, the exact opposite of the often-encouraged positive-thinking path to saintliness, this involves classic instantaneous transcendence to spirituality by passionate rejection of worldliness and an intense longing to be apart from all evil-including the evil in one's own self. It seems to be the very rare moment of true repentance when our attitude and perspective shifts to allow God in. It is the moment of being in the world but not of it, when the soul longs only for what God does also.

In November of 1981 I was wandering around a very large outdoor swap meet (flea market, to some) on a sunny, perfect Southern California day. My mood and thoughts were completely incompatible with the weather. I was very upset about some worldly injustice or another, which I cannot even remember now. At some point it merged with all my other peeves, including fate's sometime cruelty to helpless children and animals, and erupted in a kind of emotional critical mass. Oblivious to the lighthearted environs, I was now experiencing a runaway inner rage and disgust with virtually all things Earthly. I resented even my own complicity with the mess for existing as a part of it.

Literally in a split second, my perspective changed completely. I found myself suddenly flooded with joy and a totally different outlook on everything, At age thirty-seven I was having my first classic transcendent experience while wide awake…at a swap meet! I realized that the typically human viewpoint of life is a gross distortion of proper perception, and that misunderstanding is where much human pain and cruelty originates. There are greater and lesser realities. When one thinks from awareness of the greater realities, problems of the lesser realities have a way of miraculously resolving themselves. Jesus discussed this in his Sermon on the Mount. Mystics of most religions and eras have expressed the same. But I was not read in all that yet.

The greater realities are that there *is* a God of Love, that we are spirit and only temporarily experiencing being human, and that we should not let forgetfulness of this result in destructive cares and worries. This physical world is a temporary and lesser reality. The natural causes that science studies are, under certain circumstances and conditions, superceded by the metaphysical cause and effect forces of a greater reality. When the spirit behind human mind and brain transcends to touch Divine Mind, miracles can and do happen. And these miracles, sometimes labeled synchronicity, prove the mystical experience to be much more than mere ecstasy created by the release of endorphins in the brain under stress. I experienced such miraculous synchronicities for weeks after this brief experience, just as I had previously following my one "in the Light" out-of-body experience. Periods of mystical transcendence are very brief, but the greater truths and laws of existence momentarily glimpsed are never ending.

About Mark Ziegler

Mark is an artist who does illustration and animation work.

CHAPTER 7

ANIMAL ANGELS

"Until one has loved an animal, a part of one's soul remains unawakened."

—Anatole France

An angel is described as a "messenger of God." I consider animals, especially our pets to be within the scope of those so-called messengers of God. Let me explain. When I had my transcendent mystical encounter with the Light of God, I experienced such unconditional love, the likes of which no mortal human being on earth has experienced or will experience from this earthly existence we inhabit. When we cease living in our physical bodies, we will live again in another realm/reality. I was there twice - once when I died, and another time when I had my near-death-like mystical experience while delivering a eulogy. Both times my spirit-self encountered the Light of God and the ineffable unconditional love that emanated from the Divine Presence who welcomed me. The absolute beauty of love's perfection in its gentleness upon my soul silenced me in awe and reverence. It was a gift of the Divine for which I feel profound gratitude. Therefore, I feel qualified to speak about God and unconditional love from that higher spiritual perspective.

Unconditional love is pretty foreign to human beings. At

least that is what I discovered when I learned what unconditional love is, coming from the Divine Source. We think of love as an emotion, that it has to be deserved - if you are good to me, then I will be good to you. That is conditional love, one we are all very familiar with. We think we love unconditionally, but we always have strings attached to our love because we have egos whose primary interest is security, survival, self-esteem, power, and control. The ego doesn't want to change, despite its sufferings and fears. Consequently, the ego is sort of a bully, wanting its own way, demanding explanations, and looking for someone or something else to blame for its misery. Ego will judge others, criticize them, and see their flaws. Ego will withhold our love from someone if they disappointed or hurt us in some way.

Unconditional love is the love of God for God IS LOVE! This love is not interested in hatred, revenge, jealousy, violence, egotism, fear, or anything other than *simply to love for love's sake.* This type of love *transcends* the ego! Unconditional love is all about caring about someone else's happiness without expecting or wanting anything in return - no strings attached.

When we are able to transcend our ego needs for all circumstances, all identity, all desires, then what we begin to experience is the very essence of our truest self, the self that is unified with the Divine Presence within. But all too often, we feel too vulnerable to explore our true self, so we cover it up with the mask of a false self or the ego. Unconditional love is resting in God. It is the source of our purest self. What we need then, are teachers of unconditional love so we can learn to recognize what it really is. Mother Teresa was such a teacher.

I am suggesting that one of our surprising teachers of unconditional love is the human-animal-Divine connection. During one part of my mystical experience, my Great Teacher the Light of God informed me that *everything* ever created has within it, a portion of the Divine Light. Everything from the quarks, atoms, cells, tissues, organisms, plants, animals, soil, water, humans, etc. has the Creator's Light, whose Spirit is at the very core of its essence because **everything** was created from the Light of God- from itself. **Everything!** This Light is not ordinary light as we know it, but Light that lies beyond the space-and-time universe. Its Source is the Godmind that guides our growth, our unfolding, and is our life force.

Divine Light dwells in animals. Our pets are similar to the way a mystic lives his or her life. If the mystics, near-death experiencers, the saints, return from their Light experiences knowing the nature of the Light is LOVE, then it is no stretch of the imagination to suggest that our pets transcend all ordinary awareness by having direct knowledge of their own Source. They radiate their Light from the perspective of the Divine which also created them, and who loves and provides for them. Animals know who created them, it's humans who want to forget.

There is an interesting passage in the Bible. Job 12:10 says: *"For the soul of every living thing is in the hand of God, and the breath of all mankind."* Notice it said **every living thing**. Animals are included and are loved by the Creator. He commanded Noah to save the species by putting their kinds in Noah's ark in pairs. The Bible also talks about the Creator's love for His animals and how He provides sustenance for them. When He created them, He gave them heightened sense reactions: hummingbirds navigate across vast distances to seek warmth and shelter from the cold, ants and bees cooperate and work together to form well-organized colonies, hawks have sharp eyes that can spot mice scurrying through fields in the dark night. Every species has been provided for from the good-heartedness of God's Providence, which looks after the whole creation and adorned them with a variety of essences, powers, energies and perfections for their well-being and survival. All of creation is called to glorify the Creator according to its ability because all are a reflection of His goodness.

There are accounts in the near-death experience research

literature of individuals who crossed over to the other side of the
veil, who were greeted by their animal angels, the pets they had
loved and with whom shared their lives. One account is that of a
woman who during surgery was met by her two deceased dogs,
who then jumped on her and kissed her face with such joy in the
reunion they shared. The Light told her that when it was time
for her to stay on the other side, her dogs would be there once
again. Another account tells of seeing all the pets the individual
had had as a child. She is firm in her belief that animals survive
death. Another account gave the person comfort in knowing
that her beloved dog would be with her again when she returned
to the Light. Roy of Siegfried and Roy recalled the memories of
his near-death experience; his tigers were with him during that
time. "No doubt, when it is my time, my cats should greet me -
they are my family!"

Read about Roy Horn's near-death experience: http://www.
mercurynews.com/mld/mercurynews/news/local/states/cali-
fornia/counties/alameda_county/9674613.htm?1c

I should add that these witnesses to the continuum of life tell
us that all life is sacred, and all return to that sacredness. What a
comfort that should be for all of us whose beloved animal angels
have returned to our Source, and who will be welcoming us with
wet sloppy tongue kisses!

Thus, it is our love for animals that is nourished from the
depths of our heart, by the deepest longing of our soul to unite
to our own Beingness of Light which is the natural form within
us. In the words of the German mystic Meister Eckhart: *"The eye
by which I see God is the same eye by which God sees me."* With our
animal companions we journey together in selfless love, which
consists of the purest thoughts in this state of grace and blessed-
ness. As Bruce Schimmel says, *"The little furry buggers are just
deep, deep wells you throw all your emotions into."*

We can learn so much from our animal angels. They go with
the flow, accepting and adapting readily. They have no other

agenda but to love us. We are invited into their world of love and steadfast devotion simply by being with them. These animal angels or those messengers of God's love bring us that love through wet, sloppy kisses on our face when the world seems to be crashing down on us. Our spirits are immediately raised when we look into their luminous, loving eyes.

"There is no psychiatrist in the world like a puppy licking your face."

—Ben Williams

While talking to my vet one day, I told her I was writing a book and one chapter would deal with how animals have so much to teach us. She replied, "Yes, they do. My husband gave me this example the other day. He said, 'Put your dog and your wife in the trunk of your car and then close the trunk door. Wait five minutes, then open the trunk and watch what happens. The dog will come out so excited and happy to see you. Notice what the wife does!' (No explanation needed - you get the picture.)

It is no wonder that the spelling of the word dog is the word God spelled backward.

WORDS OF WISDOM

"O God, enlarge within us the sense of fellowship with all living things, our brothers to whom Thou hast given this earth as their home in common with us.
May we realize that they live not for us alone, but for themselves and for Thee, and that they love the sweetness of life even as we, and serve Thee better in their place than we in ours."

—St. Basil the Great, 370 A.D.

Now, let's look at what some people have to tell us about their animal angels.

A BALL OF LIGHT IN A FURRY LITTLE BODY

Martha St. Claire, Washington

As long as I can recall, I have been sensitive to things that others are not necessarily aware of. When I was very little, I thought everyone saw pretty glowing colors around others or magical things or felt the pure essence of animals. As I grew, I learned to not talk about the "invisible" since that seemed to work out best.

In 1974, as a young adult, I had a truly fortunate life-changing near-death experience. I nearly drowned while water-skiing when I fell, and the tow-rope twisted around my left arm, dragging me behind the speeding boat while my friends were not paying attention.

Twenty years later, through becoming connected with other experiencers and also from my own research, I realized that my premature birth and a later childhood trauma were childhood near-death experiences; thus, explaining the heightened aware-ness I had while growing up, including my deep connection to animals.

After years of integration, I feel more blessed regarding my life-long challenging sensitivities, and yet, I remain surprised by what happens to me in unique ways and how it can involve others, even my pets.

One example of this still touches my heart. My dear elderly Aunt Julia had too many cats on her large country property in Monmouth, Oregon. All of them lived outside and even though upon occasion, a relative would catch a few and have them "fixed," they still multiplied like rabbits.

Although I had two beloved cats at home, one day I decided to rescue an especially adorable runt of the litter and took home newly named "Baby Kitty," who was cute as a bug and tugged at my heartstrings.

In a way, Baby Kitty looked like something other than a cat, making him especially endearing. He had yet to grow into his huge ears, giving him a bat-like look, and something about his free spirit reminded me of a wild baby animal. He had a white spot on his dark nose that looked like he'd gotten into powdered sugar and his long rich fur was a mixture of beautiful fluffy white with black tabby stripes mixed in. Beneath his curious nature, his soulful, big, round, green eyes seemed to peer deeply into mine, and I fell in love. Even my kitties at home seemed to be fascinated by him, and all was well.

A few months later, I was lecturing on near-death experiences on the east coast and was staying with friends in Vermont, while my neighbor, Denise, looked after my cats at home in Lake Oswego, Oregon.

One evening, while visiting with friends, I felt a sudden hot feeling physically, literally on my chest and within my heart. It felt as if someone had placed a hot radiating stone there or something warm and penetrating, like a heating pad but with an intense feeling of love. It seemed that a glowing energy of golden love and light suddenly was in my heart communing with me, which was not an everyday occurrence.

I felt such warmth, particularly over my shoulders and chest. The most intense loving emotional feeling came over me, and suddenly, I had a strong urge to call my home voice mail. In doing so, I discovered that Denise had very emotionally, just minutes before, left a message saying that she had found Baby Kitty lying on my side of the bed (how he jumped up by himself remains a mystery), looking very sick with a swollen stomach, and breathing far too fast. She was racing him to the vet.

By the time I was able to speak with the doctor, I was told that my precious kitten had passed away soon after arrival. As I asked the vet assistant to please save some of his fur for me before cremation, my mind raced with thoughts like, "I should have been home," or "How could I have not known he was sick?"

Looking back on it, Baby Kitty did seem to be a bit less than perky in the days leading up to my trip, and he did have a big tummy, but kittens often do. I had taken him to the vet upon adoption caring for him properly, and now he was "dead." It turned out that he had an illness that could not have been prevented; still I had huge regret and sadness that I was not there for him in his last moments, while he was energetically there for me.

My heart ached to think he found comfort choosing to rest on the side of the bed where we snuggled at night; clearly he wanted to be near my energy, while his spirit had something more majestic in mind.

Soon after the vet conversation, I was on the phone speaking with Denise, trying to take the sting out of her upsetting experience as I shared the amazing love I'd felt that was still physically with me.

While my heart was broken, I also felt incredible joy since I absolutely knew that Baby Kitty's spirit had come to me with his love and gratitude, literally touching my heart with his presence on his way to Heaven. I continued to feel his deeply loving essence during my long flight home that night, while I exhaustingly picked up his ashes from the animal hospital in the wee hours, and while I sobbed upon entering my bedroom.

In spite of my natural human grief, I wish everyone could have such an amazing experience when a loved one passes because what I felt from him was the most incredible feeling of pure divine love, intense reassurance, and connection, not unlike what I felt during my last near-death experience. Think of being enveloped in a tangible bubble of pure warm expansive energy that contains the most wonderful feeling of radiant peace, joy, wholeness, well-being, and bliss imaginable - times infinity. Baby Kitty was and is that divine presence and so are we all a part of the whole, the whole of creation, that oneness beyond measure.

Our pets are deeply special souls and just like humans, have varied levels of soul growth and attainment. Some are truly spiritual masters in non-human bodies, and Baby Kitty fit this category, having had the insight and consciousness to share with me in a remarkable way.

Throughout my life, I have been blessed with wonderful comfort both in dreams and in real time of feeling the presence around me of many loved ones, including multiple pets, who have passed on. Such experiences are a vivid, enormously comforting reminder of the reality and tangibility of our access to heavenly dimensions and vice versa.

Our loved ones, including our precious pets on the "other side" are never truly gone or lost from us. Our heavenly pets love us deeply, often try to contact us, and indeed hear our words, thoughts, and prayers. In many cases, they want to remain in contact and hope that we will respond and understand that we can still have an actual relationship with them. In other cases, their souls may need to move on, but they are concerned for our well-being and also may need to let us know that they are fine.

It is up to us to open fully to receive the great love that comes our way. Animals are far more than just "animals." They feel, they know, they see, and they do their sacred part on earth and in Heaven. Their consciousness is ever expanding, endless, and eternal whether in physical form or in spirit bodies. Their loving nature reigns supreme, and they remember our love for them. Pets are essentially designed to be a pure expression of divine unconditional love, given to us by the Creator.

One day, perhaps when you least expect it, love could land on your doorstep in the form of a light-filled masterful being in disguise, here to open your heart even more, bringing untold heavenly wisdom and uniting you with the oneness of eternal life.

About Martha St. Claire, M.A.

Martha's counseling offers a client deep awareness for the soul, along with practical guidance and spiritual insight for daily life and during major life transitions, including the death of loved ones and pets. She has a natural angelic attunement and gift of mediumship, seeking to bring awareness, connection, and comfort regarding loved ones who have passed over. Martha loves to lecture on near-death experience and related topics and welcomes your inquiry. Her purpose is to bring awareness and healing regarding any fear of death and to co-create heaven on earth.

If you wish to learn more about Martha St. Claire and her work, please visit her website: www.marthastclaire.com She can be reached at: Martha@marthastclaire.com

CHAIN OF DIVINE INTERVENTIONS OF THE CANINE VARIETY

Amy J. Randall, Ohio

From the time I was a baby until now, multiple decades later, I have had more than my share of failed human relationships. It isn't for lack of trying, or that I am not a loving person, it has just been the path I have traveled. Some of my failed relationships were designed by fate, such as with my parents; some were through my own choice, such as my seven-year and then my 17-year marriages. But my relationships with dogs have always been rewarding and happy ones. Sadness only appearing when my lovely furry companions passed on.

I'm old enough to have been through the loss of several canine companions. While not all have been a part of the chain of doggie divine intervention, the chain does exist. It began with Emily Anne. She was my first dog as an adult. She was a Dalmatian. She came from a linage of champions but had a few quirks which would prevent her from being worthy of "showing." I bought her from reputable breeders who were so caring they interviewed buyers before they would decide who would earn the privilege of purchasing one of their dogs. I named Emily nearly a whole year before I met her and fell in love with her the minute I finally did meet her.

Through the years, Emily and I survived many difficult times. My second marriage was ending, and I felt I wanted my life to do the same. I was even having thoughts about how I would bring that plan to fruition. But when those thoughts moved into the afterlife, I realized I could not leave this Earth, for who would take care of my dear Emily. I speak of this lightly, in only a few sentences, but the truth is I was on the virtual edge of life, and my love for my dog lassoed me in.

Emily was diagnosed with lymphoma when she was only 10 years old. She did very well for a couple months, but suddenly there was a change, and I knew it was time to spring ahead of the agonizing death she was facing and have her euthanized. It was a beautiful, respectful and loving passing. Emily and I laid on blankets on the floor of my veterinarian's office. I stared at her face, trying to memorize every spot, her beautiful blue eyes, and the smell of her fur. We held to each other tightly until I felt her spirit lift, and she was gone from this Earth.

After Emily passed, I had several occurrences that made me keenly aware that she was watching over me from Heaven. I used to get a rash along the side of my face whenever I hugged her. One day, I was on the back of my husband's motorcycle when I felt her flying next to me. I asked Gregory to pull over, and when he did, I explained through my tears, that I had felt Emily with me. He shared that he felt the same thing. When I took off my helmet, there was the familiar rash along the side of my face.

Gregory was my third husband, and we are no longer married, but he loved Emily. The first three days after her passing, I couldn't go to work, couldn't eat or drink, and I couldn't leave the chair where I sat clinging to her favorite toy - a stuffed Dalmatian. On the third day, when Gregory came home from work, I asked him to sit down and look at the antique photograph we kept on our bookshelves. I wanted him to tell me what he saw so that I could assure myself that I had not lost my mind. The photograph was of a handsome young man. We didn't know who he was, so we affectionately named him Lloyd. In the photograph, Lloyd was standing next to an old Indian motorcycle which was parked in front of the woods. Gregory gasped. He saw what I saw. There in the photograph, next to Lloyd, was Emily's face. As I am writing this, it has been ten years since Emily passed, and yet you can still see her image in that photograph.

Six months after Emily passed, I was at my veterinarian's office with Niddy, one of my Siamese cats who was receiving fluid boluses for kidney failure. The folks there seemed a little extra happy to see me and explained that it was because they wanted me to meet someone. They took me back to the kennel area where I met Sara. She was a 4-year-old husky mix, very much underweight and with a few other issues. Apparently she had been there a few months recovering from a life of neglect. My heart was still broken over Emily, but a loud voice boomed in my head telling me to ignore my heart since it was too broken to feel anything and to listen to my mind. I knew I could provide a good home for this lovely animal. Gregory and I were still married then, so I went home and told him about her. He agreed to meet her, and when we went back to the veterinarian's office, they led us to the kennel area, where Sara sprang upon Gregory and peed all over him. I was sure this had sealed her fate, which it had, just not in the way I expected. Gregory said that he believed that Sara peeing on him was a sign that we should take her home with us and so we did.

When Sara came to live with us, it was unsettling how good she was. I was worried she was not normal as she never did anything wrong. She also did not understand what "play" meant and found doggie toys completely confusing. One day, I came home and sat on my bed. With head in hands, I began to sob, missing my Emily. Sara jumped up on the bed, stood on her back legs, and reached up to my nightstand where I kept Emily's prized stuffed Dalmatian. Sara delicately placed the toy in her mouth and sat down next to me nudging it into my lap. Oh my goodness, I knew then that a chain of events had taken place. I knew that Sara was God's way of letting Emily pass the torch to the next dog who would look over me.

Sara lived with us for quite a few years. One day she was diagnosed with Cushing's disease, and it was really only a matter of days before this would lead to her demise. And, like was the case

with Emily, it was brutally evident when the time came to intervene with death's painful plans. Somehow I managed to gather
Sara into my arms after she collapsed, and I was able to get her to
my veterinarian's office before any agonizing torture had begun.
My veterinarian said we made it in the nick of time. Again, I
found myself lying on the floor, holding my lovely doggie while
she passed on to the next world.

I know that they say that God never gives us more than we
can handle. I believe that, and yet when I look to the future of
the possible difficult things that could happen, there are some
I view as impossible to survive. This is what I felt when I knew
Sara's passing was on the horizon. When the time came, it felt
unbearable. I remember trying to get ready for work the next day
and being barely able to find my way to the shower. When I did,
I was suddenly overcome with the strong feeling that God was
embracing me. I also felt Sara's presence, and she was speaking to
me loudly and boldly, telling me to hurry up and get on the road
that there was something she needed me to do.

I believed that I had lost my mind, and yet I hurried to get
dressed and get in my car. As I was traveling along the back
country roads that would take me into town and my job, I
rounded a curve just in time to see a small dog sitting in the
middle of the road next to a bottle of water. As was customary
for me to do, I honked my horn trying to instill fear of the road
into the animal's mind. And like a flash of light, Sara was in my
head telling me to stop. I was jerked into the realization that
this was part of the plan. So I stopped my car, put on the hazard
lights, and got out. I began to call into the woods for the little
dog to come to me. What I heard in response was not a dog, but
rather a puppy. I heard the little yelping of a 7-week old puppy,
white with brown ears and brown spots, and one blue eye, one
brown. He shyly peeked around the trunk of a little tree and
let me scoop him up into my arms. As soon as I realized I was
holding a boy, I named him Moses for the bottle of water in the

middle of the road had kept his attention until I drove by to find him. Sara's message that I needed to hurry was no doubt because of the fact that Moses was not really visible there in the road - a road which is traveled by fast-moving cars. He definitely would not have survived long.

Since Moses has come to live with me, I have observed him doing some things Sara did. He likes to sing to certain songs on the stereo and those I play on my fiddle. From the first moment I held him, I knew that he was part of the plan. That plan was designed by God and Sara and was an intervention to keep me distracted from my grief over Sara's passing. As I am writing this, I realize it was more than that. For he came into my life just a matter of months before my 17-year marriage with Gregory ended. I am grieving the end of my marriage though it was my choice. I am having a tough time on some days to handle this. But Moses is still into puppy things and has proven a lovely distraction. He has played a significant role in my ability to move forward into healing.

Emily, then Sara, and now Moses. Clearly a chain of divine interventions of the canine variety.

About Amy J. Randall

Amy is the Director of Continuing Education at the Columbus, OH Bar Association. She is also a writer and the author of *Wicked Dreams*, and *The Hills of Circleville*. Her website is: www.amycooperonline.com

PETS AND ANGELS WALK TOGETHER

Mary Ellen "Angel Scribe", Oregon

When I was twenty-five years old, I began exploring spirituality. Most of us know God is out there, some can feel God, but how can we see God in our lives? You might call me a believing-skeptic!

That summer my husband and I rented a camper and took our two shaded-silver Persian cats, Channel and Camalot, on vacation. We caught the ferry off Vancouver Island in Canada and headed to Lake Chelan in Washington State. After a six-hour drive at the campsite, we put the cats on their harness-leashes. The next time we turned around Camalot had wiggled free of his harness. He was no where to be seen. We were devastated!

Of all the animals I had ever owned and loved, this shy-gentle creature who had been raised in a cage by a breeder had not learned to fend for himself, he relied and trusted me for protection. We spent our entire "vacation" walking around the small town of Lake Chelan calling, "Liver, liver, liver." It was his favorite treat, and he always came to it except this time.

Between naps, we wandered the streets day and night going to the radio station, newspaper, and local schools searching and alerting people about our precious missing kitty. The town folks predicted that the cat would be up a tree somewhere. But I knew this innocent cat did not have survival skills, and would be hiding under a bush somewhere.

Three days later, on our last morning of intense searching, just as the sun was rising, we were still wandering the quiet dark streets calling, "Liver, liver, liver." Exhausted at 4:00 a.m., we knew it was our last chance to find Camalot as our "vacation" had run out. We never even got to sight-see or swim in the lake.

We had done everything humanely possible to find Camalot, and it was obvious locating him was out of our hands.

At this point, I passed my heart into the hands of God and said, "Dear God, if you are really out there, if you really exist, please show me where my cat is." The most unusual thing happened next! Invisible hands of God or hands of loving angels were placed on my back and directed me in the opposite direction that we'd been searching. These hands applied pressure at street crossings on which way to turn. We turned to the right and walked another block, then they guided me to the end of the street.

I followed their direction for a quarter of a mile to a location that we had not yet searched when the feeling of the guiding hands lifted. The sun rose. I stood there in confusion. What was that all about? I called "C-a-m-a-l-o-t" one last time, and under a bush, twenty feet ahead, a scared, thinner, fluffy Shaded Silver Persian meowed.

Camalot crawled out from under a bush and stood still, waiting to be picked up. He blinked his huge green Disney eyes. My soul soared; my heart melted. Is there a God out there? We all have to make that decision in our own way, in our own time. Taking the time to ask seems to be the key. Maybe if my cat had not slipped from his harness, I may never have discovered prayer, God, and the angels. Maybe when something bad happens to us, it is just part of a greater plan that we do not see at the time.

The story of our missing cat had spread around the entire town. (I had seen to that!) When we pulled out of the motor home park, we told the gate keeper we had found our cat, and she burst into tears. She said it was her twenty-first birthday, and it was the best present she could have, to have the cat safe again. There are some kind people all over the world. Oh, and Channel? When we carried Camalot back to the camper and put him in front of the water bowl, Channel walked right over to him and smacked him on the head with her paw, with a look to say, "You sure caused a lot of trouble."

As upsetting as Camalot's disappearance was during a vacation where we never got to have one, it appears that Camalot was meant to get lost so that we could find and understand that a Divine power is at work in our lives. And now, thirty years later, it is still an amazing true story and one to offer you hope in your life. May you too, find what is missing in your life. And if you are going through a rough time, may you ride it to the end and discover its deeper meaning.

About Mary Ellen "Angel Scribe"

Mary Ellen "Angel Scribe" is the International author of *Expect Miracles* and *A Christmas Filled With Miracles, Pet Tips 'n' Tales*. She is a newspaper columnist and an award-winning photojournalist. Her highly popular "Angels and Miracles" E-newsletter is filled with inspiration, humor and beautiful photography to uplift readers' hearts and souls. Recently, she transformed her warm and fuzzy pet newspaper column into an E-newsletter. To date her work has been featured in fourteen books.

Mary Ellen teaches that we have miracles waiting to be claimed. There are three steps to manifesting miracles in your life. (1) Set your intention as a vehicle for miracles to move through you (2) Let God and the angels know you are willing. (3) Show up! Miracles often do not look like what you think they will. They are often disguised as acts of kindness. You may be an answer to someone's prayers.

Join her Angels and Miracles and Pet E- newsletters at: www. AngelScribe.com

Email: AngelScribe@msn.com

DILLON

Pat Stillisano DDS, Ohio

My greyhound, Dillon, jumped out of the SUV after a walk in the park with his housemate greyhound, Justice. He limped a bit, but I didn't think much about it except that I should get him a ramp because he's eleven years old. After a few days, instead of getting better, the limp got worse, and I started to worry about osteosarcoma to which greyhounds can be susceptible. I took him to a specialty vet clinic, and an x-ray was negative for the bone cancer. However, the orthopedic and neurologist both palpated a mass in his right armpit that they were very concerned with so he went for an MRI.

This showed a large mass through his pectoral muscle that had a differential diagnosis all for cancer. The vets did a biopsy that proved inconclusive but was devastating for Dillon. The biopsy itself did not even require a suture but Dillon's right front leg swelled to three times it's normal size, and he had swelling from his chest to his scrotum. Prior to the biopsy, he had much difficulty walking, but now he couldn't walk at all and was that way for at least three days. The vets thought it was because of a condition that some greyhounds have called vasculitis, or they had possibly nicked an artery in the biopsy. They wanted to open him up and remove the tumor and his leg. If he did in fact have vasculitis as well as the tumor, the operation could kill him. I didn't want his leg removed because his rear legs were not in good enough condition that he would be able to stand, so the surgeon recommended removing as much of the tumor as he could, biopsy it, and send him to radiation after he hopefully recovered. Not a lot of options.

I've known Nancy Clark for decades. We asked her if she

would use her gift of healing with Dillon. In the 80's, I had a four-pound dog with many birth defects, the worst of which was a rotated first cervical vertebrae. This would sometimes cause a pain in her neck so that she could not move her head. I would give her prednisone. When she was five, the prednisone wouldn't work; it had been a month. It was time to call it quits, but first I asked Nancy if she could do anything. She did a healing. There was an audible snap, and Sarah could move her head and was pain free. She died at age fifteen.

Nancy agreed to come to the house for Dillon. We went out to the backyard with Dillon laying down. Nancy got on her knees to pray. She wanted to be on her knees to humble herself before God. For a period of time, she was praying and minimizing herself so that she could be filled with God and get Nancy out of the way. She then joined hands with me and Mark, my friend and Dillon's co-owner. We were to direct our love to Dillon in order to raise him to God. How easy that was. She then petted and prayed for Dillon.

There was never a doubt in my mind that Dillon would be healed if it was God's will. Nancy had mentioned years prior to this that it had to be God's Will for a healing to work. But this time she was quite certain that it was the Will of God. I had not seen that certainty before so it was quite joyous for me. When this was diagnosed, Dillon could hardly make it down the driveway; now, we've been to the park again.

How does this affect me spiritually? I'm more than thrilled to get more time with my wonderful dog. But peel back this superficial layer and examine what happened: I'm nobody. And this very ordinary woman came to my nobody house and summoned the Supreme Power of the universe and humbly asked Him to heal my dog. For the moment, the Universe revolved around this ordinary woman and my nobody dog as God focused His attention on them and healed him. Why? Because Nancy asked Him to. Nancy is the new Adam. This is what we were intended

to be - absent from the original sin of ego. We can all have these
gifts if we can empty ourselves of our selves and align our wills
with the Will of God only. And not in a spirit of sacrifice, but in
a spirit of Joy as Nancy does. In speaking of His miracles Christ
said, "You will do greater things than these." But first we have to
recognize the Christ within us and become Him.

About Pat Stillisano DDS

Pat Stillisano is a retired dentist living in Powell, Ohio. He
was first introduced to mysticism as an undergraduate at the
University of Notre Dame and continues that study today.

ROCKET

Asia Voight, Wisconsin

The instances where animals act as our guides and guardian angels helping us to grow and heal are numerous. Asia Voight, an internationally renowned Professional Animal Communicator, recalls how her relationship with a beloved pet, her horse Rocket, changed her life by helping her transcend a major trauma in her life and heal.

In the icy Wisconsin air, my hands sweated as I grasped the woven leather rein readying Rocket for our daily ride. The sun was blinding, and I pulled my arm up over my head to shield my eyes as I viewed our trail. The minute hill directly outside of the stable would seem insignificant to any other rider. But to me, the thought of racing to the top of it on Rocket's back was as treacherous as climbing a mountain like Everest in which only the bravest succeed. Closing my eyes and taking a deep breath for strength, my body trembled as flashes of twisted metal, black smoke and flames swirled in front of my face.

Nine years ago a semi-trailer crashed into my van as I waited for a light at the intersection to change, and I was trapped inside. An inferno of flames engulfed my vehicle, and I struggled to find a way out of a partially opened window. Miraculously, I did survive by jumping through the fire. But my injuries took me a year to recover from, and now the thought of any kind of speed in a car or on a horse terrified me. Speed always took me instantly back to the collision, and the time I had spent in the hospital. Anxiety raided my body of stability, and I felt like a tight rope walker who longs for solid ground.

Would I ever be free of this dread? My chest collapsed as again, I accepted this fate as part of my life. Snapping my eyes open, I wiped the tear off my chin before it fell to the dirt beneath his hooves. Earlier that day as I stood with Rocket, ever in tune with my thoughts and emotions, he sensed my anxiety and had his own views on my healing process.

We're disappearing over that hill today," Rocket said to me as the morning light shown on his adorable pony-like face. "What do you mean? Like galloping? No way!" I said, shaking my head side-ways in horror with my jaw held tight.

"It's time for you to be free," he responded pushing his wet fuzzy nose into my stomach, prodding me. "You're ready."

Looking around the large stable as I brushed his palomino and white fur, I became self-conscious and wondered if any other boarders could hear us. *Gosh, that's right,* I thought. *They can't hear animals talking to them.* Since the age of two, I've communicated with animals, nature, and spirits. I remember dancing giddily in circles at this amazing connection, my long blonde hair spinning out around me like rays of the sun. Each strand of hair a filament connecting me to rocks, trees, angels and of course, the animals. We were part of a giant Oneness in which each was an honored part of the unique and special aspects of the other. And now as I stood admiring Rocket, my little 14 hands Paint, I knew he was part of this incredible union. What did he know about me that made him so sure that I was ready for this? Maybe he thought it was a good idea, but I was not convinced.

"I can't go fast Rocket, you know that; I'm too scared," I said standing next to him now as I continued with the currycomb.

"I know you can do this Asia. Today's the day."

"What if your leg falls in a hole while we're running? You could trip," I said as my voice rattled. "There's no way I'm ending up in that hospital again."

"We'll walk the track first and you can see that it's safe," he said.

Rocket believed in safety. I knew that from our group-riding lessons earlier that year. I remember putting on his black English saddle as we went into the dimly lit sand arena, sitting on him and allowing my hips to swing in rhythm to his effortless walk. I even recall breathing in a strong smell of manure that stung my nose, and how I tried to breathe deeply and relax.

"Rocket and Asia to the outside of the arena. It's time to trot!" my riding instructor had yelled out.

"*Oh, no, I'm going to die*, I thought, as I heard the sound of my heartbeat in my ears.

Rocket and I had spent most of our lessons standing in the middle of the arena. I'd claimed his advanced age of eighteen meant he needed to rest, but everyone knew the truth as they saw the angst pouring out of me. And I remember thinking to myself, *What am I doing here anyway?*

"Move it, Asia! Get him going," my instructor shouted. Her voice bounced off the walls of the arena like an echo chamber.

Remembering that I could talk to Rocket, I decided to ask him to trot *slowly, which he didn't mind.*

"It's because of your leg, that you want to go slowly?" I asked remembering the trauma of his leg getting caught in a fence years ago." It's easier for you, huh?"

"No," he said. "I want to go slowly because I know that you're scared."

I remember how I sucked in my breath and tears rolled down my flushed cheeks as we trotted through the sand. My confidence only lasted once or twice around the 120x60 foot arena, and then I found another excuse to stop in the center.

Blowing horse snot on me, Rocket startled me back to the present moment, and I flung my head around to avoid another puff.

"Stop it!" I finally said, wiping my glasses on my dirty t-shirt, and I kicked at the stall wall with my boot in irritation.

"You really can do this." he assured me. I stared mutely back at him with my arms crossed.

"Let's get ready," he said looking at me with his dark lined eyes.

So reaching around the corner of his stall, I pulled the tan leather bridle off the metal hook. Standing next to him and placing the reins over his flaxen mane, he lowered his head and willingly took the silver bit into his mouth.

His brushed coat glistened in the sunlight, ready for his green saddle pad and basket weave stamped leather saddle. Slowly and purposefully drawing the girth through my hands and around the gold metal ring, I pulled his tack all together. It felt as important as tying down everything you owned on a car's luggage rack for all I needed was one loose tie or my life would once again crash apart on the highway.

Deliberately watching that the rope didn't get too taut, I felt for the right balance, while Rocket's face remained peaceful. Taking hold of the reins in my right hand we walked out of the barn and to the trail. While still on the ground, I found myself meticulously walking the soft dirt pathway compulsively looking for holes, rocks or debris that could trip him up. None.

"Get on," he said.

I began to shake as I flung my legs up and into the saddle. Spontaneously my arms retracted tensely into my abdomen as I held the reins in my hands.

"Let's start at the bottom of the hill," he commented matter-of-factly. I turned him in that direction with an act of sheer will though the rest of my body thought about jumping off.

But instead of starting, I went into a nervous frenzy of rearranging my riding leggings, which suddenly seemed unbearably tight and uncomfortable. Yanking at them frantically, I could hear seams tearing, and I broke a fingernail. Then when I was more comfortable, I felt myself nervously organizing and rotating the reins so they were flat and lay in my hands perfectly, which I thought definitely essential to a safe ride. Rocket, however, didn't care about any of this.

"Now, I know you're going to pull back on the reins when I start going fast," he said. "But I want you to know I'm not going to stop."

"I might pull back," I replied, as I rolled my eyes, feeling a wave of anxiety rush over me.

"Even if you pull back hard and yell at me I'm going to keep running," he said solemnly. "It's time to break free of this anxiety that is stifling the life force in you. I know you can do this."

"Okay," I said sitting tense in the saddle. "This is how I'm going to do this?" "Yes," he smiled back.

Up came Rocket's brawny legs, as he started into a robust walk then quickly broke into a ground-crossing trot. At the crest of the hill, his muscles tightened as he sprang into a canter. Flashes of the hill, the semi and my van crash, streamed by my eyes like a horror movie. Forcefully, I pulled back on the reins.

"No stop!" I screamed. "Please stop Rocket, I can't do this. I'm going to die."

"I'm not stopping. I know you can do this! He said, gently and steadily sending these thoughts through my fear. "I'm actually going to go faster now."

An explosive power like the volcano, Pele surged through his body as he stretched out his legs. We soared across the earth at a gallop. Internally my muscles contracted, sobs racked my mouth, and I was blinded by my tears.

Suddenly the wind blew hard on my face, and I felt a sensation like hard chunks of burnt metal plummeted off me. The muscles down my back lengthened and released while the curve of my back filled in with a softness that I had not felt in a long time. Arms and neck outstretched out as my sobs turned to laughter and joy.

"Oh, my god, you were right." I yelled out. Rocket gave a slight leap. We continued running as my body joined in the celebration with him. Moving together in rhythm, I pressed my hand into his neck and smiled.

About Asia Voight

Asia has been working internationally as an Animal Communicator, Teacher and healer for the past twelve years. She has been featured in the news programs seen on ABC, NBC, and Fox TV. She also organizes Swim With The Dolphins and Whales Expedition Trips. Her future plans are creating her own TV and radio shows. With a degree in Radio/TV/Film, her dreams one day may come true.

To learn more about this amazing woman, please go to her website: www.asiaVoight.com

Or on Facebook: www.facebook.com/AsiaVoight, Professional AnimalCommunicator

ANIMALS AS TEACHERS

Bernie Siegel, M.D. Connecticut

The following is from a discussion I had with our beloved pet house bunny Smudge.

After I told Smudge we needed another article for the web site, she looked at me with that deep penetrating look and said, "We need to help people deal with the death of their beloved pets. I keep seeing articles in all the pet magazines about how to deal with the loss of your pet. They don't use the word death they talk about loss, passing, failed health, gone to pet heaven and can't seem to face the fact that the animal died. They are as bad as most health care professionals. If I weren't here to teach you, I don't know where you'd be."

"I don't deny that you have been a teacher for me and helped me deal with loss and grief and turn the charcoal, under pressure, into a diamond."

"People need to understand why pets have shorter lives to begin with. You know our Creator has a reason for everything."

"Smudge, you mean to tell me there's a reason people have longer lives than animals?"

"Yup. You know that list you read when you lecture about starting the day without caffeine or pep pills, eating the same food every day, and not complaining, facing the world without lies and deceit, not judging people by their race, accepting criticism and blame without resentment, not judging a rich person as better than a poor person, conquering tension without medical help,and it ends with, and if you can then you're almost as good as your dog."

"Well that's why animals don't need as much time. We are complete and understand about love, kindness, forgiveness, how to survive life's difficulties, turn curses into blessings and do what we were born to do. We can die with a smile because we understand all that. How many people do you know who die laughing?"

"Truth is Smudge, except for the pets and people in our family, I don't know many who do die that way. I guess Lassie is a model in life and death for us all."

"People have to realize what animals already know. The only thing of permanence is love. Sooner or later our bodies will perish at any rate, but if they perish without love, of what use will they have been? We need to express and serve out of love and then we can die with a smile knowing we have done what we were sent here to do, and it has nothing to do with how much time one is on this planet."

"I think life and death are both parts of a circle. And though people fear death, I am not sure it is the worst outcome. When we are free of our bodies, we are perfect again and free of afflictions."

"You got it Doctor Bernie. The Noah story explains it all."

"What do you mean?"

"Haven't you ever wondered why Noah didn't bargain with God to save more people and animals? He never asked for his neighbors and their sweet Labrador to be allowed on his ark in addition to what God told him he should take."

"I never stopped to think about that. Why do you think he didn't try to sneak a few others onto the ark?"

"Because just like I said, death is not the worst outcome. Life is difficult. Who got left with a boat full of animal poop? Noah did. All the rest got a chance to be free of their afflictions and start again a lot wiser than before. So life is a school, and each time we experience it I hope we move up a grade and become more creative and loving."

"Wow so you think we keep coming back?"

"Yes, but I don't think I know our consciousness is passed on to those who follow us but let me add this. When your beloved pet dies, don't go looking for him or her to be reincarnated for your sake. This is nothing about replacing what you lost but taking in a new family member and giving them a full and unique life. Don't keep naming future pets after the one you have lost. Make them authentic."

"I have learned from you not to call our three-legged dog tripod and make his deformity what is important about him."

"Right and when Furphy was attacked and lost an eye you didn't get him an eye patch and change his name to Captain Hook."

"Boy Smudge we have covered a lot of stuff that people rarely want to look at. Any final words of advice?"

"Just that if you want to be immortal, share your love. Love is the bridge between the land of the living and the land of the dead. And our consciousness never ends though our bodies do. So be aware your loved ones are still around you because once you leave your body, time no longer exists, and they can share the journey but in another form and way. You'll believe it all when you experience it, and we all will someday. Now let's not waste our life time and go out and play until next month's article is due."

About Bernie Siegel, M.D.

Dr. Bernie Siegel is a world-renowned physician and best-selling author. He is internationally known as an expert on the relationship between the patient and the healing process as it evolves throughout one's life. Some of his well-known books include: *Love, Medicine and Miracles, How To Live Between Office Visits* and *Prescriptions for Living: Inspirational Lessons for a Joyful, Loving Life*.

"Bernie," as he likes to be called, graciously gave me permission to publish his story, "Animals as Teachers" for this book. Please check his website: www.berniesiegelmd.com

CHAPTER 8

AWAKENING TO OUR INHERENT TRUE NATURE

What does it mean to be awakened to our inherent true nature? Why is it important to learn who we really are? For most of us, we think we already know who we are. For instance, we define ourselves by the jobs and the socio-economic status we have. I'm a chemist; I'm a mother; I just graduated from college; I'm a cancer survivor.

We are more than our ego's characterization of ourselves. We have a powerful identity which is the very essence of life inhabiting the physical body. It is the soul, the manifestation of the Divine Presence within us. This is our *true identity*! Our ego nature is our *false self.* I am well aware that for some people, admitting that my spirit-self was taken up into God's Presence during my experiences sounds bizarre, if not downright crazy. It may be easy to surmise that I may be a lunatic. Can you put your trust in someone like me who purports to have been given knowledge of our *true and false selves* as revealed to me by my Great Teacher, the Light of God?

Typically, if we don't understand something of a supernatural nature, we have a tendency to label it and once we do that, we don't have to deal with it anymore. We think we have all the answers, but we don't. We must remember that our Creator is greater than our finite minds no matter how many PhD's we may have or how many awards we have been given for our brilliant works. If the Divine seeks us out for a purpose, and we are open to receive it, then there is nothing we can do but follow the passion in our heart to be of service to humanity.

So my advice to you is this. Draw whatever insight from my message that touches your heart. Allow the Spirit that is within the depth of your soul to speak its own truth to you. For it is in *union* with Divine Spirit and *your own soul* that God can move you to the next level, to a deeper and more intimate experience of the Sacred within.

I learned from my Great Teacher during my transcendent experience that man's true destiny is to realize the truth of the Divinity of one's self, ever present within the self. The reality of the Presence is so all-encompassing and magnificent that it defies any possible imagined idea of ecstasy. Trying to describe the Divine is like trying to describe a color to a blind person. Many have attempted such an explanation, but all have failed; because the Divine is beyond our finite minds, and beyond the language humanity has created.

How then, do I attempt to explain the all-encompassing rainbow colors of the Divine Presence within, so that people will begin to create a vision of the Ultimate Reality? I can't. No one can. The best I can do with our current language is to inspire people to awaken to the knowledge that is placed directly within every single person, so they can discover *for **themselves*** the existence of this truth that I personally awakened to. This discovery must be personally experienced; there is no other way. No amount of factual knowledge will convince anyone of its truth unless we inwardly perceive that it is true.

My Great Teacher gave me the seeds of Light to scatter, but I realize that some seeds will fall on fertile, and some on rocky soil. Many teachers strive to instruct others in this quest for understanding the innermost mystery, but we must remember that each person is unique. Just as there are no two fingerprints that are exactly alike, so too are all individuals set apart in their uniqueness. Each person can perceive only what they are capable of perceiving at whatever level of growth they happen to be at the time. I will describe some of the teachings my Great Teacher infused into my heart during my journey to Heaven's door so that you may begin to take responsibility for your own life transformation, should you choose to embark upon this magnificent Light-filled journey.

A rich and purposeful life is to be found *within oneself,* no matter what the exterior world throws our way. Make no mistake, when the veils are removed and we finally "see the Light" (pardon the pun), then this glorious Light *within,* sings its song of overflowing love, joy and everlasting peace. A new world has been revealed to us and we now dwell within it. The outer world now has no power over us to cause our struggle, suffering, and fears.

Believe me, prior to my journey to Heaven's door, I knew nothing about ego, spirituality, and our true nature. I was an ordinary woman, and I am still. I was vigorously trained in the scientific method to accept as fact, only that which is verifiable by science and objective reality. However, when I was taken up into the bosom of God, that was subjective "proof" for me that a far greater reality beyond our sense world exists. From the deepest Source of Divine Love, I was illumined with the knowledge of man's true nature, for the purpose of helping others become *aware* of something we simply forgot.

Before I discuss the Light and our relationship to it, we must first understand our ego's role in the way we relate to life, our thoughts and feelings, and how our ego causes *separation* from our awareness of our *true identity, the LIGHT within.* The ego is highly motivated to dominate our lives by using fear to condition our minds to claim authorship of all our subjective experiences.

Ego reinforces our need to be "right" at any cost and voraciously clings to its cherished beliefs. We invested a lifetime of living from an egoist perspective because everyone is attached to the ego's hope and expectations, failings, gains and losses, and the resultant human suffering. The 'I' self identifies with roles, titles, and behavior, but this creates the illusion of an independent, separate self. Probably the most tragic consequence of our ego's need for dominance is the fear that 'I' will one day be faced with the prospect of death. This makes the ego very fearful. We haven't been taught that the ego is our false self, an illusion we have about ourselves.

My Great Teacher taught me that there is only one true, authentic Self, our Higher Self, the Divinity that we came from, belong to, and return to. I was shown how we must peel away the layers of illusion we have about our false self, like layers of an onion, until we reach down to the core of our true being. There, at the core of our being, the manifestation of perfection shines forth. We have come "home" to the indwelling Divine pure love, power, healing, and knowing. From this perfection of our true identity, comes self-acceptance, self-expression, and our justification for being, all expressed as the Divine Presence through our true Self on the human level.

How do we peel away the layers of illusion of our false self so we can begin to live a life we were created to live? Remember this: our ego will resist change. The ego wants to be in charge at all times, that's its nature. It is simply a collection of thoughts, feelings, memories, data, and beliefs, but ego also tries to convince us that this is who we are. Ego motivates us to become insistent, desiring, yearning, greedy, spiteful, fearful, challenging, resentful, angry, contriving, and other negative and destructive traits that dwell in the illusion of our false self.

I don't mean to imply that ego is a bad thing to have, or that we need to get rid of it. Certainly, ego has a purpose to fulfill in our daily lives if we are to live in this world of information and knowledge. Our minds need to experiment with ideas, probe, listen, and absorb. The ego only becomes a problem when it convinces us that the world we live in is threatening and chaotic by the various negative thoughts and feeling we become ***attached to***. We have been taught from an early age that we are separate individuals who need to protect, defend or advance ourselves in some way. We try to impose our agenda on life to satisfy our ego needs at all costs, but in doing that, we experience suffering.

It is our birthright to become detached from the sorrows of our outer life experiences by living inwardly with the awareness of the Kingdom of Heaven within. This so-called "Heaven" is our true self, the Divinity that is the Light of the world. Every loving thought, word and deed arising from our true self unites our two worlds together, the physical with the spiritual. Our lives become a manifestation of God's love, healing, harmony, wisdom and power in the midst of all activity on the earth. No matter what our exterior life experiences will be, our interior world embodies all the qualities of the living Light of the Divine. In reality, we are each Divine, not separate, but united as one. This awareness is essential to a deeper and more profound experience of the Divinity of existence.

Knowing our oneness with the Divine and with all, transforms our egoist life into a life of peace and wisdom. Our inner being has become fearless, aware, and oh, so loving! It is as natural as the sunrise revealing itself in the early morning, shining Light into the shadows of the darkness that prevailed only moments earlier.

Intellectual understanding of our oneness with the Divine and with all, will not result in the consciousness necessary to dwell in this glorious state of awareness. The mind or our ego is not the soul. The soul must *experience* this sacred truth for itself. We cannot force ourselves to believe this. We cannot use willpower to try to destroy the ego's hold over us. The ego is very cunning and clever. It will discourage us at every step of the way to pull us away from experiencing the Divine Presence within.

What is needed is simply to understand that the ego holds mistaken beliefs about who we really are. So give the ego a break. Forgive the ego for what it doesn't know. Then all we need to do is learn how to loosen the ego's grip over our lives. We do that through our willingness to go deeper within the mystery of our self to surrender our self to the One who calls us "home." I do not believe we can do this by intent, or by trying to achieve these results on our own, because that only reinforces perception through the ego. Rather, the awareness of the reality of our true nature is facilitated by humility, faith, trust, and the realization that God's Grace will bring the result we seek through the various processes necessary for one's spiritual development.

When we invite the Beloved to work with us to shed the illusion of our false self, we can be assured the Eternal Power which created us can heal us into wholeness in every nook and cranny of our being. The sweet gentleness of Spirit within, will express the intrinsic qualities of the Divine through all the pathways of our life as we walk lovingly forward with a new life, a life of joy, a life of peace, and a life of Grace.

This is not idle talk. This is truth as revealed to me during the miracle of my encounter with the Beloved. It can be your personal truth as well if you accept it. A musician composes exquisite music to be shared with others, not to harbor it all for herself in the silence of a soundproof room. The musician must share the gift received, otherwise it would not be heard, ever enriching our lives in such a beautiful melodic way. So hear your own music! Know your music! **Be** your music! You will then know the revelation of what it means to be yourself, your spiritual identity.

We have each been given the connection to the Divine to compose the rest of our lives from the symphony of Holy Love, the portal to the unification of Heaven and earth. This is our ultimate fate even if we are presently unaware of this. We are each channels for Light to lift the consciousness of all people. Every word, thought or deed carries the potential for bringing Light into the world, with hearts being opened to a strong infiltration of Divine Glory.

Let us each begin the process of self-discovery, to expand our capacity to recognize the power of the Divine Presence within, the life that will bring new life to the old life. Let us each open our hearts to find our own love center, the greatest love we have ever known. Begin by claiming the truth that the Divine is individualized in every soul-being, and that this is given to us by Grace. When we can consciously realize this Presence as our true nature, we will no longer condemn any part of our being- or anyone else for that matter. The miracle that exists within us is a powerful source of pure, unconditional love. Accept it and grow with it. Our selfhood is Divine. Know it and honor it. Let nothing separate you from this truth!

Every day take the time to reflect upon your Divinity and your true worth, and be grateful to the One who created the masterpiece which is YOU. When ego sneaks in through the back door of your mind, trying to deceive you through false judgments, work to rid yourself of your preconditioned ideas of how life ought to be. Forgive the ego for trying to separate you from the truth of your being, and allow Spirit's Voice within to speak to your heart, to heal you of that mistaken notion.

Just as automobiles sometimes need front-end alignment, our thoughts also need alignment to clear our mind from old beliefs and to release us from past experiences. When we begin to align our life with the Presence within, and heal our ego's need for control, we *Will* begin to experience the promise given to us by the One who loves us beyond our imagination, *"Lo, I am with you always, even unto the end of the age."*

Go with love, knowing that within you is the wisdom and

the guidance to help you begin a new way of living that transcends the old way.

WORDS OF WISDOM

"All truth goes through three stages.
First it is ridiculed.
Then it is violently opposed.
Finally it is accepted as self-evident."

—Schopenhauer

CHAPTER 9

WHAT'S LOVE GOT TO DO WITH IT?

"The day will come when, after harnessing the winds, the tides and gravitation, we shall harness for God the energies of Love. And on that day, for the second time in the history of the world, man will have discovered fire.

—Teilhard de Chardin

During my transcendent encounter with the Light of God, my Great Teacher instructed me to help others know the truth of their being, and to open themselves to an outpouring of greater love than they have ever known. I have gone about my Great Teacher's business by writing and speaking with the hope that I can help someone to begin or continue their search for spiritual understanding, without trespassing on their level of consciousness. My deep love for the One who gifted me by Grace is a love that goes beyond human love. It is love felt with my entire soul - the expression of the Spirit of God, the oneness that expands within me. It is this kind of blessed love that indwells within all of us, no matter who we are or what we have done.

The time has come when the Light is calling each of us to be aware of our Divine nature so that humanity will know the Creator is real, alive, and working with us to forgive, to love, to lift, to heal, and to know the great JOY of the Eternal One present within us. This is the miracle; the revelation of the Divine Power expressing through us on the human level.

Love is the sustainer of our Being. It is the true essence of our Divinity, and it is our call to identify ourselves with the meaning and purpose of life. When we recognize our true self as soul, we awaken to direct inner experience of the Divine. This is the great spiritual potential created by God for us to experience, a true source of the happiness that we all crave.

Human nature (ego) created conditional love that disconnects us from the kind of loving beings we were created to be. When we feel betrayed by others, we withdraw our love from them. We see ourselves as victims, and we don't want to give up our ego's need for judgment, fear, hurt, or resentment. As a result, we suffer. Whether we realize it or not, we have a false belief that our happiness will be found somewhere within the world and the things we want to obtain. But we will always suffer when we pursue that false belief.

The experience of unconditional love is the only true way of satisfying our deepest longing for peace and happiness. When we begin to transcend human or ego-based love, we enter into another reality. We merge into our real self, the self that is our Oneness with the Divine, the Source of pure, perfect love. It is here that the soul brings forth its Light into the world, the Infinite Source that is individualized in and through us.

When we realize the indwelling Presence is perfect love, our true being that is breathing through us, thinking through us, radiating love through us, we realize the wonderful gift we have been given, to know the perfection of ourselves. We are a projection of Spirit filled with the Creator's Grace to love ourselves and others without qualification.

Divine unconditional love asks us to have a willingness to open our hearts, let go, and let love flow in and out through every fiber of our being. The love that passes between one another is a blessing to behold, for it is through oneness that the love of Spirit moves. Let us decide to make ourselves a deep channel of love to all humankind. From this moment on, we have the power to transcend our own limitations, our fears, our thinking. Let our desire to love supersede any other desire, for it is then that our outer experiences will reflect the truth of our being.

Love will then dissolve all barriers, for there is nothing that can separate us from this Infinite Love. We can face our trials and tribulations knowing the enfolding power that comes from Source within will lift us from the darkness and carry us gently and lovingly into the Light. Love is the key to universe. Love is the answer. Love is the way! Love is the only way we will lift humanity to the potential and the truth that we can move forward into a life that can be lived in the power of pure love. This is our glorious purpose, the purpose for which we were created. Learn this, and teach it to others by the way you live.

WORDS OF WISDOM

"What does love look like? It has the hands to help others. It has the feet to hasten to the poor and needy. It has the eyes to see misery and want. It has the ears to hear the sighs and sorrows of men. That is what love looks like."

—Saint Augustine

CHAPTER 10

THE FINAL CHAPTER

"The choice in life is not between pain or no pain. The choice in life is between the pain of loving or the pain of not loving."

—Bishop Joseph Gallagher

Just a few days prior to writing this final chapter, my high school sweetheart and dear husband of forty-nine years died. He died of complications of kidney disease. When you learn someone you love is dying, you enter into an experience you are never quite prepared to deal with. It hurts so much to see your loved one suffer and not being able to help; it hurts so much to see your family members hurting so much, and it hurts to feel your own heart being assaulted with pain that never seems to cease.

Only in the agony of parting do we look into the depths of love.

—George Elliot

I wanted to add this final chapter to let others know that no matter if someone has "seen the Light" through a spiritually transformative experience or a near-death experience, we are still human beings who must face events in our lives that sometimes will bring us to our knees in heartache and sorrow. I admit I am not a professional counselor who can give people the best advice on handling grief. After all, this is the first time I am personally experiencing the loss of a beloved husband. However, I have personally known what it is like to be on the other side of the veil and to experience the love from Divine Source that is beyond human comprehension. I know my beloved husband will experience this. While this is a **tremendous comfort** to me, at the same time I feel so fragile, lost, and I am in unbearable pain.

I feel as if my heart has split in half with one half wrapped around my husband's spirit as he traveled homeward. The raw pain of losing someone you love so deeply is devastating. I can weep so hard at times, and then I can feel comforted by an unknown sympathetic understanding surrounding me, at times brief, and at other times lasting long enough to gain some relief from my suffering. This is the roller coaster ride of uncontrolled emotions I am experiencing even as I write this.

I was a caregiver for my husband for many years and while it was difficult at times, it was a privilege to care for him to ease his suffering and give him the hope to look forward to another tomorrow. Through his illness, he taught me many lessons such as patience, compassion, laughter during those moments of sometimes embarrassing predicaments he found himself in. And yes, even the love and joy of caring for him when I was sometimes too tired to care for myself, he taught me the importance of selflessness.

Meeting the challenge of working through my grief to heal the deep wound my heart has sustained will be a challenge in rebuilding my life. But I recall the words of Robert Anderson, playwright of *I Never Sang For My Father*, who beautifully states, "Death ends a life, not a relationship." There is nothing in the entire world that can destroy the memories of our loved one.

Those memories will continue to live on in our hearts to bring warmth to our recovering hearts so that our loved one remains an integral part of our life.

I began this chapter acknowledging that even though I have been on "the other side" and know that life is a continuum gifted with the greatest love imaginable, the "home" of all homes, it does not shield those of us left to remain on this physical dimension from our human heartaches. To be fully human, we must acknowledge our humanness without placing expectations upon ourselves or from pressure from outside forces to be something we are not, at least not in the present moment. No two persons will be at the same place along our human journey. Wherever we are in our journey, we are there because we need to be. Pain and suffering are all part of the human journey because in that suffering, there **IS** underlying spiritual good to be found. There **IS** meaning to be found in all life's experiences, the good and the tragic. **This is what I absolutely know to be true as revealed by my Great Teacher, the Light of God during my transcendent experience.**

Divine Wisdom leads us through those good and tragic events to prepare us for our particular work or "mission" in life. We were created to be incomplete so that we would need one another. We share what God has given to us so that we can reach out to others and share the immensity of Holy Love that is from God. The mysterious way in which the Divine works beneath the surface of our daily lives to realign our thoughts to gain new insights into ourselves and others is truly a miraculous process of self-discovery. This is true even in the tragic events in our lives. It makes God's presence in humanity so real.

I have no doubt whatsoever that losing my beloved husband will catapult me into a new life, one in which I will continue to write and to speak of what my Great Teacher taught me. I will find meaning in my husband's death and will go on to fulfill my earthly "mission." I will depend upon the Divine Presence within to lead me forward toward my highest good. No matter if my life brings me roses or thorns, I will always be reminded of what my Great Teacher told me during my experience: *"As long as you hold onto my hand and don't let go, I shall lead; you shall follow. The path ahead of you shall be prepared for you."* I have no doubt that God is determined to see my work through to completion. And, I truly believe that message was not only meant for me, **but for everyone as well!**

I can be confident that this is not "The Final Chapter," but the beginning of a new one. One that will bring my appointed "mission" to fulfillment as I continue to help others to facilitate an even deeper intimacy with the Divine within in preparation for our entrance into God's presence at the end of our journey through life. I am comforted in knowing my husband was called home and is enjoying the eternal ecstasy of God's presence. While my tears will continue to be shed for awhile, I will allow them to gently fall upon my cheeks knowing that God is shedding his own tears with me because God shares all our sorrows, our fears, as well as our joys. Whatever we feel, God feels it as well. Isn't that the best friend we can have on our life's journey?

May I remind everyone that those of us who have "seen the Light" through spiritually transformative experiences should not be put on a pedestal to be viewed as being superior to anyone else or being spared the heartache of losing a loved one. Remember, we are all spiritual beings having a *human experience* and it is in living our authentic self as human beings that we can each share our love, our joys, and yes, our sorrows with one another as children of the Divine. To be otherwise would negate the reason for our earthly existence and the reason we are here.

Before closing this "Final Chapter" I want to tell you what happened one month following my husband's death. I had been praying for a sign or some type of message communication from my husband. Knowing that this type of communication termed after-death communication is a very real phenomenon and has been documented for many years, I believed that one day my husband would contact me in some way. After all, the percentage of widows experiencing an after-death communication is as high as 70 to 80 percent. The way my husband chose to contact me was through synchronicity.

Synchronicity was first described by Swiss psychologist Carl Gustov Jung in the 1920's. His idea was that life was not a series of random events but rather an expression of a deeper order having elements of a spiritual awakening. Jung believed synchronicity held some personal significance for the experiencer and he noted that among his patients, synchronicity often happens during circumstances of emotional intensity and upheaval. Certainly, the death of my beloved husband constitutes intense emotional upheaval in my personal life. From the religious perspective synchronicity shares similar characteristics of an "intervention of grace."

For many of us, we tend to doubt and deny aspects of experience that aren't verifiable. We are prone to dismiss these events by saying, "Oh, it's just a coincidence." But for the person experiencing this phenomenon it is very significant and meaningful, just as Jung has described.

The following is what took place after opening myself up to the possibility that my husband would bring me a message to comfort me. It begins with a month of daily prayers asking both God and my husband that I be allowed to receive some sign from my husband on our anniversary. That morning I prayed as usual and held my closed Bible over my heart asking God to lead me to a passage that would speak to my heart. My usual custom for doing this prayerful communion with the Divine is to close my eyes and place my index finger about two to three inches above the closed pages in the Bible. I move my index finger back and forth until I see a white light in the corner of my left eye. When I see that, I immediately poke my finger into the closed pages, open my eyes, and then I open the Bible and begin reading the verses on both pages.

The verse that stood out to me was Hebrews 12:35. *"And some women, through faith, received their loved ones back again from death."* I interpreted that to mean that my husband's spirit would be with me that anniversary day. How reassuring that passage was for me! So I decided that I would put my grief aside for that day and plan an anniversary dinner for the both of us. I bought one small five-ounce lobster tail, (which I haven't had in years), some fresh green beans and a salad along with our favorite white wine.

My husband always bought me yellow roses for our anniversary and my birthday since they are my favorite roses, so I decided to buy yellow roses for the centerpiece on our dinner table. I searched all over town for them and I couldn't find any. Disappointed, I went to WalMart and purchased a thirty-inch long-stemmed artificial silk yellow rose. Not the real thing, but I figured it would serve the purpose.

I purchased the yellow rose with some other items and when I was transferring my items into the car, the yellow rose was not there. Where did it go? I bought it; I had the receipt for it. It was a windy day so I thought perhaps it blew out of one of the bags, but heck, I would have seen it since the cart is in front of me. I looked all around the adjacent parked cars but it wasn't there. I went back to the check-out counter and asked the man if I left the yellow rose there but he told me I didn't. Where did it go?

Now I am really disappointed! I was resigned to the idea that the yellow roses that my husband loved to give me on our anniversary wouldn't be on the dinner table that evening. As I was leaving the parking lot at WalMart, I suddenly had a thought. "Nancy, go to that small grocery store around the corner to buy some red peppers." Why would I think of something like that of all things I wondered? I didn't need red peppers, but I went to that store anyway. I bought some red peppers and an avocado and proceeded to the check-out counter. There at the check-out counter was a display of bouquets of fresh flowers. In the middle of the pack was a bouquet of six yellow roses smiling up at me as if to say, "I love you Nancy."

How is this a meaningful coincidence or synchronicity that I believe was my husband's message to me? I believe with all my heart that he had a hand in this episode from the time that silk rose vanished. He had always insisted I have fresh yellow roses and when he was alive, he would order them from the florist weeks in advance to make certain they arrived for my special occasion. I have to tell you that my husband detests artificial flowers - big time! When I bought that one yellow silk rose, I knew he must have been blowing a fuse. I could hear his voice inside my head scolding me for buying it and saying he would NEVER buy me artificial yellow roses! Somehow that artificial one disappeared and I was led by the voice in my head to the one place that had the REAL yellow roses waiting for me to pick them up and place them on our anniversary dinner table.

My spirits were uplifted that day because of the synchronicity of the Bible passage that began in motion, the events that would take place to allow me to receive a sign from my husband on our very special anniversary day.

For dinner, I set a place for my husband and even poured his wine for him. He didn't get anything to eat of course, but I figured I could drink two glasses of wine that night. After all, it's our anniversary, right?

I played some soft music in the background from a CD called "Music of the Angels." Appropriate, right?

We had a lovely candlelight dinner, the REAL yellow roses and some nice conversation about how wonderful a marriage we had together. No, I didn't hear his audible voice, but I knew what he was saying. I felt his love, or I wanted to so much. When he was still alive, at the end of our daily dinners, my husband used to pick up my hand and kiss it to thank me for the nice dinner, so I put my hand out for his spirit to kiss my hand and I felt loved again.

The grief process will be played out in its own unique way for me as no two people experience grief the same way. But through the process, I will stay close to the Divine Presence within me for strength and comfort. I will ask that my life will continue to be used in the service of the Divine and my fellowman until that day when I will be reunited with my soul mate once more. To all those whose loved ones have gone before you, there is nothing more beautiful than the attributes of a loved one which death cannot terminate. There is one thing I know for sure. Love never dies. LOVE NEVER DIES!

WORDS OF WISDOM

I can never lose one whom I have loved unto the end; one to
Whom my soul cleaves so firmly that it can never
Be separated does not go away but only goes before....

—St. Bernard of Clairvaux

THE AWAKENING

To awaken one day,
As Rip van Winkle,
And you see your life with new eyes;
-to see
-to know
-and feel
That God/Spirit and the Angels
Are somehow working through you,
or with you,
Is a revelation.
And you ask,
"How can I create a better bridge,
A stronger bridge
For this Divine energy?"
And we say,
"Where you stand,
Where you sit,
Raise your hands and arms
Towards the heavens
And say
"Dear Holy God,

Dearest Angels of Light,
I raise my energy,
I open my hands, arms
And heart
To be an Earth Angel on earth.
I need not see you,
I need not hear you
To be guided
To do your will
And show your love on earth.
Guide me to be a vehicle
To answer other's prayers,
To show that God/Spirit and the Angels
Really do hear."
Often a miracle takes place
When one person is in need
And a second party shows up
To complete their request.
"I raise my arms
And open my heart today,
In this moment,
To demonstrate to you
And to myself
That I am no longer sleep-walking in life,
That my intention is to be a vehicle
For your loving energy to open
And awaken
And touch gently
The hearts of others."

And as you lower your arms
And you smile from heart to soul...
Knowing deep, deep within,
At a soul level...
That today
You are finally awake
And it is no longer an ordinary life,
But an extraordinary day
In the space of eternity."

—Authors: Mary Ellen "Angel Scribe" & her angels
www.AngelScribe.com

Have You Had a Spiritually Transformative or Near-Death-Like Experience?

The author is looking for spiritually transformative experiences and near-death-like experiences as part of her ongoing research. Near-death-like experiences have the same characteristics of a classic near-death experience with the exception that the person was **NOT** close to death, suffering serious illness or physical trauma at the time of their experience. Some individuals were simply resting in a chair, taking a walk, driving their car, etc. when their near-death-like or spiritually transformative experiences occurred.

Features of these experiences may include several but not necessarily all of the following:

- Lifting out of the physical body
- Entering into a transcendent or other-worldly reality
- Seeing a Light, deceased spirits, spiritual beings, demons, animals, landscapes, buildings, the cosmos, etc.
- Telepathic communication
- Sense of timelessness
- Life review or life preview
- Attaining some type of knowledge or message
- Experiencing unconditional love; bliss, joy, peace, fear
- Seeing colors, hearing music, voices

Central to the individual's experiences is the resulting awakening in one's personal consciousness and in the way he/she responds to the world. The old self is no longer there. The old patterns have been cleared away and with it comes a simpler, more purified way of living. There may be the inexpressible awareness of divine love, ecstasy, and an overwhelming awareness of the divine oneness of all things.

If your experience fit's the criteria the author is looking for, your story will be documented in her next book. All person's anonymity will be protected at all times. When sharing your story with the author, **be sure to tell what you were doing at the time of your experience and be sure to include how you believe this experience affected you afterwards, whether it was spiritual, physical, psychic, affirming or changing your beliefs, etc. Please end your account with a message you would like others to know, based upon what you learned from your experience.** Write your experience between 500-1,000 words, and email it to Nancyclarkauthor@gmail.com. The author answers all emails. Or if snail mail is preferred, you can mail your account to: Nancy Clark, PO Box 835, Dublin, OH 43017. If you would like the author to reply, please include a SASE. Without this, the author will be unable to reply. Again, all person's anonymity will be protected at all times.

ABOUT THE AUTHOR

Nancy Clark is the national award-winning author of *Hear His Voice* and *My Beloved: Messages From God's Heart To Your Heart*. She graduated from Women's Medical College at the University of Pennsylvania as a cytologist, (study of cells). Trained in the scientific method, she was a cytology instructor and worked as a cancer researcher at a major university before retiring to devote her life to the spiritual work that is so important to her.

She is the founder and facilitator of the Columbus, Ohio International Association Near-Death Studies; member, Academy of Spirituality and Paranormal Studies; and National League of American Pen Women. Nancy has been featured in the following renowned near-death-experience researchers books: Kenneth Ring, PhD, *Heading Toward Omega, and Lessons From The Light*; Charles P. Flynn, PhD, *After The Beyond*; PMH Atwater L.H.D, PhD (Hon.), *Beyond the Light; and Near-Death Experiences: The Rest of the Story*; and Barbara Harris Whitfield, *Spiritual Awakenings*. Nancy is also featured in Josie Varga's books, *Visits From Heaven* and *Journey To Heaven*. She has also served as a consultant for journalists and the media.

Her inspiring talks have been delivered to universities, professional conferences, churches, hospitals, community organizations, book clubs, metaphysical groups, as well as being interviewed on radio and television.

To schedule personal appearances and speaking engagements

with the author, please contact the author at nancyclarkauthor@ gmail.com You may also want to consider writing a review of her book, *Divine Moments* on Amazon.com if you think her book may be helpful to others. The author appreciates your support!

CPSIA information can be obtained at www.ICGtesting.com
Printed in the USA
LVOW061404171012

303215LV00001B/127/P

9 781421 886398